AQA

KS3

Activate

Know • Apply • Extend

2

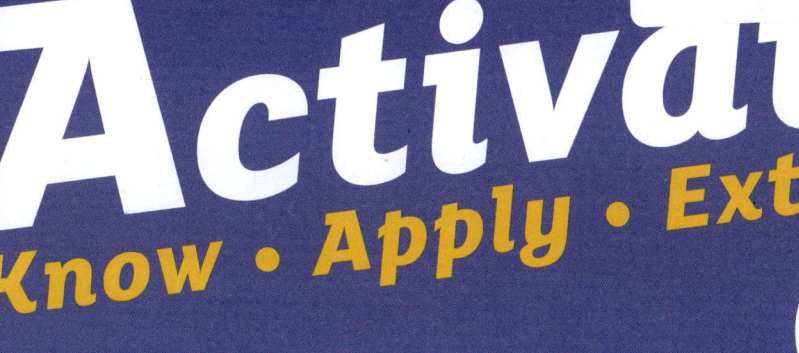

Philippa Gardom Hulme
Jo Locke
Helen Reynolds

Assessment Editor
Dr Andrew Chandler-Grevatt

Approval message from AQA

This textbook has been approved by AQA for use with our qualification. This means that we have checked that it broadly covers the specification and we are satisfied with the overall quality. Full details of our approval process can be found on our website.

We approve textbooks because we know how important it is for teachers and students to have the right resources to support their teaching and learning. However, the publisher is ultimately responsible for the editorial control and quality of this book.

Please note that when teaching the *AQA Key Stage 3 Science* course, you must refer to AQA's specification as your definitive source of information. While this book has been written to match the specification, it cannot provide complete coverage of every aspect of the course.

A wide range of other useful resources can be found on the relevant subject pages of our website: www.aqa.org.uk.

OXFORD
UNIVERSITY PRESS

Contents

Enquiry processes

6	More on planning how to answer a question	2	10	Critique claims and justify opinions	10
7	More on analysing and evaluating	4	11	Risks and benefits	12
8	Communication	6	12	Review theories 1	14
9	Evidence and sources	8	13	Review theories 2	16

1: Forces Part 2 Opener 18

1.3 Contact forces

1.3.1	Friction and drag	20
1.3.2	Squashing and stretching	22
1.3.3	Turning forces	24

1.4 Pressure

1.4.1	Pressure in gases	26
1.4.2	Pressure in liquids	28
1.4.3	Stress on solids	30
	Part 2 Summary and Questions	32

2: Electromagnets Part 2 Opener 34

2.3 Magnetism

2.3.1	Magnets and magnetic fields	36

2.4 Electromagnets

2.4.1	Electromagnets	38
2.4.2	Using electromagnets	40
	Part 2 Summary and Questions	42

3: Energy Part 2 Opener 44

3.3 Work

3.3.1	Work, energy, and machines	46

3.4 Heating and cooling

3.4.1	Energy and temperature	48
3.4.2	Energy transfer: particles	50
3.4.3	Energy transfer: radiation and insulation	52
	Part 2 Summary and Questions	54

4: Waves Part 2 Opener 56

4.3 Wave effects

4.3.1	Sound waves, water waves, and energy	58
4.3.2	Radiation and energy	60

4.4 Wave properties

4.4.1	Modelling waves	62
	Part 2 Summary and Questions	64

5: Matter Part 2 Opener 66

5.3 Elements

5.3.1	Elements	68
5.3.2	Atoms	70
5.3.3	Compounds	72
5.3.4	Chemical formulae	74
5.3.5	Polymers	76

5.4 Periodic Table

5.4.1	The Periodic Table	78
5.4.2	The elements of Group 1	80
5.4.3	The elements of Group 7	82
5.4.4	The elements of Group 0	84
	Part 2 Summary and Questions	86

6: Reactions Part 2 Opener — 88

6.3 Types of reaction

6.3.1	Atoms in chemical reactions	90
6.3.2	Combustion	92
6.3.3	Thermal decomposition	94
6.3.4	Conservation of mass	96

6.4 Chemical energy

6.4.1	Exothermic and endothermic	98
6.4.2	Energy level diagrams	100
6.4.3	Bond energies	102
Part 2 Summary and Questions		104

7: Earth Part 2 Opener — 106

7.3 Climate

7.3.1	Global warming	108
7.3.2	The carbon cycle	110
7.3.3	Climate change	112

7.4 Earth resources

7.4.1	Extracting metals	114
7.4.2	Recycling	116
Part 2 Summary and Questions		118

8: Organisms Part 2 Opener — 120

8.3 Breathing

8.3.1	Gas exchange	122
8.3.2	Breathing	124
8.3.3	Drugs	126
8.3.4	Alcohol	128
8.3.5	Smoking	130

8.4 Digestion

8.4.1	Nutrients	132
8.4.2	Food tests	134
8.4.3	Unhealthy diet	136
8.4.4	Digestive system	138
8.4.5	Bacteria and enzymes in digestion	140
Part 2 Summary and Questions		142

9: Ecosystems Part 2 Opener — 144

9.3 Respiration

9.3.1	Aerobic respiration	146
9.3.2	Anaerobic respiration	148
9.3.3	Biotechnology	150

9.4 Photosynthesis

9.4.1	Photosynthesis	152
9.4.2	Leaves	154
9.4.3	Investigating photosynthesis	156
9.4.4	Plant minerals	158
Part 2 Summary and Questions		160

10: Genes Part 2 Opener — 162

10.3 Evolution

10.3.1	Natural selection	164
10.3.2	Charles Darwin	166
10.3.3	Extinction	168
10.3.4	Preserving biodiversity	170

10.4 Inheritance

10.4.1	Inheritance	172
10.4.2	DNA	174
10.4.3	Genetics	176
10.4.4	Genetic modification	178
Part 2 Summary and Questions		180

Glossary — 182
Index — 188
Periodic Table — 190

Introduction

Learning objectives

Each spread has a set of learning objectives. These tell you what you will be able to do by the end of the lesson.

- the first learning objective tells you what you will **Know** by the end of the lesson
- the following learning objectives tell you how you will **Apply** what you know.

Key Words

The key words in each spread are highlighted in bold and summarised in the key-word box. They can also be found in the Glossary.

Link

Links show you where you can learn more about something mentioned in the Big Idea.

Summary Questions

1. 🧪 Questions with one conical-flask symbol are the easiest.

2. 🧪🧪 The questions get harder as you move down the list.

3. 🧪🧪🧪 The question with three conical-flask symbols is the hardest. In these questions you need to think about how to present your answer. You may need to write more, or solve a more difficult problem.

Welcome to your *AQA Activate for KS3* Student Book. This introduction shows you all the different features that will support you on your journey through Key Stage 3 Science.

Being a scientist is great fun. As you work through this Student Book, you'll learn how to work like a scientist, and get answers to questions that science can answer.

This book is packed full of fantastic (and foul!) facts, as well as plenty of activities to help build your confidence and skills in science.

Q These boxes contain short questions. They will help you check that you have understood the text.

Maths skills
Scientists use maths to help them solve problems and carry out their investigations. These boxes contain activities to help you practise the maths you need for science. They also contain useful hints and tips.

Literacy skills
Scientists need to be able to communicate their ideas clearly. These boxes contain activities and hints to help you build your reading, writing, listening, and speaking skills.

Enquiry Processes
Scientists work in a particular way to carry out fair and scientific investigations. These boxes contain activities and hints to help you build these skills and understand the process so that you can carry out enquiry processes.

Fantastic Fact!

These interesting facts relate to something in the topic.

Opener
Each Big Idea begins with an opener spread. This introduces you to some of the key concepts that you will cover in the Big Idea.

You already know
This lists things you've already learnt that will come up again in the Big Idea. Check through them to see if there is anything you need to recap on.

Big Questions
These are some of the important questions in science that the Big Idea will help you to answer.

Picture Puzzlers
These puzzles relate to something in the Big Idea – can you work out the answers?

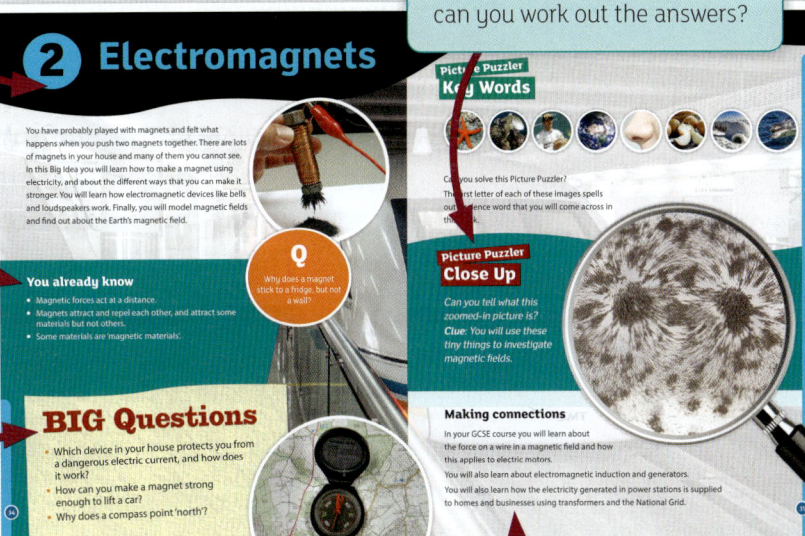

Making connections
This shows how what you will learn in each Big Idea links up with the science that you will learn in other parts of the course.

Section spreads
Each lesson has a double-page spread containing learning objectives, practice questions, key words, and task boxes to help you work through the Big Idea.

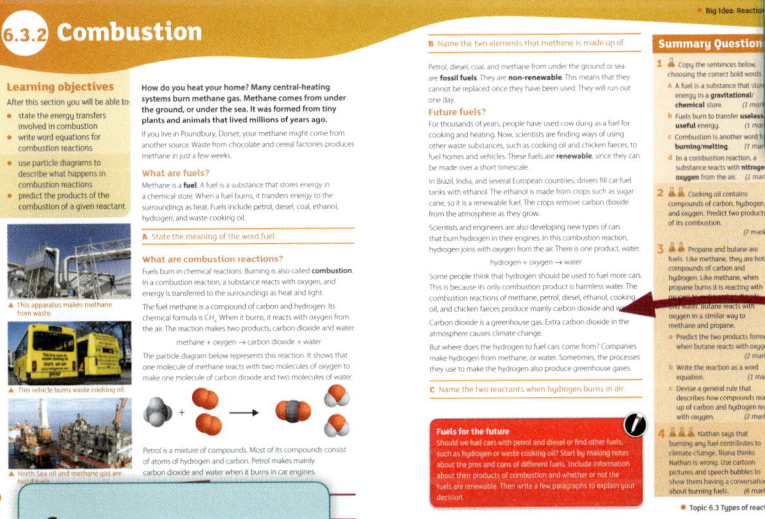

Summary
This is a summary of the Big Idea. You can use it to check that you have understood the main ideas in the Big Idea and as a starting point for revision.

Big write/Maths challenge/Case study
This is an activity that you can do at the end of the Big Idea. It will help you to practise using your scientific skills and knowledge.

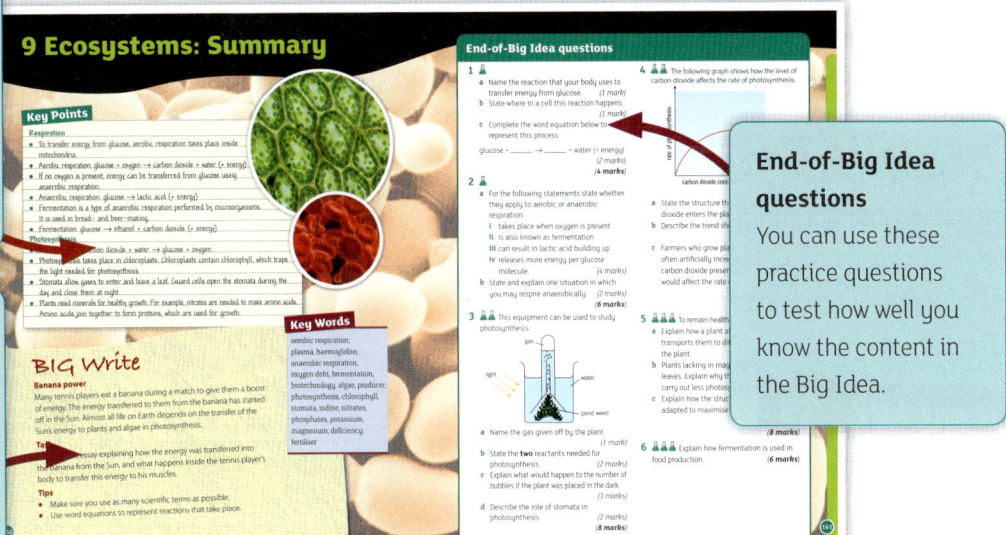

End-of-Big Idea questions
You can use these practice questions to test how well you know the content in the Big Idea.

6 More on planning how to answer a question

Learning objectives

After this section you will be able to:
- explain why and how we test hypotheses
- explain why controlling variables is important
- explain why it is important that someone else repeats your experiment.

You can bungee jump off bridges and at fun fairs. Bungee jumping can be exciting. The organisers need to know about the bungee cords to make it safe for you to jump. They need data.

◀ Scientists collect data about bungee cords that organisers use when you jump.

Deciding how to answer a scientific question

Katie and Tom's teacher has shown them a video about bungee jumping. The video shows the bungee jumper getting on scales first.

She asks them to devise a question. They can use a piece of elastic to model a bungee cord.

Katie and Tom produce a table to show some of the possible questions, and the best type of enquiry you can use to answer them.

I wonder how bungee jumping works?

We need to think of a scientific question and a way to answer it.

Link

You learnt about variables and scientific enquiry questions in Book 1, 1 Asking scientific questions.

Fantastic Fact!

The highest bungee jump in the world is from a bridge in Colorado USA. You fall a distance of 321 m and reach a speed of 110 mph.

Key Words

hypothesis, independent variable, dependent variable, repeatable

Question	Which type of enquiry is best, and what would you do?
How are sites for bungee jumps different from each other?	An observational enquiry. You *collect data* about different sites and analyse it in terms of height, location, cost of jump, etc.
Which is the best type of elastic?	This is not a scientific question because you cannot define 'best'.
How does the thickness of the piece of elastic affect the length of it when you stretch it?	A pattern-seeking enquiry. You *collect data* by changing the thickness, measuring the length, and looking for a pattern.
How are bungee cords different from each other?	An observational enquiry. You *collect data* about the physical properties of different cords.

You can investigate a question scientifically if you can collect data. Data can be observations or measurements. If you cannot collect data then the question is not scientific.

A Write down another scientific question about elastic that you could answer with a pattern-seeking enquiry.

● Enquiry processes

Deciding which data to collect

Katie and Tom decide to investigate the link between the thickness of a piece of elastic and the length.

Their **hypothesis** is:

'If the thickness of the piece of elastic is greater, the extension will be smaller when you stretch it. If we double the thickness, the extension will halve. There are more bonds for the force to stretch.'

They make a list of variables. In their plan they:

- Identify the **independent variable** (the thickness) and **dependent** variable (the length)
- Identify all the variables they need to control, and say how they will control them.

I think that's true. We don't need to test it.

If we test it and it is true then it will be a stronger hypothesis. If we don't then it's just a guess.

Why is controlling the variables so important?

If we don't then we don't know which variable has made a difference. We can't be confident in our conclusion.

B Write down one of the variables that Katie and Tom need to control.

Katie and Tom discuss what data they are going to collect. Here is part of their discussion.

- A bigger range means our conclusion can be more general, a small range will limit what we say.
- A smaller interval between measurements will help us to see the pattern very clearly, but will take longer.

Tom realises that they cannot control things like the temperature in the room. They will still be able to draw a conclusion because the temperature will not change very much. In your investigation there may be variables that you cannot control, and you need to assess the impact they might have on your conclusion.

Repeating the experiment

Katie and Tom will repeat their experiment to help them identify results that don't fit the pattern (outliers) and to increase their confidence in their conclusion. Other people in the class also do the same investigation, and Katie and Tom can compare their results with those of other groups. If they are similar, then the experiment is **repeatable**.

Repeatability is very important in science. The results of all experiments need to be checked by other scientists to make sure that the results are accurate. This increases confidence in the conclusion of the experiment.

Summary Questions

1 Copy and complete these sentences:

If you compare your results to someone else's and they are similar we say they are _____. This means that you have more _____ in your conclusion.

(2 marks)

2 A student wants to investigate how the thickness of cotton thread affects the force needed to break it.

a Identify the variables in the investigation. *(3 marks)*

b Explain why this is a scientific question. *(1 mark)*

c Explain why you need to control variables in an investigation. *(1 mark)*

d Describe a variable that the student might not be able to control, and how this affects their conclusion. *(2 marks)*

3 Manufacturers of plastic bags use a range of material. Think of a scientific question, and describe in detail how and why you would test a hypothesis based on this question.

(6 marks)

7 More on analysing and evaluating

Learning objectives
After this section you will be able to:
- identify ways to use data and line graphs
- explain how to evaluate investigations and ask further questions.

Safety is the most important consideration when you want to do a bungee jump. How do the organisers know it will be safe for you to jump?

◀ Before you do a bungee jump you have to stand on some scales. The company uses the value of your weight to work out how to adjust the cord for your jump.

Analysing data using a graph

Katie and Tom look at their results table. Here is part of it:

Thickness (mm)	Length of piece of elastic (cm)	Length of piece of elastic (cm)	Length of piece of elastic (cm)	Mean length (cm)
0.7	11.8	12.2	12.0	12.0
1.2	10.1	10.0	10.2	10.1
2.0	7.2	7.2	7.3	7.2

To find out if doubling the thickness means that the length halves Katie and Tom plot a line graph. To find the relationship the starting point for each axis needs to be zero.

You need to decide which **line of best fit** to draw on your graph. This line is a curve. If you drew a straight line a lot more of the points would be further from the line.

A Write down the length when the thickness is 1 mm and 2 mm.

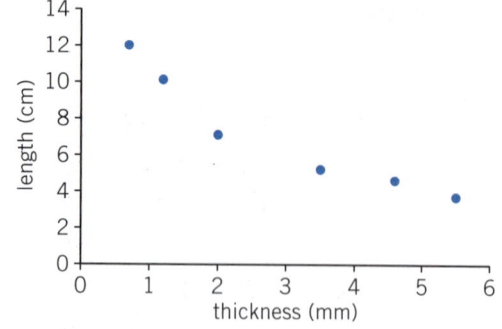

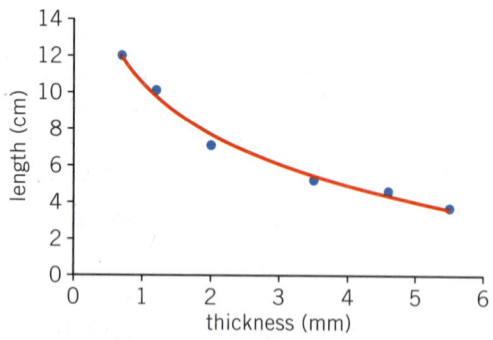

▲ Katie and Tom decide to draw a curved line, not a straight line, as their line of best fit. A straight line would not fit the data.

Katie reads the length when the thickness is 1 mm and 2 mm. She notices that if you double the thickness the length is more than half.

Our hypothesis was partly right. The length decreases if you increase the thickness, but it does not halve if you double the thickness.

Key Words
line of best fit, secondary data

Katie and Tom could still draw a limited conclusion even though part of their hypothesis was wrong, and the results did not match their prediction. Their conclusion is more believable because they now have data to support it.

B Write down what you do if your results do not support your prediction.

Conclusions and limitations

Tom was concerned because they only had a limited number of thicknesses in their results table. This meant that their conclusion would be more limited than if they had a larger range. They had taken many readings, so they were confident that their data were accurate. The range and interval for the variables that you use can depend on the equipment available, the measuring instruments, or the time available.

Using secondary data and other questions

Katie wondered what real bungee cords were like. She looked up some data on the internet and found a graph of the same experiment. Graphs or data that someone else has collected is **secondary data**.

C Write down what secondary data is.

The data show the same pattern as their graph. This made her feel more confident about their conclusion.

When you do an investigation it may prompt you to think of other questions that you could investigate. Tom and Katy could investigate other types of elastic cord.

Zero or non-zero?
You cannot make a statement about two variables being directly proportional if the axes of your line graph do not both start at zero.

Having axes that do not start at zero changes the pattern on the graph. Find a graph in a newspaper, bring it in, and compare the scales.

Link
You learnt about analysing data, writing conclusions, and evaluating in Book 1, 4 Analysing patterns and 5 Evaluating data.

Summary Questions

1. Copy and complete these sentences by selecting the correct word or words:

   A line of best fit goes through **all/most** of the points, with **fewer/more/the same number of** points above and below the line. Data that you use in your conclusion that you did not collect are called **primary/secondary** data. Testing a hypothesis by collecting data makes any explanation of it more **believable/true**.

   (4 marks)

2. Look at the graph on page 4.
   a Use the graph to calculate the ratio of lengths for thickness of 1 mm and 2 mm. (2 marks)
   b Explain why the graph starts at (0,0). (1 mark)
   c Another student used fewer pieces of elastic and drew a straight line of best fit. Suggest which thicknesses he used. (1 mark)
   d Suggest another question that arises from doing this investigation, and how you might investigate it. (2 marks)

3. Manufacturers of plastic bags use a range of material. Discuss how you might test a hypothesis about the strength of the bags, including the factors that might affect the choice of range and interval of variables, and why they are important.

   (6 marks)

8 Communication

Learning objectives

After this section you will be able to:
- describe how to plan to communicate effectively
- describe how to adapt your style to different audiences.

People write for a wide range of purposes, and for lots of different audiences. What makes communication effective?

Planning what to write

When you need to communicate ideas you need to think about how you are going to do it. Here are some questions that you need to think about:

- Who is the **audience**?
- What is the purpose?
- What is the best structure?
- How can I make it clear, concise, correct, and coherent?

Concise writing means that you describe or explain as much as possible using the minimum number of words. Writing is coherent if it is logical, well organised, and easy to understand.

A Write down two things you need to consider when you decide on the style of your writing.

Writing for a scientific audience

When you write up an investigation you are writing for a particular audience, which is probably your teacher or other students. A report of an investigation involves a particular type of writing.

▲ The audience for some scientific writing is the general public. There are articles about science in newspapers and magazines. Scientists publish their research in journals, which are only read by other scientists.

Katie and Tom need to make sure that they use the correct scientific vocabulary. There are many words in science that have a different meaning when you use them in everyday life, like force.

It should be clear from their report which evidence they are using to back up their conclusion.

B Write down one thing you need to remember when you write up an investigation.

Fantastic Fact!

There are over a million pieces of research published in scientific journals every year.

Key Word

audience

● Enquiry processes

Writing for other audiences
There are many other types of audience. You will communicate effectively if you adapt your writing to suit the audience. Here are some examples.

What you are writing	How to adapt your writing
an information leaflet for primary pupils	• use simpler words • use shorter sentences
a newspaper article for the general public	• illustrate ideas with real-life examples • use vivid words, describing real things • if you are making a claim, make sure that you clearly state the evidence that you are using • make a list of the points and cover one in each paragraph
a report of an investigation for your teacher	• use diagrams to make the meaning clear • use scientific vocabulary, units, and chemical notation accurately

C Write down one thing that you include in a newspaper article but not in an investigation report.

Writing well for any audience
Good communication has certain qualities whoever is writing and whomever the audience is. The writer will do particular things to ensure that the communication is effective. They will:

- use clear language and well-formed sentences
- read what they have written and rewrite anything that is not clear
- check there are no mistakes in spelling, punctuation, or grammar
- put paragraphs in a sensible order
- use link words to help the reader connect sentences and paragraphs
- use diagrams/charts/graphs to communicate a lot of information more easily
- include everything that the reader needs to understand but leave out unimportant details.

All these ideas help to make sure the reader understands what the writer is saying, and why the writer is saying it.

Check it out
You might find it difficult to work out where the meaning of your writing is not clear. Next time you write something ask someone else to read it and underline sections that they don't understand.

▲ You need to consider the needs of your audience when you write.

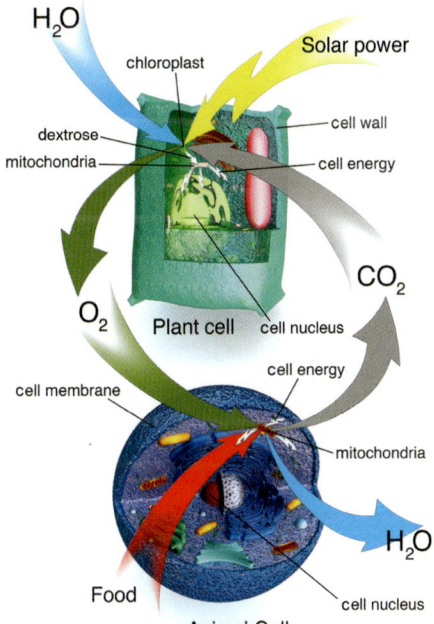
▲ Diagrams are very important if you want to communicate clearly. It would take many paragraphs to describe what this diagram shows.

Summary Questions

1. 🧪 List four of the strategies that you should use when you are writing about a science investigation.
   (4 marks)

2. 🧪🧪 Compare writing for a science journal with writing for the general public.
   (4 marks)

3. 🧪🧪🧪 Write a leaflet aimed at primary school students based on Katie and Tom's investigation into elastic bands and describe how your writing is suitable for the audience.
   (6 marks)

7

9 Evidence and sources

Learning objectives

After this section you will be able to:
- describe what peer review is
- describe how to assess sources of evidence.

Historians use evidence to make conclusions about the past. Police need evidence to convict people of crimes. In science there is a process that ensures that scientific evidence is believable.

How good is the evidence?

Not all **evidence** carries equal weight. For example, you may hear someone say:

'I know what they say about smoking, but my grandfather smoked every day for 80 years and he didn't get cancer'.

This is not scientific evidence. It is called anecdotal evidence. You cannot reason from this one example that smoking doesn't cause cancer. Scientific evidence is checked by other scientists.

▲ Evidence is important in science.

What is a peer-reviewed journal?

Scientists make hypotheses, devise ways to test their hypotheses, collect evidence, and write up their investigation. This is not the end of their work. They submit their work to a scientific **journal**. The editor of the journal sends it to other scientists working in the field. Those scientists judge whether the work is correct. This is called **peer review**. Other scientists try to repeat the work to make sure that the results are correct.

This is a checking system to make sure that the work is accurate, and that you can believe the conclusions that they have made. Work that has not gone through this process is *not* scientific evidence.

◄ Journalists for science magazines often use the peer reviewed articles that scientists publish in journals for their articles.

A Name the type of publication where scientists publish their results.

How do you interrogate sources?

How do you know if evidence is worth taking into account? To judge the reliability of evidence you need to consider the answers to a range of questions:

What do look for	Questions to ask
Who are the authors?	• Are they qualified scientists? • Is this their field of study?
Where is the research published?	• Has it been published in a peer-reviewed journal?

Link

You learnt about effective communication in 8 Communication.

Key Words

evidence, journal, peer review, funder, bias

● Enquiry processes

What were the findings of the research?	• Does it agree with current scientific thinking? • Did the author give a scientific explanation of the findings?
Does the scientist have a vested interest in the results?	• Who is the **funder** of the research? • Does the scientist work for a company that would like the conclusion to be a certain way?
Were there enough data to justify the conclusion?	• How many data points were collected? • What was the range and interval of measurements? • Was the sample big enough? • Did the sample involve all the categories (of age/gender etc.) that should be included?
What does other research into this area say?	• Are the findings backed up by other research? Who did that research?

▲ Companies making medicines need to test them in laboratories.

Answering these questions will enable you to judge the reliability of the source.

B Write down three things you need to comment on when you judge the reliability of a source.

Who funds scientific research?

Scientists need money to do research. They need to pay for equipment, pay themselves a salary, and possibly employ other people. Where does the money come from? Here are the main sources of funding:

- Governments. Governments set up funding councils. Scientists write grant proposals to get money to do research. Scientists in universities may get funding, but this has come from the government. The government gets its money from people who pay taxes.
- Companies. A car company might fund research into the emissions of their cars.
- Non-profit organisations, such as charities. The British Heart Foundation might do research into the effect of a particular diet on the risk of heart disease.

What is bias?

If someone has a **bias** it means that they have a preference, which can be unfair.

- A scientist doing research into the side effects of a drug may have a bias about the results if they work for the company producing the drug.
- A journalist may have a bias when they are reporting the results of the scientist's research if they have a family member who has suffered side effects because of similar drugs.

Summary Questions

1 Copy and complete the sentences below.

When other scientists check a scientist's work we say it has been _____ _____. This makes the evidence in the work more _____. Evidence may be _____ if the person doing the research could benefit from it, or if the _____ of the research could make money from certain results.

(4 marks)

2 In 1972 John Sawyer, a meteorologist, published evidence in the scientific journal 'Nature'. It said there is a link between man-made CO_2 and a rise in global temperatures.

  a Explain why this evidence is probably reliable. *(2 marks)*

  b Explain why a journalist may be biased in their reporting of this claim. *(5 marks)*

3 Suggest how the funding of the research into new medicines affects the reliability of the evidence produced by the research.

(6 marks)

10 Critique claims and justify opinions

Learning objectives

After this section you will be able to:
- describe how to critique a claim
- describe how to justify your opinion.

Can you believe what you read in the newspapers?

You need to look at evidence ▶ and where it comes from to work out if a claim may be true.

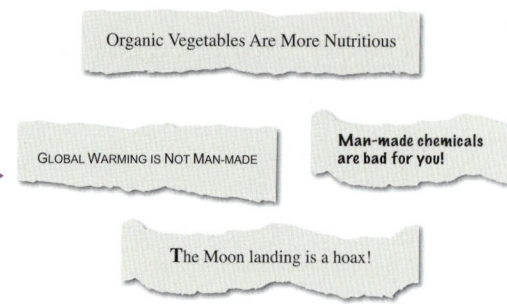

What do you do when you 'critique a claim'?

When you critique a **claim** you need to look at the claim, the **evidence** for the claim, and how the evidence was collected. Then you can work out if the evidence supports the claim.

What is the claim, and the evidence for the claim?

Identifying the claim may be difficult because claims are not always clearly stated. If you read that eating a particular food is 'better for you', you need to immediately ask yourself 'better in what way?'

To critique a claim, you need to state the claim precisely.

It is important to look at the type of evidence the author has used to make the claim. You may have less confidence in the claim if the article says:

'Studies show…' but it doesn't say which studies, or who did them.

'Scientists say…' but it doesn't say which scientists, or what they have done.

In some articles there will be a list of references at the bottom. This is where you can look to find the evidence for the claim.

▲ Some people think that the moon landing is a hoax, but the evidence shows that it did happen.

A Write down a place to look for evidence of a claim in an article.

You are looking for details about the experiments or research done – the data collected, how it was collected, the range of data, who collected it, and whether it has been published in a scientific journal.

How good is the evidence, and the reasoning for the claim?

The evidence should be scientifically accurate and relevant to the claim. The claim should follow logically from the evidence. You can explain how believable you think the claim is by presenting the evidence and **reasoning**.

▲ People make lots of decisions every day. What is the evidence that genetically modified food is harmful?

● Enquiry processes

B Write down two things you are looking for when you assess the evidence for a claim.

Sometimes the reasoning is not clearly linked to the evidence. For example, scientists have found that your brain does adapt as you get older, but this does not mean that using brain training computer games makes you smarter.

How do you justify your opinion on an issue or decision?

Evidence from science can help people to make decisions, or to form an opinion on an issue. You should start by stating the issue or decision, and all the options.

You can use scientific evidence to justify your opinion. You should state your opinion clearly and list all the facts, ideas, or data that support your opinion. It should be clear which is the most important piece of evidence, and you should use one or two pieces of supporting evidence.

C Give an example of an opinion that someone might hold about organic food.

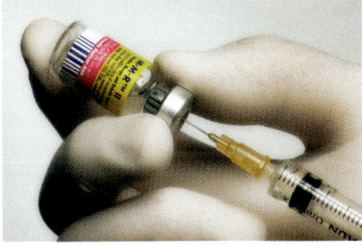

▲ Many parents stopped vaccinating their children against MMR because they thought it causes autism. There is no scientific evidence for this opinion.

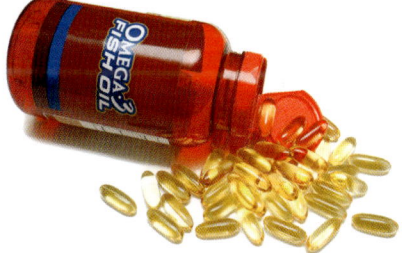

▲ There have been claims that giving fish oil to students increases their examination results.

There will always be other options. You should identify those options, and explain how the evidence supports your opinion, and does not support the other opinions.

Your reasoning should be clear, but you can indicate how someone may have a different opinion based on the same evidence. Think about what you would say if someone criticises your opinion.

Key Words

claim, evidence, reasoning

Link

You learnt about peer-reviewed journals in 9 Evidence and sources.

Summary Questions

1 🧪 Put these statements in order to show how to justify your opinion.

state your opinion

acknowledge other opinions

list all the data supporting your opinion

identify the most important piece of evidence

state the issue or decision to be made

explain how the data support your opinion *(7 marks)*

2 🧪🧪
  a A company claims that a particular diet supplement they sell is good for losing weight. Ten of their customers lost weight when they used it. Comment on the reasoning in this claim. *(2 marks)*

  b State your opinion about using fossil fuels in power stations and justify it. *(2 marks)*

3 🧪🧪🧪 Suggest and explain how you would critique a claim that giving fish oil supplements to school children improves their grades.

(6 marks)

11

11 Risks and benefits

Learning objectives

After this section you will be able to:
- describe how to assess the impact of an invention or discovery
- describe which types of groups need to be considered
- explain how a decision might be reached.

A scientific discovery or invention can lead to an application that we use in society. The invention of the laser led to the use of barcodes.

Estimate risks

To make a decision about whether to use a discovery or application you need to weigh up the **benefits** and risks. Here are some examples:

Application	Benefits	Risks	Probable decision
taking a drug for a headache	your headache goes away	there are side effects to every drug	take the drug, but not too often
having an X-ray to see if your ankle is broken or sprained	you get the correct treatment	the X-rays can cause damage to cells in your body, which may cause cancer	have the X-ray

In many medical situations, such as the X-ray, the benefits outweigh the risks. In all situations that affect you personally you need to weigh up the risks and benefits when you make a decision. It helps to list the risks, and to look not just at the consequences, but at the probabilities as well. Then you can explain why you made the decision.

A Explain why someone would choose to have a dental X-ray.

Examine consequences

Decisions about applications of science can affect individuals (including you), families, communities, and whole countries.

Some people might benefit, and some may lose out. This means that their perception of the risks or the benefits, or both, will be different. They would come to a different decision about what should be done.

Imagine that a small city wants to allow people to use driverless electric cars. The table on the next page shows some of the groups and how they may be affected.

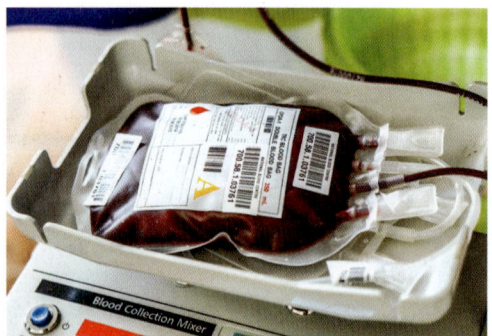

▲ Barcodes on donated blood help to ensure that it can be correctly identified.

Key Word

benefit

Link

You learnt about risk assessment in Book 1, 2 Planning investigations.

● Enquiry processes

Group	Risks	Benefits
owners of driverless cars	• there is a cost for the car, and for installing a charging system at home • the car's battery might run down	• you are less likely to cause an accident • you can do other things on your journey
taxi companies/drivers	• fewer people would need taxis – loss of profit • drivers could lose their jobs	• none
bus employees	• drivers and other workers could lose their jobs	• none (unless they had an electric car)
other drivers	• a driverless car could cause an accident with you • there could be more congestion as driverless cars could drop people off then drive home	• there could be fewer accidents as most accidents are caused by driver error, so fewer delays
local residents	• there could be more cars, and more congestion	• less pollution from burning fossil fuels (petrol)
environmental groups	• there could be increases pollution if you use fossil fuel power stations to generate electricity for the cars • animals living in habitats affected by pollution (e.g., acid rain) may be affected	• there would be less pollution in the local area due to less petrol being burned. • animals in the local environment would benefit

◀ A driverless concept car.

It is important to work out the risks and benefits for each group. There are many other groups that are not on the list – people who repair cars that have been in accidents, insurance companies.

B Identify a group that benefited, and one that did not benefit, from the invention of hands-free mobile phone kits.

When you examine consequences you should:
- consider people, including yourself
- consider the environment, including air quality and animals
- consider the money, including the financial consequences for the groups concerned.

Listing the risks and benefits means that you can predict the views that people might have about the introduction of a new invention or discovery.

There is no 'right' answer. You can try to select a choice that maximises the benefits and minimises the harm.

You can also list 'we should' or 'we should not' rules that you think everyone should follow.

Summary Questions

1. Copy and complete these sentences.
   When you examine the consequences of an invention or discovery you need to consider the _____, the _____ and the _____. Two different groups may reach different decisions depending on whether they benefit the _____ or the _____. *(5 marks)*

2. You can now buy self-cleaning glass for windows. Describe and explain:
   a a group that could gain financially from this invention *(1 mark)*
   b a group that could lose financially from this invention *(1 mark)*
   c how this invention could affect you in the future. *(1 mark)*

3. In the future all devices could be powered electrically without having to plug them in, a bit like Wi-Fi. Examine the consequences of this invention, identifying groups who would benefit positively and negatively, and give your opinion and justify it. *(6 marks)*

12 Review theories 1

Learning objectives

After this section you will be able to:
- describe what a scientific theory is
- describe the link between theory and evidence in the development of a theory.

When there is a sudden unusual event you might hear someone say 'I have a theory about that'. When a scientist says 'I have a theory' it does not mean the same thing.

◀ Some people think events happen because of things like astrology. There is no scientific evidence that astrology predicts what will happen.

What is a theory?

A theory is not just an idea. It is an idea that is supported by scientific **evidence**.

There are lots of different words to describe what scientists have worked out about the universe we live in, and how it works. You may have met some already. Here are some examples:

- a **model** – the model of the atom, the model of the Solar System
- a **theory** – theory of evolution, theory of combustion, the Big Bang theory
- a **law** – the law of conservation of energy, Hooke's Law.

A model is a way of representing something that is too difficult to display, usually because it is too big, too small, or too complicated. The mental image it gives you enables you to explain the results of experiments, or to predict the outcome of other experiments.

▲ A lot of laws in physics are written as mathematical equations.

A Write down a theory that you have used in science lessons.

A theory is an explanation for patterns that we see in observations or data. It is *supported by scientific evidence*, and repeated experiments show that it is true. A theory can be a statement in words or a mathematical formula.

A law is a theory that you can express with a concise statement, such as 'Energy is always conserved.'

▲ You learnt about Hooke's Law in 1.3.1. The equation for Hooke's law is $F = kx$, where F = force, k = spring constant, and x = extension.

• Enquiry processes

Both laws and theories are supported by scientific evidence. Kinetic theory explains the behaviour of gases using the idea of particles, and Einstein's theory of relativity explains observations of the night sky.

To see the role of evidence in producing and supporting a theory it is useful to look at the history of some theories.

Changing scientific theories

The table below shows how theories have changed the ideas that people have about living things, matter, and the Universe.

Theory	Before	After	Critical evidence
germ theory	diseases are caused by a miasma (bad air) which comes from rotting organic matter	diseases are transmitted by microorganisms (e.g., viruses and bacteria)	studies of diseases spreading, and experiments using heat to kill microorganisms
theory of natural selection	species were not related or connected, and had always existed the way they were; the Earth is about 6000 years old	there is variation between animals, and those that survive and reproduce pass on the characteristics to their offspring	modern animals are similar to fossils, or to other species that are extinct
theory of combustion	anything that burns contains a fire-like element called phlogiston that is released during combustion	the air contains oxygen that combines with the matter when it burns	when metals react with air their mass increases
kinetic theory	the idea of four elements (earth, air, fire, and water) had been adapted by alchemists who wanted to turn ordinary metals into gold	matter is made of particles, and gas pressure is produced by the collision of gas particles with its container	air has mass/weight, and decreasing the volume of a gas increases its pressure
the Big Bang theory	the Universe is in a steady state – it is unchanging and has always been this way	the Universe has been expanding since the Big Bang about 14 billion years ago	galaxies are moving away from the Earth, and more distant galaxies are moving faster

B Write down a piece of evidence that you have learnt that showed that everything does not orbit the Earth.

There are many unanswered questions in science. Some examples are:
- what is the link between the brain and what we think?
- what will happen to our Universe?

There are lots of scientists working on these and other questions to produce a theory that explains the evidence.

Key Words
evidence, model, theory, law

Link
You learnt about the heliocentric model of the Solar System in Book 1, 7.2.4 The Moon and changing ideas. You learnt about evolution in 10.3 Evolution and combustion in 6.3.2 Combustion.

▲ An old theory said that wood releases phlogiston when it burns.

Summary Questions

1. Write down the definition of a theory.
   (1 mark)

2.
   a Name a theory that has changed and a piece of evidence for it.
   (2 marks)

   b Explain why theories are used in science.
   (2 marks)

3. Describe the role of evidence in supporting theories.
   (3 marks)

13 Review theories 2

Learning objectives
After this section you will be able to:
- describe the role of argumentation in the development of a theory
- explain why some theories take a long time to be established.

A scientist proposed that the continents of the Earth were moving over 40 years before the theory was accepted. Why does it take so long for ideas to change?

How do ideas change, and how long does it take?
The information in the table in 12 Review theories 1 might make you think that one piece of scientific evidence is enough to change from one theory to another. This is not how science works. It takes a lot of debate, **argumentation**, and time for a new theory to be accepted.

The role of evidence
In the examples in the table there is a brief description of some of the evidence that led to a change in the theory. Some of the evidence was generated by new technologies, like microscopes and telescopes. Other evidence came from new types of experiment or ways of thinking. In all of the examples there was a range of evidence that led scientists to move away from one theory and accept the new theory. This happens when:

- there are new observations or data that the old theory cannot explain
- the new theory is better at explaining observations or data than the old theory, or gave a simpler explanation
- the new theory is better at predicting what would happen in new experiments.

New evidence is critical. Without it there is no reason to move away from the old theory.

▲ The evidence for Alfred Wegener's theory of continental drift was gathered after he died. We know from underwater volcanoes that the continents drift by about 2 cm per year.

▲ This is how Alfred Wegener thought the world looked millions of years ago before the continents drifted.

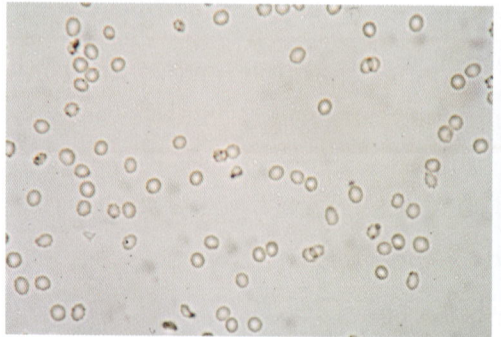

▲ The first person to see red blood cells probably saw an image like that in the left. Now more powerful microscopes can image microbeads on a single blood cell.

• Enquiry processes

A Write down one reason why a new theory can be better than an old theory.

It often takes years or decades for a new theory to be accepted. This is for a variety of reasons.

- Scientists are people. They hold on to ideas that are familiar to them, and can be unwilling to accept new ideas.
- There are cultural or religious reasons for not accepting a new idea. You learnt about that when you studied the changing model of the Solar System.

The role of argumentation

For a theory to change the scientific community has to accept the new idea. This means that the scientist or scientists who believe that the new idea is correct have to convince other scientists. They can try to do that in a variety of ways:

- publishing their work for other scientists to read
- discussing the new theory, and the evidence for the new theory, at meetings.

The role of argumentation is extremely important in science. Argumentation is not the same as having an argument. Scientists meet to share what they have learnt, and to challenge each other about the evidence.

B Write down what argumentation means.

▲ This cartoon, which appeared in a newspaper in 1874, was drawn by someone who did not agree with Darwin's theory.

Key Word

argumentation

◀ Scientists meet at a conference to discuss the evidence for new ideas.

It is essential that a new theory is tested, and scientists try to find out why it could be wrong. They might point to:

- evidence that contradicts the new theory
- phenomena that the new theory does not explain very well.

This means that when the theory is accepted it is much stronger.

Summary Questions

1 Explain why it takes new evidence to change an existing theory.

(1 mark)

2
 a Write down two reasons why a new theory may be accepted.
(2 marks)
 b Write down two reasons why a new theory may not be accepted.
(2 marks)

3 Suggest what might happen if argumentation was not a part of the development of scientific theories.

(3 marks)

1 Forces

You may have seen videos of skydivers jumping out of a plane and landing safely. Their motion changes between jumping and landing. Understanding the forces acting on an object allows you to explain how it is moving, or not moving.

The air skydivers move through is a fluid – it is like a spread-out liquid. In this Big Idea you will learn about pressure in fluids (gases and liquids) and relate it to floating and sinking. You will also learn about the pressure of one solid object, like the skydiver, on another solid object, like the ground.

Q How do brakes on cars and bikes work?

You already know

- Some forces need contact between two objects.
- Friction, air resistance, and water resistance act between moving surfaces to slow things down.
- Most forces require direct contact.
- The shapes of solid objects made from some materials can be changed by squashing, stretching, bending, and twisting.

BIG Questions

- Why is there so little friction on some surfaces, like ice, but not others, like wood?
- Why do you get put on weighing scales before you do a bungee jump?
- Why don't earthmovers sink?

Picture Puzzler
Key Words

Can you solve this Picture Puzzler?

The first letter of each of these images spells out a science word that you will come across in this book.

Picture Puzzler
Close Up

Can you tell what this zoomed-in picture is?
Clue: Friction is very important when you use one of these to start a fire.

Making connections

In your GCSE course you will learn about work done against frictional forces and the effects of work done. You will interpret braking distances in terms of friction.

You will also learn about elastic and inelastic behaviour, and the work done in stretching a spring.

You will also use a simple model to explain the variation of pressure with the height of the atmosphere.

You will also learn how to calculate the pressure of a column of liquid and how that pressure varies with the density of the fluid.

1.3.1 Friction and drag

Learning objectives

After this section you will be able to:
- sketch the forces acting on objects when there are contact forces acting
- describe what happens to a moving object when the resultant force acting on it is zero
- describe the factors that affect the size of the drag forces and friction, and how friction and drag can be reduced.

▲ You need friction to move across surfaces.

Link

You learnt about contact forces and newtons in Book 1, 1.1.1 Introduction to forces, and about resultant forces and equilibrium in 1.1.2 Balanced and unbalanced forces.

Fantastic Fact!

In 1995 Fred Rompelberg travelled at 167 mph.... on a bicycle! He did it by cycling behind a lorry where there was very little air resistance.

Slide your finger along the desk. Does the surface feel smooth or rough? Even really smooth surfaces exert a force.

What is friction?

A surface such as a metal slide in a playground looks and feels really smooth. Now imagine zooming in on it – you will see that it is actually rough.

When a book is resting on the table you can push on it but it may not move. **Friction** grips objects. As you increase the force by pushing harder the book will start to move. If you remove the force the book slows down and stops. This is because the rough surfaces can no longer move past each other.

A State whether friction is greater on a rough or a smooth surface.

What is drag?

As you learnt in Book 1, 1.1.1 Introduction to forces, friction and air resistance are **contact forces**. They act when surfaces are in contact. Forces are measured in **newtons**.

If an object is moving through a fluid, such as air or water, the force slowing it down is called a **drag force**. A dolphin swimming through the water and a surfer paddling through water will both experience **water resistance**. As a snowboarder jumps through the air he will experience **air resistance**.

◄ When you move through water you experience water resistance.

To understand drag forces you need to think about the particles in the air and the water.

Big Idea: Forces 1

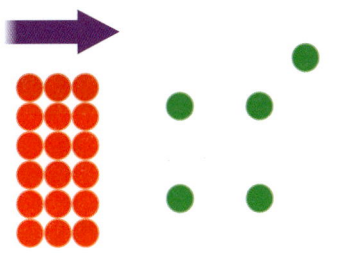 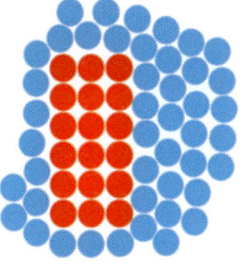

A solid moves through a gas.   A solid moves through a liquid.

▲ A moving object is in contact with air or water particles.

As a dolphin moves through the water it pushes the water particles out of the way. This produces a drag force, which slows it down.

B Sketch a diagram showing the forces on a stone falling through water.

How do drag forces and friction affect motion?

As you learnt in Book 1, 1.1.2 Balanced and unbalanced forces, an object will keep moving at a steady speed in the same direction (or stay still) unless a **resultant force** acts. So if friction or drag forces are acting you need to apply a force to cancel them out, not to keep an object moving.

The resultant force on an object moving with a steady speed in the same direction is zero. The object is in **equilibrium**.

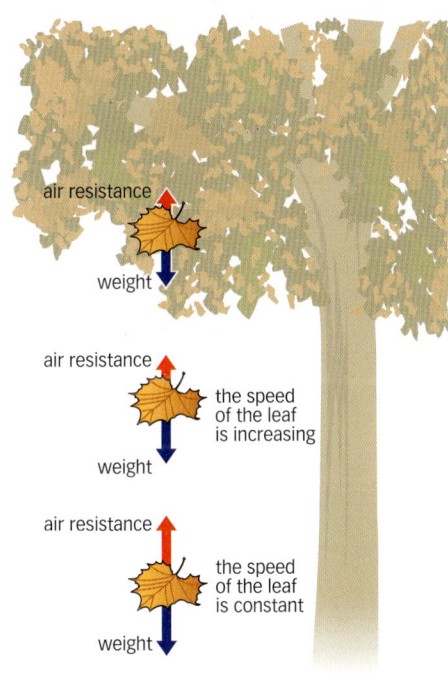

▲ When the resultant force is zero the leaf falls with a steady speed.

C Write down two things that an object does when the resultant force on it is zero.

How can you reduce drag forces and friction?

An Olympic cyclist will tuck her arms in close to her body as she cycles. She will even make sure that her thumbs are as close to the handlebars as possible. This makes her more **streamlined**, which reduces the force of air resistance. One way to reduce friction is by using oil or grease. This is called **lubrication**.

Key Words
friction, contact force, newton, drag force, water resistance, air resistance, resultant force, equilibrium, streamlined, lubrication

Testing a parachute
A company wants to compare different materials for making parachutes. Name **three** ways that they could make it a fair test.

Summary Questions

1. Copy and complete the sentences below.

   The force of _____ acts between two solid surfaces in contact that are sliding across each other. The surfaces are _____ and will grip each other. This is why you need to exert a _____ to make something move. There are two drag forces: _____ and _____. When a moving object is in contact with _____ or _____ particles it has to push them out of the way. *(7 marks)*

2. Describe the factors that affect the size of the frictional force. *(2 marks)*

3.
   a Explain how a bird diving through water can be in equilibrium. *(2 marks)*
   b Sketch a force diagram for the bird in equilibrium. *(2 marks)*

4. A dragster is a car that uses a parachute as a brake. Use the ideas on this page to compare the forces of drag and friction on the car when it accelerates and when it brakes. *(6 marks)*

● Topic 1.3 Contact forces

1.3.2 Squashing and stretching

Learning objectives

After this section you will be able to:
- describe how forces deform objects
- explain how solid surfaces provide a support force
- use Hooke's Law
- explain what 'linear relationship' means.

▲ Even a solid golf ball changes shape when you hit it.

Foul Fact!

When a footballer heads a ball the forces deform both the ball and the footballer's head.

Link

You can learn more about particles in solids, liquids, and gases in Book 1, 5.1.1 The particle model.

Key Words

deformation, compression, tension, reaction, extension, elastic limit, Hooke's Law, linear relationship

Why don't you fall through the chair you're sitting on? The chair changes shape, or deforms, when you sit on it. This produces the force that pushes you up.

Changing shape

Forces can change the shape of objects. This is called **deformation**. Your weight is the force that causes the chair to deform when you sit on it.

When forces squash an object, they cause **compression**. When they stretch an object, they cause **tension**.

A Describe what happens to a tennis ball when it hits the ground.

How can the floor push you up?

The floor pushes up on you when you stand on it. It seems strange to talk about the floor exerting a force on you. You can't see anything happening.

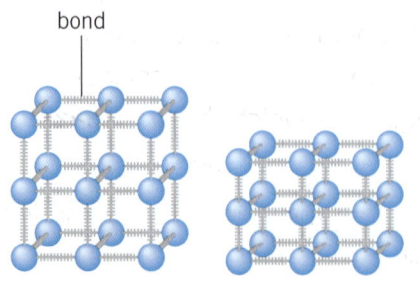

◀ These diagrams show what happens when you exert a force on a solid object.

You compress the bonds when you exert a force.

The floor is a solid. Solids are made up of particles arranged in a regular pattern. The particles are joined strongly together by bonds. This is what happens when you stand on the floor:

- Your weight pushes the particles together.
- The bonds are compressed.
- They push back and support you.

Solid materials are only compressed a very small amount when you apply a force to them. A support force from a chair or the floor is called the **reaction** force.

Stretching

Bungee cords, springs, and even lift cables all stretch when you exert a force on them. The amount that they stretch is called the **extension**.

Big Idea: Forces 1

A bungee cord stretches as the jumper falls. When the bungee cord has stretched as far as it will go, it pulls her back up.

◀ The shape of a bungee cord changes when you stretch it.

What happens when you stretch a spring?
Springs are special. If you *double* the force on the spring the extension will *double*. You can use the length of the spring to measure the size of a force. When you remove the force the spring goes back to its original length.

What's the limit?
At some point the spring will not go back to its original length when you remove the force. This is the **elastic limit**. Trampoline springs are designed to never go past their elastic limit.

Hooke's Law
If the extension doubles when you double the force then the object obeys **Hooke's Law**. The graph of force against extension is a straight line, through the origin (0,0), which shows a **linear relationship**. The force and extension are proportional.

Hooke's Law is a special case. Not everything behaves like a spring when you stretch it. If you double the force on an elastic band the extension may not double.

B Write down what happens to a spring as you increase and then decrease the force on it.

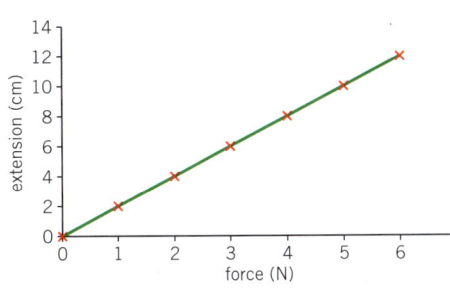

▲ This graph shows how the extension of a spring changes as you pull it.

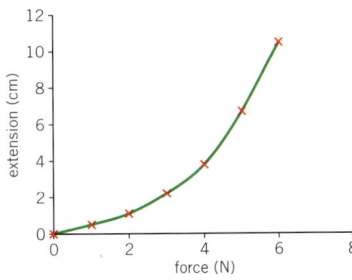

▲ This graph shows the relationship between force and extension for poly(ethene). It is not linear.

A straight-line graph
Using the graph for the extension of the spring below, find the extension when the force is 3 N and again when it is 6 N. Does this spring obey Hooke's Law? Explain your answer.

How long?
You have a spring that is 4 cm long. When you exert a force of 3 N it stretches to a length of 6 cm. What is the extension? What would the extension be if you doubled the force?

Summary Questions

1 Copy and complete the sentences below.

Forces can change the shape of objects or _____ them. Solid surfaces are made of _____. The bonds between particles are compressed when you apply a force. They _____ back on you. This provides a _____ force called the _____ force. When you sit on a wooden chair you _____ it. When you sit on a swing, you _____ the chain.

(7 marks)

2 Describe and explain what happens to the extension of a spring when you double the force on it. *(2 marks)*

3 Use the graphs to the left to compare the behaviour of a spring and poly(ethene).

(6 marks)

● Topic 1.3 Contact forces

1.3.3 Turning forces

Learning objectives

After this section you will be able to:
- describe what is meant by a moment
- calculate the moment of a force

▲ Tightrope walking at Monte Piana, Italy.

▲ You need to apply a turning force to open a door.

Key Words

pivot, moment, newton metres, law of moments, centre of gravity, centre of mass

A tightrope walker uses a long pole to help him to balance.

A force that turns

Whenever you open a door you are using a turning force. A turning force acts a certain distance from a **pivot**.

The turning effect of a force is called a **moment**. The moment depends on the force being applied and how far it is from the pivot.

moment (Nm) = force (N) × perpendicular distance from the pivot (m)

You measure force in newtons (N) and distance in metres (m). You calculate a moment in **newton metres** (Nm).

A State the unit of a moment.

The law of moments

You sit on the left of a see-saw with your friend at the other end. It balances.

The moment of your weight acts anticlockwise. The moment of your friend's weight acts clockwise.

When an object is in equilibrium the sum of the clockwise moments is equal to the sum of the anticlockwise moments. This is the **law of moments**.

▲ These apples are in equilibrium because the clockwise moment equals the anticlockwise moment.

B State the law of moments.

Big Idea: Forces 1

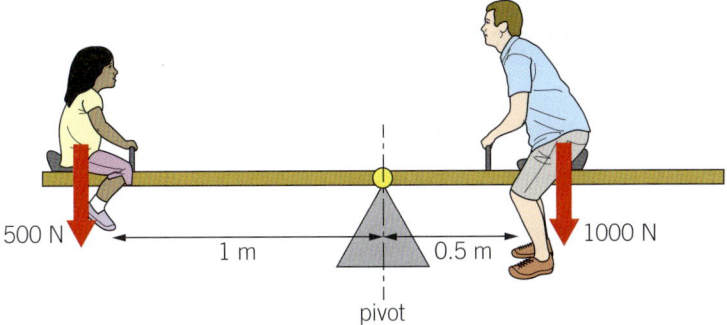

▲ The see-saw doesn't turn if it is in equilibrium.

You can work out if a see-saw is going to be balanced by calculating the clockwise and the anticlockwise moments.

clockwise moment = force × distance on the right
= 1000 N × 0.5 m
= 500 Nm

anticlockwise moment = force × distance on the left
= 500 N × 1 m
= 500 Nm

The moments are the same. The see-saw balances.

Falling over

When you lean back and tip your chair slightly, there is a turning force that brings your chair back. That turning force is your weight acting about the point where the legs touch the floor. If you lean back far enough you will topple over.

All the weight of an object seems to act through a point called the **centre of gravity** (or **centre of mass**). If the centre of gravity is above the pivot there is no turning force. If the centre of gravity is to the left or right of the pivot there will be a turning force.

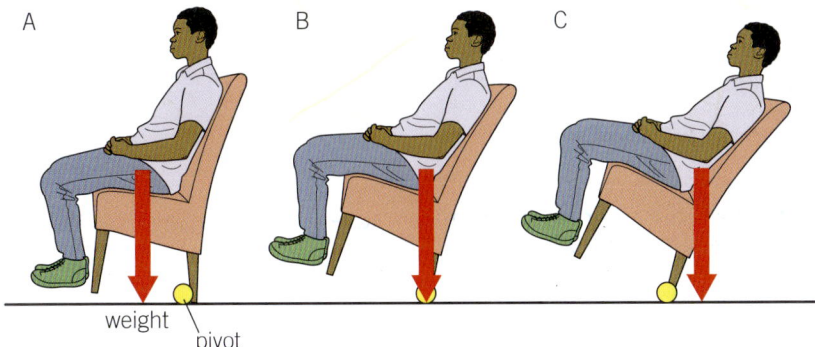

▲ There is a turning force in A and C, but not in B.

C Describe what is meant by centre of gravity.

Sitting on a see-saw

A mother and daughter are on a see-saw 2 m long. The mother has a weight of 600 N and the child has a weight of 150 N.

Calculate where the mother must sit to balance the child who is sitting at the other end.

Fantastic Fact

The world's largest see-saw is in New York. It is just over 24 metres long. It lifts you higher than a house.

Summary Questions

1. Copy and complete the sentences below.

   The _____ effect of a force is called a moment. You can calculate the moment of a force by multiplying the _____ by the _____. If the anticlockwise moments equal the clockwise moments the object will be in _____. This is the _____ of moments. The _____ of an object acts through a point called the centre of _____.

   (7 marks)

2. A girl applies a force of 5 N to close a door. The handle is 0.75 m from the hinge. Calculate the moment of the force.

   (2 marks)

3. Design a balancing game that children can play. Explain in terms of the law of moments and centre of gravity how to play it.

   (6 marks)

● Topic 1.3 Contact forces

1.4.1 Pressure in gases

Learning objectives

After this section you will be able to:
- describe how fluids exert a pressure in all directions
- calculate fluid pressure
- explain the behaviour of objects using ideas of pressure
- describe how atmospheric pressure changes with height.

Have you ever blown a balloon up until it bursts?

◀ The moment when a balloon bursts.

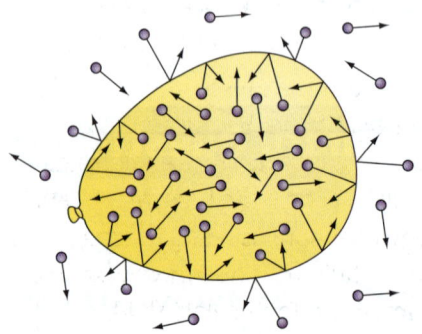

▲ If there are more collisions on the inside than the outside the balloon gets bigger.

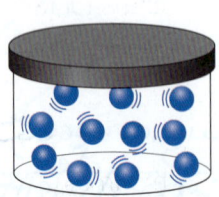

▲ In a smaller volume gas molecules will collide more often with the walls of the container.

Balloon pressure
A student wants to investigate how the volume of a fixed amount of air in a balloon changes with temperature. Write a plan for the investigation.

What is a fluid pressure?

You are surrounded by a **fluid** called air. A fluid is a substance with no fixed shape, like a gas or a liquid. Gases and liquids contain atoms or molecules that collide with the surfaces to produce fluid **pressure**. Pressure in a gas or a liquid acts in all directions, so when you blow up a balloon it inflates in all directions.

Lots of collisions of air molecules, such as inside a balloon, make a high gas pressure. There is a big force over a small area.

Calculating fluid pressure

You calculate the pressure of a gas or liquid using this equation:

$$\text{fluid pressure (N/m}^2\text{)} = \frac{\text{force (N)}}{\text{area (m}^2\text{)}}$$

You measure force in newtons (N) and area in metres squared m^2.

For example, inside a balloon the force exerted by the gas on an area of 0.0001 m^2 is 11 N.

A Write down the direction, or directions, that pressure in a gas acts.

$$\text{fluid pressure (N/m}^2\text{)} = \frac{\text{force (N)}}{\text{area (m}^2\text{)}}$$

$$= \frac{11 \text{ N}}{0.0001 \text{ m}^2}$$

$$= 110\,000 \text{ N/m}^2.$$

Big Idea: Forces 1

This is equivalent to a force of 110 000 N acting on a m² of the balloon. This force is the same as the weight of about six cars!

B Write down the two quantities you need to know to calculate fluid pressure.

You increase **gas pressure** if you squash or heat a gas. The same amount of gas in a smaller volume results in more collisions between air molecules and the container walls, so the pressure is higher.

Atmospheric pressure

There is air all around you. The air exerts a pressure on your body all the time called **atmospheric pressure**. You do not feel the pressure. It is cancelled out by the pressure of the gases and liquids in your body pushing out.

◀ Marshmallows contain pockets of air that expand when you pump out the air around them.

Changing atmospheric pressure

The atmospheric pressure near the ground is bigger than the pressure higher up. Near the ground there is more air above you, so the weight of air above you is heavier. The pressure is higher.

The gas has a higher density at sea level because gravity pulls the air molecules towards the Earth. This makes it harder for mountain climbers to breathe because there is less oxygen.

Mountaineers often take oxygen tanks when they climb high mountains such as Everest. The tanks contain oxygen gas that has been compressed into a small volume.

C State what happens to the atmospheric pressure as you go up a mountain.

Key Words

fluid, pressure, gas pressure, atmospheric pressure

Foul Fact

Think of your favourite famous person. When you breathe in you are breathing in at least 10 air molecules that they have breathed out.

Link

You can learn more about gas pressure in Book 1, 5.1.7 Gas pressure.

Summary Questions

1. 🧪 Copy the sentences below, choosing the correct bold words.

   A gas exerts a pressure on the walls of its container because the particles **collide with/stick to** the walls. The pressure is exerted in **all/one** direction. As you go deeper into a fluid the pressure **decreases/increases**. To calculate fluid pressure you need to know the **force/mass** and the **area/temperature**.

   (5 marks)

2. 🧪🧪 Draw diagrams to explain the size of the marshmallows before and after you remove the air around them.

   (2 marks)

3. 🧪🧪🧪 A climber climbs a mountain.
   a Explain why he might take a cylinder of oxygen with him.

   (3 marks)

   b There is 200 N on each 0.002 m² of a mountaineer at the bottom of a mountain. Calculate the fluid pressure. Describe and explain what happens to the force on this area as he climbs.

   (3 marks)

● Topic 1.4 Pressure

1.4.2 Pressure in liquids

Learning objectives

After this section you will be able to:
- state how liquid pressure changes with depth
- explain why some things float and some things sink, and how area affects upthrust
- calculate pressure in liquids in a range of situations
- explain how hydraulic machines work.

How do you squash a polystyrene cup without touching it? Take it deep beneath the sea and the pressure in the water will do it for you.

Liquid pressure

Water is a fluid. When you swim underwater it exerts a pressure on you. The water molecules are pushing on each other and on surfaces, and this **liquid pressure** acts in all directions.

When you squeeze a bag with holes in it the water is pushed out of all the holes because of liquid pressure. The water comes straight out of each hole and then falls because of gravity.

If you put water in a syringe, cover the end, and try to compress the liquid you will find it impossible. Liquids are **incompressible**. This is because the particles in a liquid are touching each other and there is very little space between them.

Liquids pass on any pressure applied to them. We use this property of liquids to make hydraulic machines, like brakes in a car.

◀ The cup on the left was taken down to a depth of 3000 m.

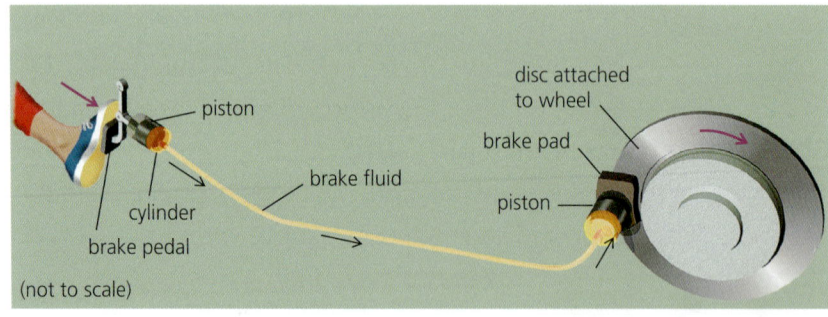

▲ The hydraulic fluid transmits the force of the driver's foot on the brake to the brake pads and discs in a car.

▲ The water comes out in all directions.

A Write down the direction, or directions, that pressure in a liquid acts.

Why does it float?

A primary-school student says that 'heavy things sink and light things float'.

Use the example of a ferry to explain to them why that is not the case.

Pressure and depth

The wall of a dam is not straight. It curves outwards at the bottom. The pressure at the bottom of the lake is bigger than the pressure at the top. The pressure at a particular depth in a liquid depends on the weight of water above it. This is like atmospheric pressure. The pressure at any point in a fluid depends on the weight of fluid above that point.

Big Idea: Forces 1

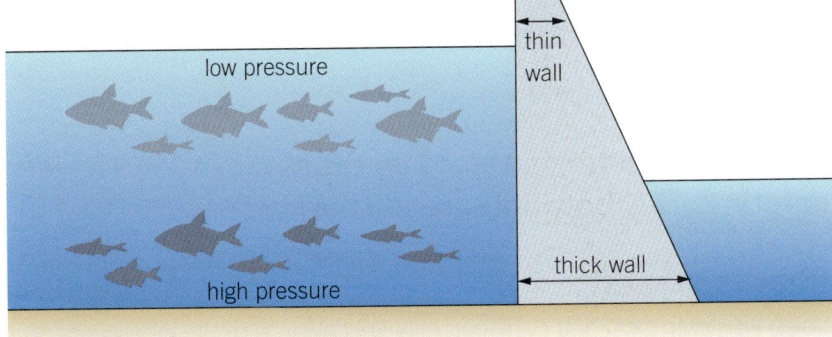

▲ A dam is thicker at the bottom.

B State what happens to liquid pressure as you go deeper in a lake.

Floating and sinking

Upthrust acts on any object that is floating, or is submerged in a liquid. It is easy to work out why a rubber duck floats. There are lots more water molecules hitting the bottom of the rubber duck than there are air molecules hitting the top. There is a resultant force acting on the duck, called upthrust. The duck sinks until there is enough upthrust to balance the weight. If the area in contact with the water is too small, there is not enough upthrust to balance the weight, so it sinks.

The underside of a boat has an area of 10 m², and a weight of 1000 N. It sinks to a depth where the pressure produces a force to balance its weight. At that depth:

$$\text{pressure (N/m}^2) = \frac{\text{force (N)}}{\text{area (m}^2)}$$

$$= \frac{1000\,\text{N}}{10\,\text{m}^2}$$

$$= 100\,\text{N/m}^2.$$

When a submarine is submerged there is a difference in pressure between the top and bottom of the submarine. That produces a force that pushes the submarine up and balances the weight.

C Write down two factors that affect the upthrust on a floating object.

Key Words

liquid pressure, incompressible, upthrust

Fantastic Fact

The water pressure at the bottom of the Atlantic Ocean is equivalent to the weight of eight cars pushing on an area the size of your thumb.

Link

You learnt about upthrust in Book 1, 1.1.1 Introduction to forces.

Summary Questions

1. Copy and complete the sentences below.
   The pressure in a liquid acts in _____ directions. The pressure _____ as you go deeper because the _____ of the water above you gets _____. The difference in pressure explains why there is a force called _____ on a floating object. (5 marks)

2.
   a Explain in terms of pressure why a boat made of modelling clay floats. (2 marks)
   b Explain why the same mass of modelling clay shaped into a ball sinks. (2 marks)
   c Calculate the water pressure when the force exerted by the water is 2000 N, and the area is 0.5 m². (2 marks)

3. You push a ping pong ball to the bottom of a bucket of water. Explain in detail what happens to the ball when you let it go. (6 marks)

4. A hydraulic machine has two pistons of area 1 cm² and 10 cm². Calculate the force exerted by the large cylinder if you exert a force of 25 N on the small cylinder. (2 marks)

● Topic 1.4 Pressure

1.4.3 Stress on solids

Learning objectives

After this section you will be able to:
- state what is meant by stress
- explain the effect of solid surfaces on each other using ideas about stress.

▲ There is no wind on the Moon to blow Neil Armstrong's footprints away.

▲ The tracks on the earthmover stop it sinking into the mud.

Key Words
stress, newtons per metre squared

When Neil Armstrong walked on the Moon in 1969 he left footprints. The footprints are still there.

What is stress?

When you stand on any surface you exert a force on it because of your weight. Your weight is spread out over the area of your foot. You are exerting a pressure on the ground, called **stress**. If you are standing on a soft surface such as mud the pressure might be big enough for you to sink.

An earthmover is very heavy. It has a weight of about a million newtons, the same as about 15 000 people! A single person standing on the same muddy ground might sink. The earthmover does not sink because its weight is spread out over a bigger area.

The stress acts in a direction that is at 90°, or normal, to the surface.

A State the direction in which stress acts.

How do you calculate stress?

Stress is a measure of how much force is applied over a certain area. You calculate stress using this equation:

$$\text{stress (N/m}^2\text{)} = \frac{\text{force (N)}}{\text{area (m}^2\text{)}}$$

You measure force in newtons (N) and area in metres squared (m^2). Stress is measured in **newtons per metre squared** (N/m^2).

Sometimes it is easier to measure smaller areas in centimetres squared (cm^2). If you measure the area in cm^2 then the stress is measured in N/cm^2.

When you do calculations it is very important to look at the units of area. If you write them next to the number in your equation then you will see which unit of pressure you need to use.

B State the units of stress.

Fantastic Fact

To produce the same stress on the floor that you exert when you push in a drawing pin, you would need over 5000 people standing on your shoulders.

• Big Idea: Forces 1

Big and small stresses

The studs on the bottom of a hockey or football boot have a small area compared with the area of the foot. This produces a bigger stress. The studs sink into the ground and help the player to move quickly.

The weight of a hockey player is 600 N.

The area of her two feet is 200 cm².

stress = force / area
= 600 N / 200 cm²
= 3 N/cm²

The total area of the studs is 20 cm².

stress = force / area
= 600 N / 20 cm²
= 30 N/cm²

▲ The stress is bigger if your weight is concentrated over a smaller area, such as your hand.

▲ The studs increase the grip on the ground.

▲ Snowshoes increase the area of your feet so the stress is less.

A solid can scratch another solid if the stress is large. You sink into soft surfaces like mud or snow if your weight is spread over a small area.

Spreading out the force over a large area, by wearing snow shoes for example, stops you sinking. Stresses can break the surface of a material, which produces a scratch.

Finding the force

Which of these is the correct equation for working out the force?

A force = stress ÷ area
B force = stress × area
C force = area ÷ stress

Summary Questions

1. Copy the sentences below, choosing the correct bold words.

   Stress is a measure of how much **force/mass** there is on a certain **area/volume**. A nail scratches a surface because the area of the nail is **big/small**. A large stress can **break/heat** a surface. The stress needed to **float on/sink into** a solid surface depends on the type of surface.

   (5 marks)

2. A gymnast has a weight of 600 N. The area of each hand is 150 cm². Calculate the stress on the floor when he is doing a handstand.

   (3 marks)

3. The point of a nail has an area of 0.25 cm², and an average person has a weight of 700 N. Explain in detail why it is possible to lie on a bed of 4000 nails, but not on a single nail.

   (6 marks)

• Topic 1.4 Pressure

1 Forces: Summary

Key Points

Contact forces
- When the forces acting on an object are equal in size and acting in opposite directions then they are balanced and the object is in equilibrium. The resultant force is zero.
- There is a force of friction when objects are in contact because surfaces are rough. Friction can be reduced by lubrication.
- Drag (air and water resistance) slows objects down because the object has to push the air or water out of the way. Drag can be reduced by streamlining.
- Forces can deform objects.
- Springs or ropes extend when you apply a force and produce a tension.
- For some objects, like springs, if you double the force the extension will double. The extension is proportional to the force. This is Hooke's Law, and is a special case. There is a linear relationship between them and the graph is a straight line through (0,0).

Pressure
- Fluids, like gases or liquids, exert a pressure on a surface because of the collisions of molecules with the surface.
- Atmospheric pressure decreases with height, and water pressure increases with depth.
- Fluid pressure or stress on a surface = force/area, measured in N/m^2 or N/cm^2. The pressure tells you how the force is spread out over an area.
- The turning effect of a force is called a moment. You calculate a moment by multiplying the force by the distance from a pivot.
- If the clockwise moments acting on an object equal the anticlockwise moments the object will be in equilibrium. This is how see-saws balance.

Key Words
friction, contact force, newton, drag force, water resistance, air resistance, resultant force, equilibrium, streamlined, lubrication, deformation, compression, tension, reaction, extension, elastic limit, Hooke's Law, linear relationship, pivot, moment, newton metres, law of moments, centre of gravity, centre of mass, fluid, pressure, gas pressure, atmospheric pressure, liquid pressure, incompressible, upthrust, stress, newtons per metre squared

Case study

Alien landing
When NASA sent a probe to Cassini, one of the moons of Saturn, they did not know what would happen. They called it 'crash or splash'.

Imagine landing a spacecraft on an unknown planet.

Task
Tell the story of the journey of your spacecraft as it approaches and lands. You need to decide:
- the type of atmosphere on the planet, and how it changes close to the surface
- whether there are oceans, and what they are made of
- whether your spacecraft would float or sink on any ocean.

What happens? Can you land safely? Do you survive?

End-of-Big Idea questions

1 Match the word or phrase and its definition.

A: Fluid pressure
B: Atmospheric pressure
C: Drag
D: Friction

1: a force opposing motion when one surface is a fluid
2: a force opposing motion when both surfaces are solid
3: produced by the collision of particles with a surface
4: caused by the weight of air above a point

(3 marks)

2 You can make a hole in a piece of wood if you bang in a nail with a hammer. If you hit the wood with the hammer it does not make a hole. Choose the best explanation for this from the statements below:

A The area of the nail is much smaller so the pressure is smaller.
B The area of the nail is much smaller so the pressure is bigger.
C The area of the hammer is bigger so the pressure is bigger.

(1 mark)

3 a Explain why it can hurt your hands when you carry heavy shopping in carrier bags.

(2 marks)

b Explain why road bikes have narrow tyres but off-road bikes have wide tyres.

(2 marks)
(4 marks)

4 An acrobat can balance on one finger. Her weight is 500 N, and the area of one finger is 0.0001 m². Calculate the stress on the floor.

(3 marks)

5 You do not see most of an iceberg because most of it is underwater.

a Explain in terms of forces why an iceberg floats. *(1 mark)*

b You model icebergs with ice from the freezer. You make two different shapes that have the same mass:

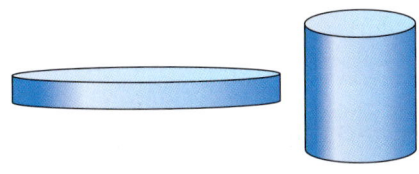

Suggest and explain in terms of fluid pressure what happens when you put your 'icebergs' in water. *(3 marks)*
(4 marks)

6 Look at the diagram of an arm holding a phone. The phone has a weight of 1.5 N.

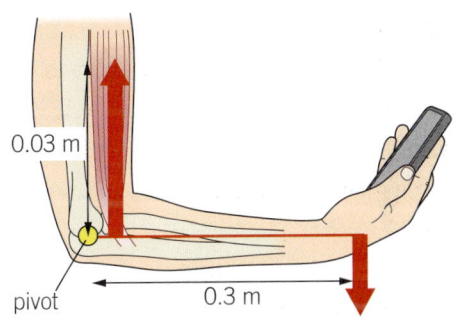

a Calculate the moment of the force exerted by the phone. *(2 marks)*

b Calculate the force that the muscle exerts to keep the phone in equilibrium. *(2 marks)*

c Explain why the force exerted by the muscle is much greater than the weight of the phone. *(2 marks)*
(6 marks)

7 You buy a bag of crisps in an airport. After take-off you take the crisps out of your rucksack. Explain in detail why the bag has expanded.

(6 marks)

2 Electromagnets

You have probably played with magnets and felt what happens when you push two magnets together. There are lots of magnets in your house and many of them you cannot see. In this Big Idea you will learn how to make a magnet using electricity, and about the different ways that you can make it stronger. You will learn how electromagnetic devices like bells and loudspeakers work. Finally, you will model magnetic fields and find out about the Earth's magnetic field.

You already know

- Magnetic forces act at a distance.
- Magnets attract and repel each other, and attract some materials but not others.
- Some materials are 'magnetic materials'.

Q Why does a magnet stick to a fridge, but not a wall?

BIG Questions

- Which device in your house protects you from a dangerous electric current, and how does it work?
- How can you make a magnet strong enough to lift a car?
- Why does a compass point 'north'?

Picture Puzzler
Key Words

Can you solve this Picture Puzzler?

The first letter of each of these images spells out a science word that you will come across in this book.

Picture Puzzler
Close Up

Can you tell what this zoomed-in picture is?

Clue: You will use these tiny things to investigate magnetic fields.

Making connections

In your GCSE course you will learn about the force on a wire in a magnetic field and how this applies to electric motors.

You will also learn about electromagnetic induction and generators.

You will also learn how the electricity generated in power stations is supplied to homes and businesses using transformers and the National Grid.

2.3.1 Magnets and magnetic fields

Learning objectives
After this section you will be able to:
- describe how magnets interact
- describe how magnetic field diagrams tell you about the direction and strength of a magnetic field
- explain observations about navigation using the Earth's magnetic field.

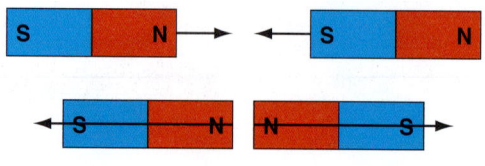

▲ Magnets can attract or repel other magnets.

Memory jogger
Remember it like this: 'Like poles repel, unlike poles attract.'

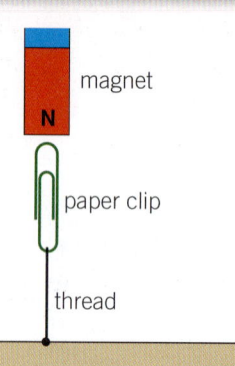

▲ There is a force on a steel paper clip in a magnetic field.

Fantastic Fact
The Earth's magnetic field keeps flipping. About 500 000 years ago the magnetic north pole was actually the south pole.

With a magnet you can make something move without even touching it.

◄ Ferrofluid is a special liquid that is magnetic.

A **magnet** has two **magnetic poles**, a north-seeking pole and a south-seeking pole.

- **North-seeking poles** *repel* **north-seeking poles**.
- **South-seeking poles** *repel* **south-seeking poles**.
- **North-seeking poles** *attract* **south-seeking poles**.

A Name the two poles of a magnet.

Some materials are magnetic. If you put iron, steel, cobalt, or nickel in a **magnetic field** they experience a **magnetic force**. This is a non-contact force. The force is stronger the closer you are to the magnet.

What is a magnetic field?
In an electric field there is a force on a charge. In a magnetic field there is a force on a magnet or a magnetic material. You can draw lines called **magnetic field lines** to represent the field. The field lines are like elastic bands that try to straighten. This is one way of explaining attraction and repulsion.

You can find out the shape of a magnetic field in two ways:
- using plotting compasses
- using iron filings

• Big Idea: Electromagnets 2

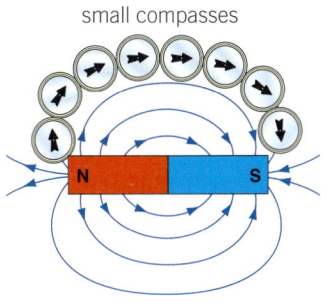

▲ The field around a bar magnet.

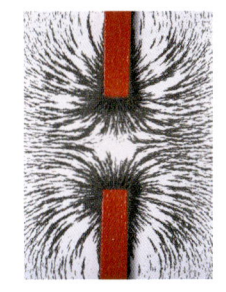

▲ Two magnets repelling.

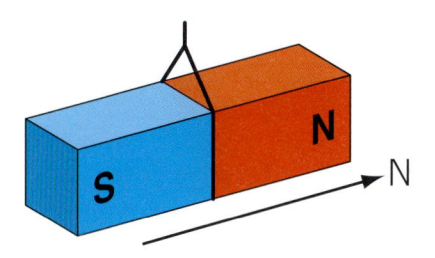

▲ A magnet lines up with the Earth's magnetic field.

The needle of a compass lines up with the magnetic field. So do the iron filings. The magnetic field lines go from the north pole to the south pole of the magnet, with arrows pointing from the north to the south pole.

- If the magnetic field lines are closer together this shows that the magnetic field is stronger.
- A **permanent magnet** is a magnet that has its own magnetic field.
- A magnetic material will experience a force if it is placed in or rolled through a magnetic field.

There is also a magnetic field around a wire with a current flowing in it.

B State two ways that you can find out the shape of a magnetic field.

The Earth's magnetic field

If you hang a magnet up it will line up in a direction pointing north to south. This is because it is in the magnetic field of the Earth.

The Earth behaves as if there is a huge bar magnet inside it. There is not really a bar magnet, and physicists are not sure what produces the Earth's magnetic field. People have used compasses, which contain a small bar magnet, to navigate for thousands of years.

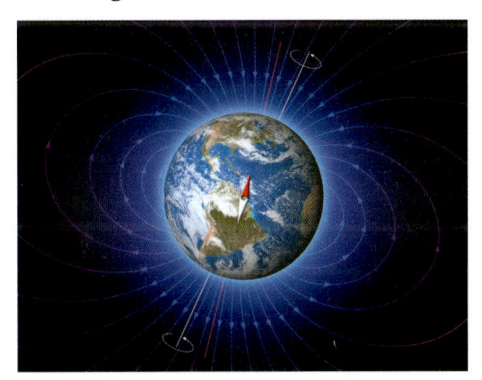

▲ The Earth's magnetic field is the same as that of a big bar magnet with the south pole at the top of the planet.

Key Words

magnet, magnetic poles, magnetic field, magnetic force, magnetic field lines, permanent magnet

How strong?
A student wants to measure the strength of different types of magnet by holding up a paperclip as shown in the diagram on the opposite page. Draw a table for their results.

Summary Questions

1. Copy and complete the sentences below.

   Magnets have a _____ pole and a _____ pole. Two poles that are the same will _____ and two poles that are different will _____. The needle of a _____ lines up in the _____ _____ of a magnet.

   (6 marks)

2. Explain why the needle of a compass always points in the same direction wherever you point it in a room.

   (2 marks)

3. Draw the pattern of magnetic field lines around attracting and repelling magnets and use them to explain why the magnets attract or repel.

   (6 marks)

• Topic 2.3 Magnetism

2.4.1 Electromagnets

Learning objectives

After this section you will be able to:
- describe how to make an electromagnet
- use a diagram to explain how to make an electromagnet and how to change its strength
- describe how the strength of an electromagnet changes with distance.

Permanent magnets are fun, but you can't turn them off.

The magnetic field around a wire
A wire with an electric current flowing through it also has a magnetic field around it. You can investigate the field with a plotting compass or iron filings. The field lines are circles.

Making an electromagnet
You can make a circular loop of wire and pass a current through it. The magnetic field lines at the centre of the loop are straight.

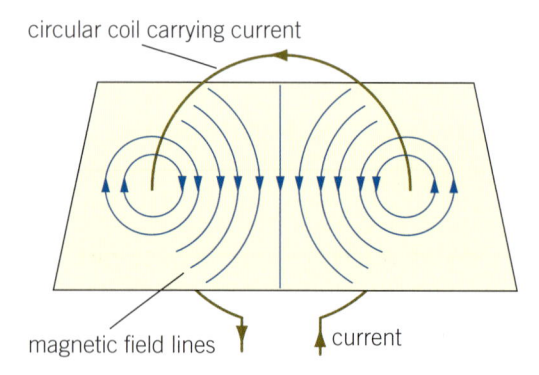

◀ The magnetic field around a loop of wire.

The magnetic field around a single loop isn't very strong. You can wind lots of loops together to make a coil, called a **solenoid**. If a current flows through it you have an **electromagnet**.

You can turn an electromagnet on and off by turning the current on and off. The magnetic field is only produced when the current is flowing in the wire.

▲ The magnetic field lines around a wire are circular.

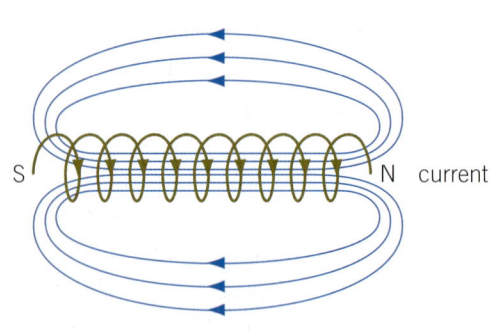

▲ The magnetic field around a coil of wire carrying a current.

Using a core
Electromagnets usually have a magnetic material in the centre of the coil, called a **core**. This makes the electromagnet much stronger. Most cores are made of iron. Iron is easy to **magnetise** but loses its magnetism easily.

Steel is hard to magnetise but keeps its magnetism. If you had a steel core in an electromagnet you could not turn the electromagnet off, because the steel would still be magnetic.

Foul Fact
Doctors in hospitals have used electromagnets to remove steel splinters from a patient's eye.

A State the type of material you can use for the core of an electromagnet.

● Big Idea: Electromagnets 2

Iron core with current ON

Iron core with current OFF

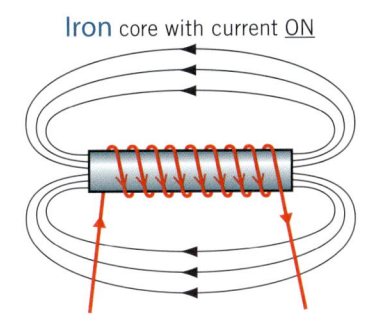

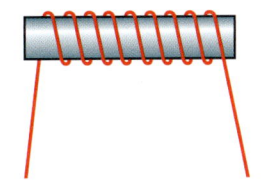

Steel core with current ON

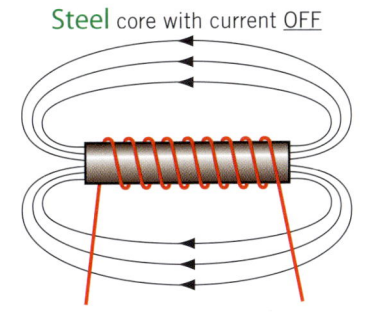

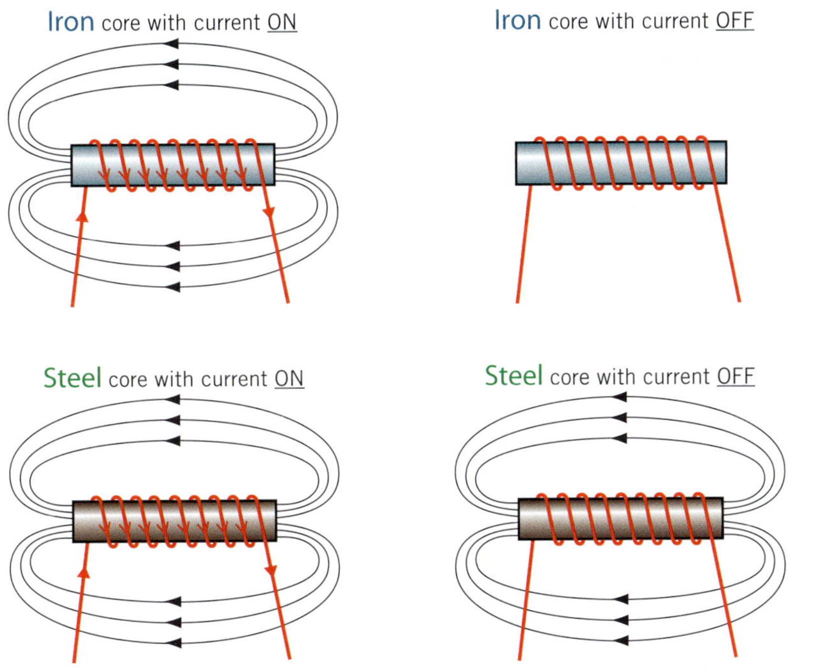

Steel core with current OFF

▲ The steel core of an electromagnet stays magnetic when you turn the current off

▲ The strength of an electromagnet depends on the number of turns on the coil, the current, and the core.

How do I make an electromagnet stronger?

The strength of an electromagnet depends on:

- the number of turns, or loops, on the coil. More turns of wire will make a stronger electromagnet.
- the current flowing in the wire. More current flowing in the wire will make a stronger electromagnet.
- the type of core. Using a magnetic material for the core will make a stronger electromagnet.

B State three things that affect the strength of an electromagnet.

How does the strength of an electromagnet vary with distance?

The strength of a magnetic field around an electromagnet decreases with distance. This also happens to the electric field around a charge, and the gravitational field around a mass.

The magnetic field around a solenoid has the same shape as the field around a bar magnet.

Fantastic Fact

The strongest magnet is an electromagnet that produces a magnetic field 10 million times stronger than the Earth's magnetic field.

Key Words

solenoid, electromagnet, core, magnetise

Summary Questions

1. Copy and complete the sentences below.

   When a _____ flows in a wire it produces a _____ _____ around it. You can make an electromagnet using a _____ of wire with a _____ flowing in it. The strength of an electromagnet _____ with distance from it.

   (5 marks)

2. Use a diagram to describe how to use a nail, a piece of wire, crocodile clips, leads, and a battery to make an electromagnet.

   (2 marks)

3. Use the ideas on these pages to explain in detail why the number of coils, the current, and the type of core affect the strength of an electromagnet.

   (6 marks)

● Topic 2.4 Electromagnets

2.4.2 Using electromagnets

Learning objectives

After this section you will be able to:

- explain why you choose an electromagnet rather than a permanent magnet for a purpose
- describe how electric bells, circuit breakers, and loudspeakers work.

Have you ever travelled on a high-speed train? Trains that use electromagnets can go faster than a Formula 1 car. They don't have an engine. How do they work?

Ringing a bell

You press a switch to make a doorbell ring. The doorbell is an **electric bell** that contains a circuit with an electromagnet, a switch, and a battery in it. The switch completes a circuit and a current flows.

Look at the diagram to the right.

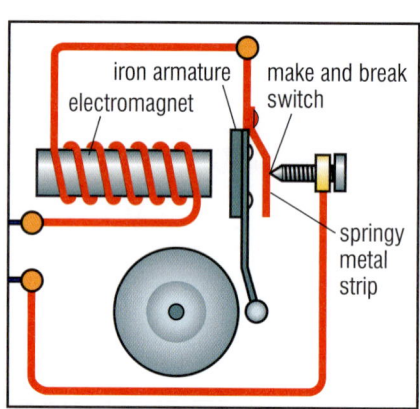

- The electromagnet attracts the iron armature.
- When the armature moves it breaks the circuit, so a current no longer flows.
- The coil and core are no longer magnetic and the springy metal strip returns to its original position, and the bell rings once.
- Now the circuit is complete again, so the armature moves and the bell rings again.

This process carries on until you release the switch.

▲ An electric bell contains a 'make and break' switch, which keeps the bell ringing.

▲ Very powerful magnets on the track repel magnets on the train, lifting it off the tracks.

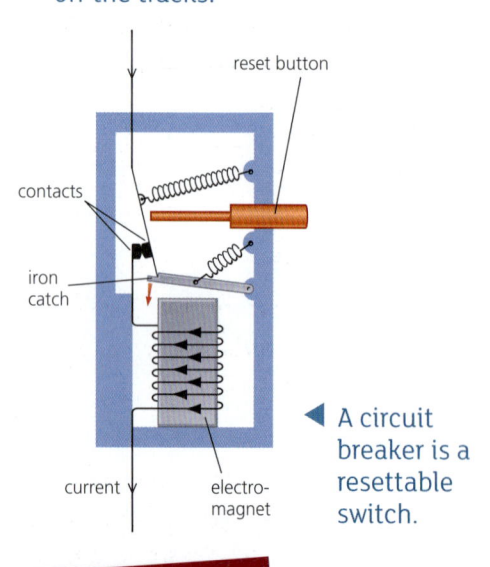

A Describe what happens to the coil of wire when a current flows in it.

Switching off

Some of the wires in the devices in your house carry a large current. If a device is faulty the current it carries could injure you, or worse.

One of the safety devices designed to prevent that is a **circuit breaker**.

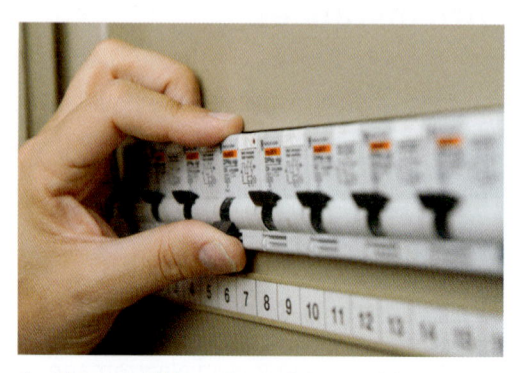

◀ A circuit breaker is a resettable switch.

▲ There will be a board in your house with lots of circuit breakers near your electricity meter. Do not touch the circuit breakers!

Key Words

electric bell, circuit breaker, loudspeaker

● Big Idea: Electromagnets 2

When a large current flows in the wire around the electromagnet, the magnetic field of the electromagnet is strong enough to attract the iron catch. The catch moves down and this breaks the circuit. This is a bit like the electric bell, but instead of 'making and breaking' the circuit, this circuit stays off.

You can turn the device on again by pushing a reset switch.

B Describe what happens in the circuit when you press the reset button.

▲ Inside your earphone is a coil, a cone, and a magnet.

Making sound

Your earphones contain tiny **loudspeakers**.

The electric current from your phone or mp3 player flows in a coil of wire inside the earphone. The coil becomes an electromagnet that changes in strength.

A magnet inside the earphone repels and attracts the electromagnet making the cone move in and out. This makes sound.

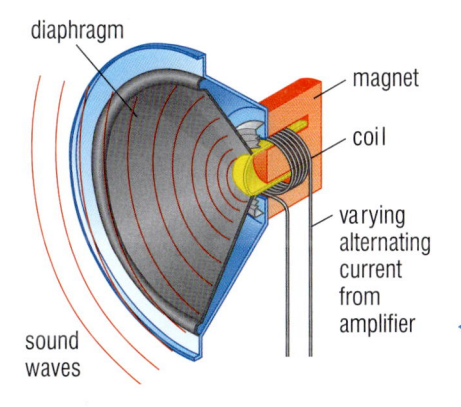

◀ A loudspeaker cone moves in and out to produce sound.

Permanent magnet or electromagnet?

A piece of magnetic material that has been magnetised is a permanent magnet. There are two main differences between permanent magnets and electromagnets:

- You can turn electromagnets on and off.
- You can make electromagnets that are much stronger than permanent magnets.

Permanent magnets and electromagnets both have their uses. You can use a small permanent magnet as a fridge magnet, but you need an electromagnet to lift a car.

C Explain why electromagnets are used to lift up cars in a scrap yard.

Summary Questions

1 Copy and complete the sentences below.

In an electric bell, circuit breaker, or loudspeaker a coil of wire becomes an _____ when a current flows. A bell contains a 'make or break' circuit that makes the bell _____. A circuit breaker is like a _____ you can _____. In a loudspeaker the _____ magnet and electromagnet _____ to make a cone move in and out.

(6 marks)

2 Describe one similarity and one difference between an electric bell and a circuit breaker.

(2 marks)

3 Design a system that uses electromagnets to hold open fire doors. The fire doors should close automatically when the fire alarm button is pressed. Explain in detail how it works.

(6 marks)

● Topic 2.4 Electromagnets

2 Electromagnets: Summary

Key Points

Magnetism
- Magnets have a north-seeking pole and a south-seeking pole. Like poles repel and unlike poles attract. Magnetic field lines go from the north-seeking to the south-seeking pole.
- Magnetic materials feel a force when they are in the region around a magnet, electromagnet, or the Earth, where there is a magnetic field. This is a non-contact force.
- The magnetic field around any magnet gets weaker as you move away.
- The magnetic field of the Earth has the same shape as that of a bar magnet. For thousands of years people have used the magnetic field of the Earth to navigate using compasses. A compass needle is a small magnet that lines up with the magnetic field of the Earth.

Electromagnets
- If a current flows in a coil of wire (called a solenoid) it produces a magnetic field in which a magnetic material will feel a force. This is an electromagnet.
- You model magnetic fields with field lines that show the strength and direction of the field.
- You can turn an electromagnet on and off. You cannot turn a permanent magnet off.
- You can make the electromagnet stronger by using a bigger current or having more coils on the solenoid. You can also use a core made of a magnetic material like iron or steel.
- Electromagnets are used in electric bells, loudspeakers, and circuit breakers.
- Electromagnets can be made to be much stronger than any permanent magnet.

Maths challenge

Mixed up electromagnets!

A student has been investigating the strength of electromagnets. He has had lots of fun changing the number of coils, the type of core, the type of wire wrapped around the core, and the potential difference across the wire. Here is his results table:

Number of coils	Potential difference	Type of core	Type of wire	Number of paperclips
10	1.5 V	iron	copper	4
10	3 V	iron	copper	8
10	4.5 V	iron	copper	12
10	6 V	iron	copper	16
40	3 V	iron	copper	20
30	3 V	iron	copper	16
20	3 V	iron	copper	12
10	3 V	steel	copper	10
10	3 V	aluminium	copper	0
30	3 V	iron	tungsten	3

Use the data to:
- make separate tables for each of the variables that he changed and plot an appropriate graph for each variable
- work out whether tungsten wire or copper wire has the biggest resistance.

Key Words

magnet, magnetic poles, magnetic field, magnetic force, magnetic field lines, permanent magnet, solenoid, electromagnet, core, magnetise, electric bell, circuit breaker, loudspeaker

End-of-Big Idea questions

1. Write down the definitions of the following:
   a. solenoid
   b. electromagnet
   c. permanent magnet
   d. magnetic field.
   (4 marks)

2. There is a magnetic field around a bar magnet.
   a. Draw a diagram to show the magnetic field around a bar magnet. *(2 marks)*
   b. Describe what would happen to the magnets in the diagrams A and B below. *(2 marks)*

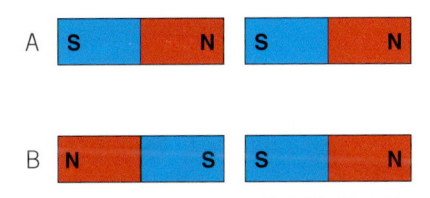

   A S | N   S | N

   B N | S   S | N

   c. State one difference between a permanent magnet and an electromagnet. *(1 mark)*
   (5 marks)

3. There is a magnetic field around the Earth.
   a. Draw a diagram of the magnetic field around the Earth. *(2 marks)*
   b. Explain how you have shown
      i. the direction of the magnetic field *(1 mark)*
      ii. the strength of the magnetic field. *(1 mark)*
   (4 marks)

4. Copy and complete the table below by ticking all of the actions that could make an electromagnet stronger. *(4 marks)*

Action	✓
use a larger current	
use an aluminium core	
wind more turns on the coil	
use a steel core	

5. Electromagnets have lots of uses.
   a. Name two things that you would find in a circuit breaker that you would also find in a loudspeaker and an electric bell. *(2 marks)*
   b. Copy and complete these sentences:
      i. An electric bell is like a loudspeaker because… *(1 mark)*
      ii. A circuit breaker is like an electric bell because… *(1 mark)*
   (4 marks)

6. A surgeon wants to use a magnet to remove metal splinters from a patient's eye.
   a. Suggest and explain whether the surgeon should use an electromagnet or a permanent magnet. *(2 marks)*
   b. Suggest and explain one problem that the surgeon might have when trying to use the magnet. *(2 marks)*
   (4 marks)

7. If you fix two magnets on the desk with poles that are repelling there will be a 'neutral point' somewhere between them where a magnetic material would not feel a force.
   a. Draw a magnetic field line pattern for the arrangement. *(2 marks)*
   b. Explain why no magnetic force can be felt at the 'neutral point'. *(1 mark)*
   c. Explain how the position of the neutral point would change if the strength of the magnets was unequal. *(2 marks)*
   d. Draw a magnetic field line pattern for this arrangement. *(2 marks)*
   (8 marks)

8. People have used compasses to navigate for thousands of years.
   a. Explain how you navigate with a compass. *(2 marks)*
   b. Suggest and explain what would happen if you rolled a strong magnet down a slope. *(2 marks)*
   (4 marks)

3 Energy

Athletes can use energy in chemical stores to run, jump, or throw. Where does this energy end up? There are lots of different ways of transferring energy between stores. In this Big Idea you will learn about doing work and transferring energy with radiation and particles.

Sometimes we want to stop energy being transferred, and you will learn about different ways of stopping energy transfer due to friction and conduction.

Q How does light enable us to see?

You already know

- Vibrations from sounds travel through a medium to the ear.
- Light travels from a light source to our eyes.
- Unsupported objects fall towards the Earth because of the force of gravity.
- Air resistance, water resistance, and friction act between moving surfaces.

BIG Questions

- How are you transferring energy as you read this?
- What happens in terms of energy when you are watching television, or charging your phone?
- How can you reduce your electricity bills?

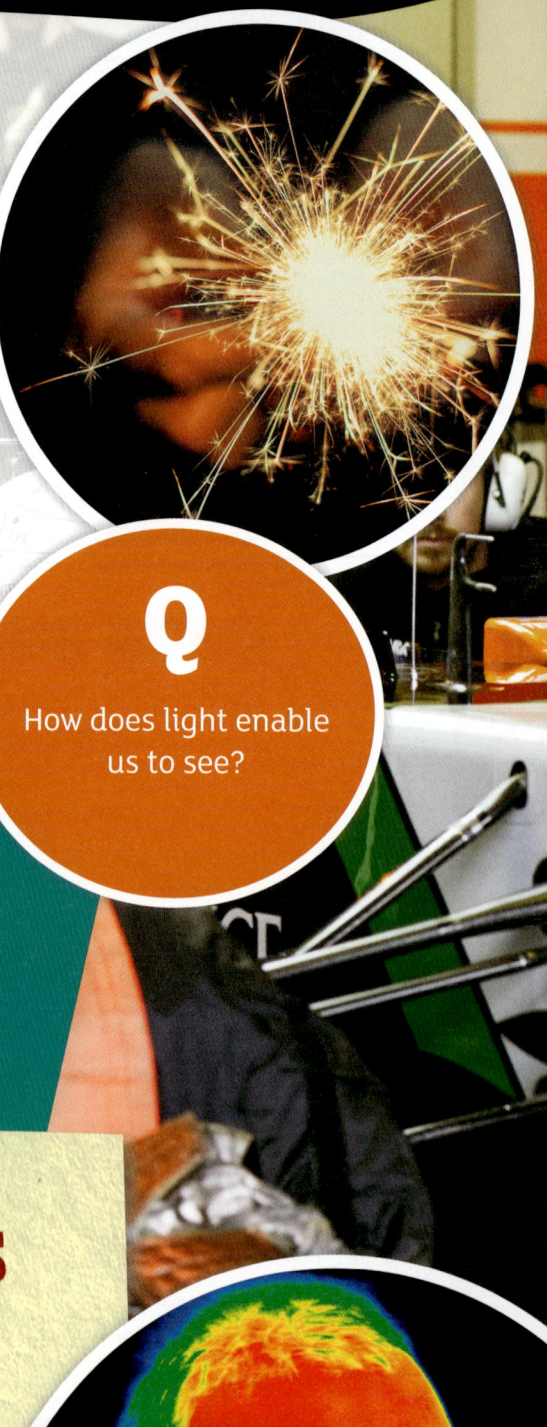

Picture Puzzler
Key Words

Can you solve this Picture Puzzler?

The first letter of each of these images spells out a science word that you will come across in this book.

Picture Puzzler
Close Up

Can you tell what this zoomed-in picture is?

Clue: Not marshmallows, but you can keep ice in this and it won't melt.

Making connections

In your GCSE course you will learn about specific heat capacity, and how to investigate it.

You will also learn about thermal conductivity and how it applies to building houses.

You will learn about black body radiation, and investigate the radiation emitted by different surfaces.

3.3.1 Work, energy, and machines

Learning objectives

After this section you will be able to:
- describe what work is
- describe what simple machines do
- use a diagram to show how a lever works
- compare the work needed to move objects different distances.

▲ You need a pulley system to be able to lower lifeboats from a ship in an emergency.

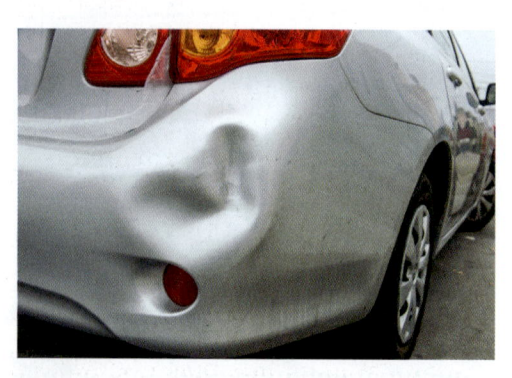

▲ You can do work to deform an object by moving a force over a distance.

Key Words

work, deform, displacement, simple machine, lever, output force, input force

In an emergency on a ship you have to lower lifeboats down to the water. This job would be almost impossible without a simple machine.

Working out work

In physics, the word '**work**' has a special meaning.
- When you lift a book you do work against gravity.
- When you slide the book you do work against friction.
- It takes work to **deform** objects, like stretching elastic or squashing your bed springs.
- When a force moves an object, or deforms it, energy is transferred between stores. The amount of work depends on the size of the force and the distance the object moves from its original position (or **displacement**).

$$\text{work done} = \text{force} \times \text{distance moved}$$
$$(J) \qquad (N) \qquad (m)$$

▲ Lifting a book.
work done = force × distance
= 2 N × 1 m
= 2 J

▲ Sliding a book.
work done = force × distance
= 1 N × 0.2 m
= 0.2 J

A State the definition of work.

Making life easier

A **simple machine** makes it easier to lift things, move things, or turn things. It reduces the force that you need to do a job, or increases the distance that something moves when you apply a force.

A wheel is a simple machine. There is less friction between a rolling wheel and a surface than between a sliding object and the same surface.

● Big Idea: Energy 3

Levers

Most people use a **lever** to open a tin of paint. If you put a screwdriver between the lid and the rim of the tin, you can open the tin with a much smaller force.

The force applied to the lid by the lever (the **output force**) is bigger than the force that you apply with just your hand (the **input force**). A lever is a force multiplier.

Your hand moves down and the other end of the lever moves up. Your hand moves much further than the other end of the lever.

◀ Using a lever can make a job easier.

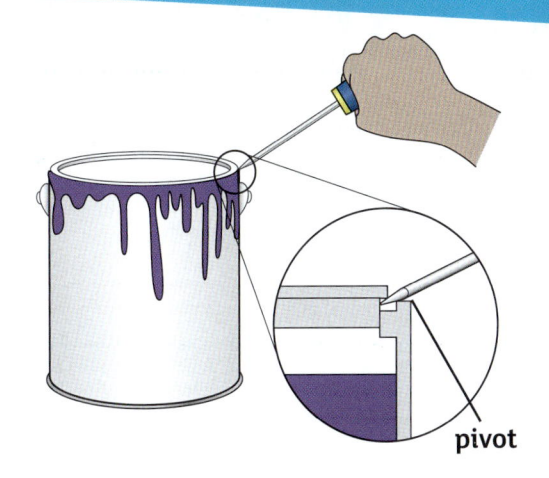

▲ The force may be bigger but the distance is smaller.

Pulleys

You can use a pulley system to lift (or lower) heavy objects.

You can use a pulley to change the direction of the force. The pulley makes it easier to use your weight, but the input and output forces are the same.

In image B on the right, the input force is smaller than the output force, but the distance that you need to move your hand is bigger than the distance moved by the weight.

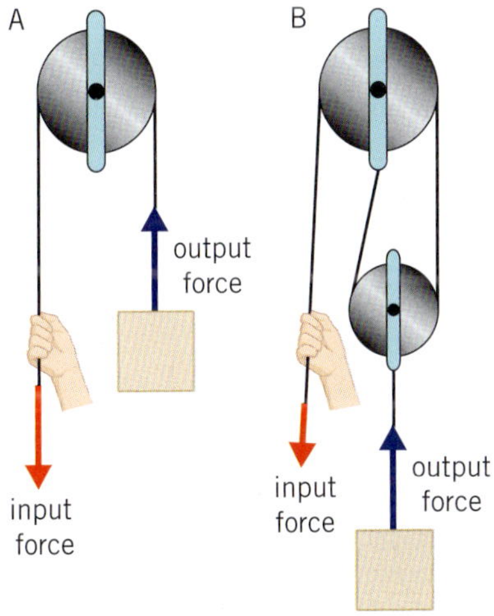

B Name two types of simple machine.

Getting something for nothing?

A small force acting over a big distance produces a big force. The big force can only move a small distance. You cannot get something for nothing.

The reason is the law of conservation of energy. If you increased the distance *as well* as the force then you would get more energy out than you put in. You cannot get out more than you put in.

Summary Questions

1. Copy and complete the sentences below.

   You do more work when a bigger _____ moves an object a bigger _____. A simple _____, like a _____, can be used to open a paint tin because it is a _____ multiplier. A _____ system can make it easier to lift a load. The force you use is _____, but the distance your hand moves is _____. (8 marks)

2.
   a Draw a diagram to show how you can use a lever to lift up one side of a heavy box. (3 marks)
   b Describe how changing the position of the pivot changes the input force and the distance your hand moves. (2 marks)
   c Explain why moving the same box on a trolley would need a smaller input force. (1 mark)

3. A person with a weight of 600 N climbs Mount Everest, a vertical height of 10 km. Compare the work done climbing Mount Everest and climbing 2.5 m upstairs to bed. (4 marks)

● Topic 3.3 Work

3.4.1 Energy and temperature

Learning objectives

After this section you will be able to:
- state the difference between energy and temperature
- state what the thermal energy of an object depends on
- explain, in terms of energy, why objects change temperature.

Hot tyres grip the road much better than cold tyres. Formula 1 drivers heat up their tyres.

What is temperature?

Something that is hotter than your skin will feel hot, and something that is colder than your skin will feel cold. You cannot measure **temperature** with your skin.

You use a **thermometer** to measure temperature. Some thermometers have a liquid inside a very thin glass tube that expands when it is heated. Other thermometers are digital.

We measure temperature in degrees Celsius (°C).

A State the unit of temperature and the unit of energy.

What's the difference?

There is a difference between energy and temperature. You can have a swimming pool and a beaker of water at exactly the same temperature.

Even though they are at the same temperature the swimming pool represents a much bigger **thermal energy store** than the beaker of water.

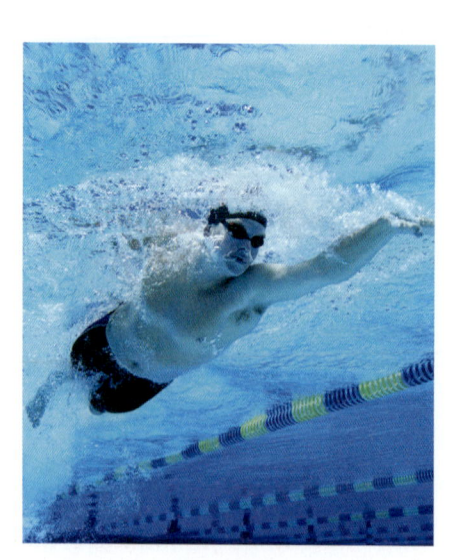

▲ Formula 1 teams heat up their tyres.

◀ Some thermometers use sensors to measure temperature.

▲ Sparks are hot, but they do not have much energy in the thermal store.

▲ There is a lot of energy in the thermal store of a heated swimming pool.

▲ There is less energy in the thermal store of a glass of water at the same temperature than in the swimming pool's thermal store.

Big Idea: Energy 3

What happens when you heat things up?

Heating changes the movement of particles. If you heat a solid the particles vibrate more. If you heat a liquid or a gas the particles move faster and vibrate more.

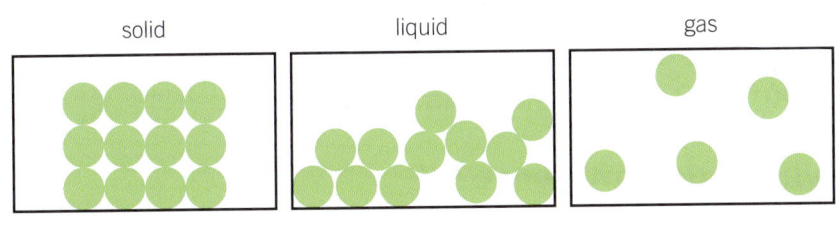

▲ Particles in solids, liquids, and gases.

Individual particles in a solid, liquid, or gas don't get hotter. They move or vibrate faster. The energy that you need to increase the temperature of a material depends on:

- the mass of material
- what the material is made of
- the temperature rise that you want.

B State three things that affect the thermal energy of an object.

Which way?

Hot objects cool down. Energy is never transferred from a cold object to a hot object, only from a hot object to a cooler object. The temperature difference is reduced and eventually both objects will end up at the same temperature. How quickly energy transfers depends on the temperature difference.

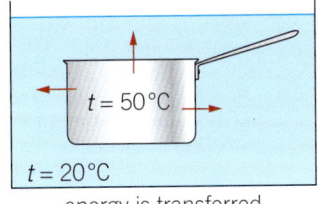

t = 50 °C
t = 20 °C
energy is transferred

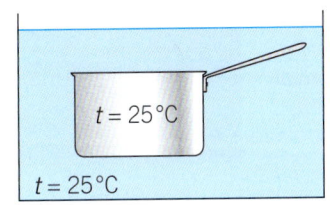

t = 25 °C
t = 25 °C
no more energy is transferred

C State what is happening in terms of energy when the temperature of an object is increasing.

Hot and cold
You might hear someone say 'Shut the door, you'll let the cold in!' Rewrite the statement so that it is scientifically correct and explain why it is now correct.

Key Words
temperature, thermometer, thermal energy store

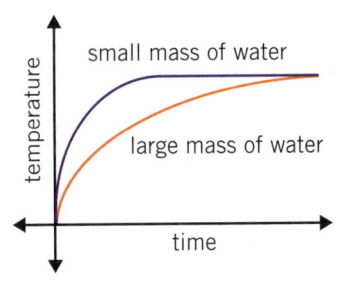

▲ A large mass of water takes longer to reach the same temperature as a small mass of water if they are heated by the same device.

Summary Questions

1. Copy and complete the sentences below.
   You measure _____ in degrees Celsius using a _____. When there is a temperature difference energy transfers from a _____ to a _____ object.
   (4 marks)

2. Sort these things in order from least energy stored to most energy stored: a saucepan full of water at 50 °C, a cup of water at 30 °C, a saucepan full of water at 30 °C.
   (1 mark)

3. Describe and explain the shape of the temperature–time graphs for the large and small masses of water shown in the diagram above.
   (6 marks)

● Topic 3.4 Heating and cooling

3.4.2 Energy transfer: particles

Learning objectives

After this section you will be able to:
- describe how energy is transferred by particles
- sketch diagrams to show convection currents
- describe how a thermal insulator can reduce energy transfer.

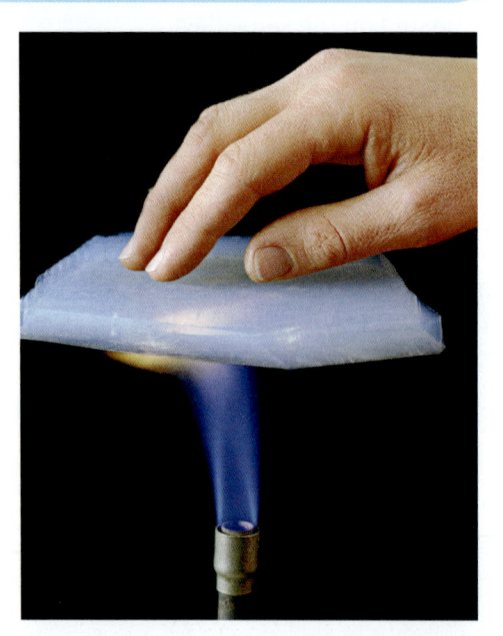

Have you ever lit a wooden splint in a Bunsen burner flame? The end of the splint is at a temperature of about 1000 °C but you can still hold the other end.

What's the difference?

When you put a saucepan of soup on the hob, the soup heats up.

The bottom of the saucepan is made of metal. Metal is a good **thermal conductor** of energy. Energy is transferred through it very quickly. This is **conduction**.

Energy can be transferred by different pathways – conduction, **convection**, or **radiation**.

A Write down three pathways that transfer thermal energy.

Particles and conduction

In conduction particles transfer energy by colliding with other particles when they vibrate. Metal are good thermal conductors because they contain electrons that are free to move.

Energy transfer happens until the two surfaces are at the same temperature. If you keep one surface warm by heating it then you will maintain the temperature difference. The solid will continue to conduct.

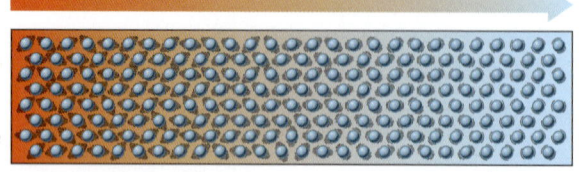

▲ This special material is called aerogel. Energy is transferred very slowly through it.

thermal store at a high temperature → thermal store at a low temperature

Solid conductor, solid insulator?

Energy is not transferred very easily through materials like wood. Wood and many non-metals are poor thermal conductors. They are **thermal insulators**. This does not mean that they do not conduct at all but that energy is transferred very slowly through them.

Insulating liquids and gases

Liquids are poor thermal conductors. Divers wear wetsuits, which use a thin layer of water against the skin as a thermal insulator to keep them warm.

▲ The capsule that brought these astronauts back is insulated so that they do not burn up in the atmosphere.

Big Idea: Energy 3

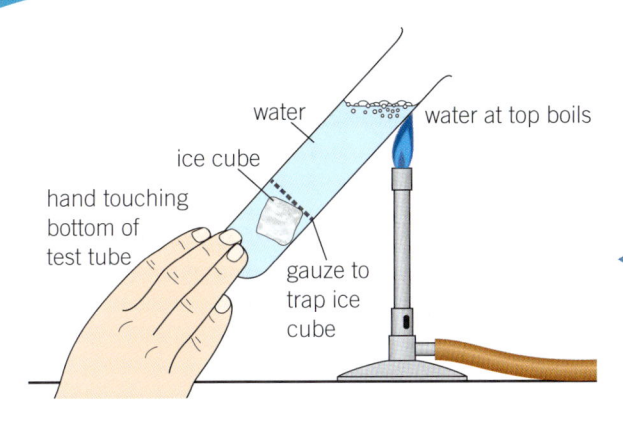

Liquid is a very poor conductor. Energy travels slowly through it.

Gases do not conduct well at all because their particles are much further apart than the particles in a solid. Duvets and warm clothing are designed to trap small pockets of air, which is a good insulator.

B State what an insulator is.

Particles and convection

When you heat soup in a pan it all heats up, not just the layer in contact with the bottom of the saucepan. This is what happens:

- The soup that is in contact with the bottom of the pan gets hotter so the particles there move faster.
- The particles in the hotter soup move further apart, so the soup becomes less dense.
- The hotter soup rises (floats up) and cooler, denser soup takes its place.

This is called a **convection current**. Convection also happens in gases.

▲ A convection current in a saucepan of water heats all of the water up.

▲ Hurricanes are produced by convection currents in the atmosphere, and the spin of the Earth.

How fast?
A student wants to investigate how the temperature of a liquid affects how long it takes to cool down. Write a plan for the investigation, including a risk assessment.

Fantastic Fact
The temperatures on the outside of a space capsule moving through the Earth's atmosphere can reach over 1200 °C, which is five times hotter than an oven.

Key Words
thermal conductor, conduction, convection, radiation, thermal insulator, convection current

Summary Questions

1. Copy and complete the sentences below.
   Energy is transferred through a solid by _____ if there is a _____ _____ between the ends of it. Liquids and solids transfer energy by _____ because the particles can _____. Energy is transferred much more _____ through an insulator than it is through a conductor.
   (5 marks)

2. Describe in terms of pathways how a thick woollen jumper keeps you warm in winter.
   (5 marks)

3. Sketch a labelled diagram to show the convection current above a radiator in your house.
   (3 marks)

4. An electric kettle contains an element at the bottom that gets hot when you switch it on. Use the ideas on these pages to explain in detail how all the water in a kettle boils.
   (6 marks)

● Topic 3.4 Heating and cooling

3.4.3 Energy transfer: radiation and insulation

Learning objectives

After this section you will be able to:
- describe some sources of infrared radiation
- describe how energy is transferred from the Sun to the Earth
- compare insulation methods in terms of conduction, convection, and radiation.

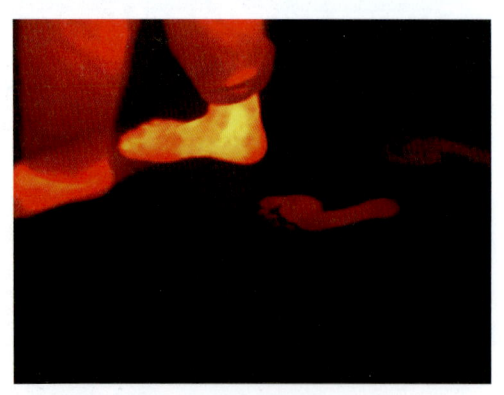

You leave warm footprints on the floor when you walk across it in bare feet. You can't see them because your eyes only detect visible light.

What is radiation?

Very hot things such as burning coal give out light as well as **infrared radiation**. Some people call infrared 'thermal radiation' or 'heat'. The Sun emits lots of different types of **radiation**, including light and infrared. Both light and infrared radiation travel as waves.

Transferring energy by radiation

You need particles to transfer energy by conduction and convection. You don't need particles to transfer energy by radiation. Light and infrared reach the Earth from the Sun by travelling through space. Space is a vacuum. There are no particles in a vacuum.

Emitting infrared

All objects (including you) give out, or emit, radiation.

- The type of radiation that they emit depends on their temperature.
- How much radiation they emit per second depends on the type of surface.
- Infrared can be transmitted, absorbed, or reflected, just like light.

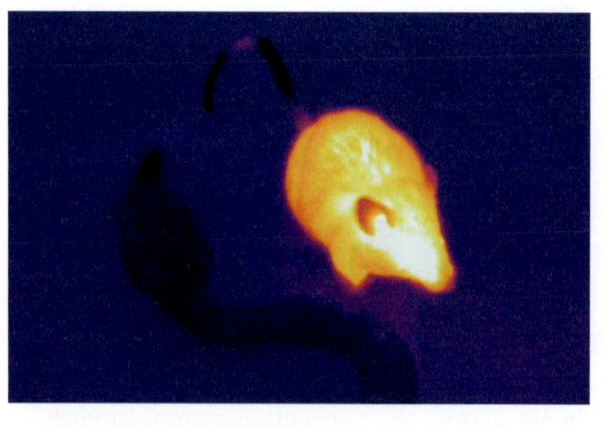

▲ A special camera detects these footprints.

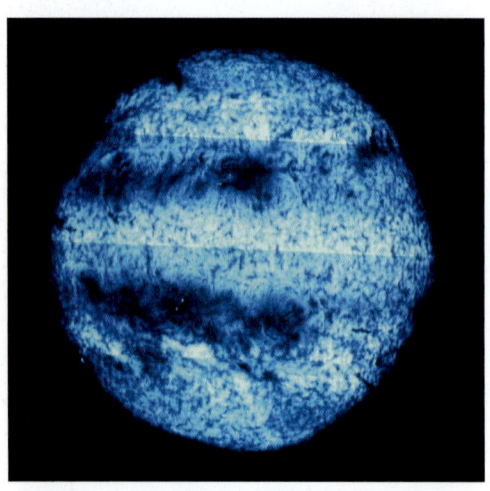

▲ This is what the Sun looks like if you can only see infrared.

◄ The mouse is warmer and emits a lot more infrared than the snake.

A Name two sources of infrared radiation.

Absorbing infrared

When the Sun is shining your skin feels hotter. Your skin detects the infrared when it absorbs it. Your skin is just one thing that detects infrared.

Big Idea: Energy 3

- A **thermal imaging camera** absorbs infrared and produces an image. The colours in the image are 'false'. The camera works out which areas are hotter and shows them redder in the image.
- A remote thermometer contains a sensor that detects infrared. It uses the radiation to work out the temperature.

You might feel hotter when you wear dark clothing. Dark colours *absorb* infrared, and light-coloured and shiny surfaces *reflect* infrared. If you hang clothes on a washing line the dark-coloured clothes will dry more quickly than the light-coloured ones.

B State what happens when infrared hits a shiny surface.

▲ A thermal imaging camera produces a coloured image of the fire.

Ways to insulate

If you want to slow down energy transfer you can use insulation. Insulators slow down the transfer of energy by removing particles, trapping particles so they cannot move, or using reflecting surfaces.

Transfer method	Way to slow down transfer	Example
conduction	use a good thermal insulator	use plastic for a kettle
convection	use materials that contain pockets of air which can't move	use foam between the walls of your house
radiation	use shiny surfaces to reflect infrared	use a foil blanket to stop a runner's temperature dropping too quickly

Cooling down

A student investigated the effect of the colour of a can on the time it takes hot water inside to cool down.

Colour of can	1st measurement	2nd measurement	3rd measurement	Mean
shiny metal	12	15	16	
shiny white	5	18	14	
matt black	11	16	13	
shiny black	23	15	10	

Temperature drop (°C)

a Identify the outlier or outliers.
b Calculate the mean temperature drop.
c Explain why it is not possible to make a conclusion from this experiment.

Summary Questions

1. Copy and complete the sentences below.

   The Sun and fire are examples of _____ of infrared. All objects emit _____ but the type of radiation depends on the _____. Infrared can be _____ from shiny surfaces, just like light. Dark-coloured surfaces _____ infrared better than light-coloured surfaces. Infrared does not need _____ to travel. It can travel through empty space, or a _____. Energy is transferred from the Sun to the Earth by _____. (8 marks)

2. Explain why:
   a energy cannot be transferred from the Sun to the Earth by conduction or convection. (1 mark)
   b you can't find people in burning buildings with a thermal imaging camera. (2 marks)

3. Explain how insulation keeps your home warm. (6 marks)

4. Compare and contrast the three ways that energy is transferred by heating. (6 marks)

Key Words

infrared radiation, radiation, thermal imaging camera

● Topic 3.4 Heating and cooling

3 Energy: Summary

Key Points

Energy costs
- You do work, and transfer energy between stores, when you use a force to move an object. You do work when you deform (squash or stretch) an object.
- You calculate work using this equation:
  Work done (J) = force (N) × distance moved (m)
- Simple machines like levers and pulleys can make it easier to do work but you do not get more energy out than you put in. The force is smaller but the distance moved is bigger.
- Wheels reduce friction.

Heating and cooling
- The thermal energy of an object depends on its mass, temperature, and what it is made of.
- When a hot object is in contact with a colder one energy is transferred from the hot object to the colder one.
- Energy is transferred by conduction in solids and by convection in liquids and gases.
- Energy travels quickly through a thermal conductor, but more slowly through a thermal insulator.
- Some insulators work by trapping air, which is a poor thermal conductor.
- Energy is transferred by radiation, which does not need a medium to travel through. All objects emit radiation. Infrared radiation can be detected by your skin or a thermal imaging camera.

BIG Write

Journey to the South Pole
Here is some data for three different types of material used to make sleeping bags provided by the manufacturer. In each of the cooling experiments a scientist covered a container of water with one of the materials and measured how long it took to cool down.

Material	Time for water at 100°C to cool to room temperature (mins)	Time for water at 20°C to freeze when put in the freezer (mins)	Mass of 1 kg (or density) (kg)
BeWarm	550	480	1.2
HeatSave	800	600	0.7
WarmerThan	840	600	0.8

Task
Write a report that compares the three materials, and make a recommendation for which material you think you should use, and explain your choice.

Key Words

work, deform, displacement, simple machine, lever, output force, input force, temperature, thermometer, thermal energy store, thermal conductor, conduction, convection, radiation, thermal insulator, convection current, infrared radiation, radiation, thermal imaging camera

End-of-Big Idea questions

1. Here are some units. Circle the two units of energy.

   joules   watts   kilowatt hours   degrees Celsius

   (1 mark)

2. Match statements below to make three correct sentences about energy transfer.

Conduction happens mainly in	liquids and gases
Convection happens in	a vacuum
Radiation can happen in	solids

   (2 marks)

3. In the days before central heating people used hot rocks to warm their beds. Complete the sentences using the words 'less' or 'more'.

   A more massive rock has _____ energy in a thermal store than a less massive rock at the same temperature.

   A more massive rock would take _____ time to heat up, and _____ time to cool down.

   (3 marks)

4. Select the correct statement about using a lever below.

   A A lever increases the output force and you get more energy out that you put in.
   B A lever increases the output force and you get less energy out that you put in.
   C A lever can produce a smaller or a bigger output force depending on the position of the pivot.
   D A lever always produces a larger output force if the pivot is closer to your hand than to the output force.

   (1 mark)

5. Calculate the work done in each of the situations below:
   a a car engine that uses a force of 500 N to move a car 200 m. *(2 marks)*
   b a shopkeeper who uses a force of 50 N to lift a box 1.5 m. *(2 marks)*

   (4 marks)

6. Here is an experiment to demonstrate convection.

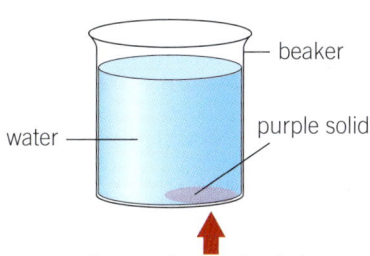

   a Describe what will happen to the purple colour during heating. *(3 marks)*
   b Draw a diagram to show what you will see in the beaker. *(2 marks)*
   c Explain why the purple colour forms a convection current. *(3 marks)*

   (8 marks)

7. Some double-glazing systems trap air between two panes of glass.
   a Explain how energy is transferred through a double-glazed window from a hot room to the cold air outside. *(3 marks)*
   b State and explain how the rate of energy transfer would change if you removed the air from the gap. *(3 marks)*

   (6 marks)

8. Explain in detail why insulating your house will reduce your energy bills.

   (6 marks)

4 Waves

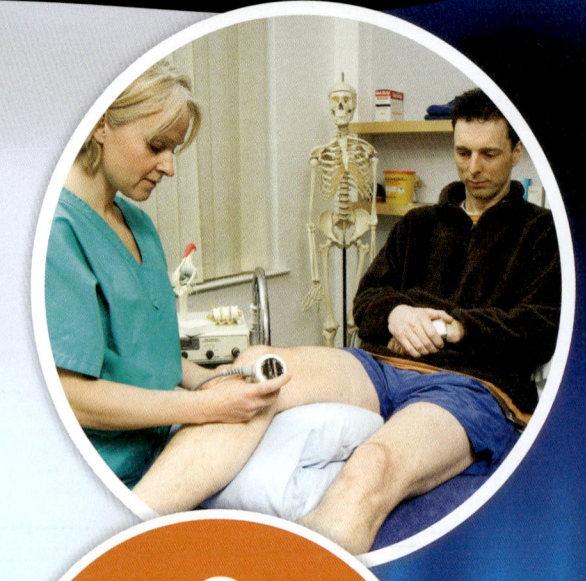

Tsunamis, sound, infrared, and light all have something in common. They are waves and transfer energy. In this Big Idea you will learn about what affects the energy that waves transfer, and how they interact with surfaces they hit and with matter they travel through. You will find out about ultrasound and some of its uses. You will learn how the wave model can help you to explain wave behaviour.

Waves can cause damage, and not just by damaging objects on a large scale. Radiation can cause damage to the human body.

Q How is your mirror image the same as you, and how is it different?

You already know

- Light from the Sun can be dangerous and you need to protect your eyes.
- Light is reflected from surfaces.
- Sounds are made by vibrating objects.
- Vibrations from sounds travel through a medium.

BIG Questions

- What is ultrasound, and how do we use it?
- What damage does electromagnetic radiation do to the human body?
- Why do bottles of water act like lenses?

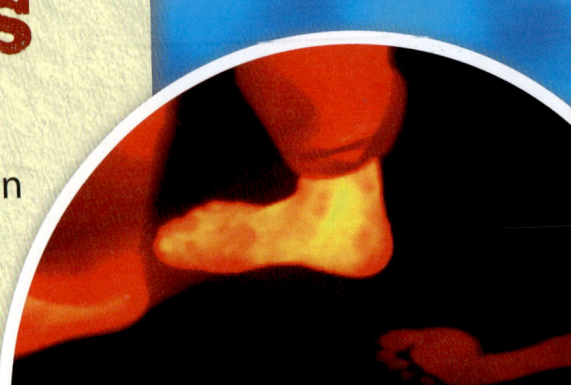

Picture Puzzler
Key Words

Can you solve this Picture Puzzler?

The first letter of each of these images spells out a science word that you will come across in this book.

Picture Puzzler
Close Up

Can you tell what this zoomed-in picture is?

Clue: You won't hear much with these tiles on the walls of a room.

Making connections

In your GCSE course you will learn more about electromagnetic waves, their frequencies and wavelengths, and how they interact with matter.

You will investigate the reflection and refraction of light.

You will also learn how images are formed using lenses, how to construct ray diagrams, and how to calculate magnification.

You will learn about how sound waves are used to detect structures we cannot see, and how we use ultrasound to find distances.

You will also learn how we use seismic waves to work out the structure of the Earth.

4.3.1 Sound waves, water waves, and energy

Learning objectives

After this section you will be able to:
- describe how sound transfers energy
- describe the link between amplitude or frequency and energy
- explain how a microphone and loudspeaker work.

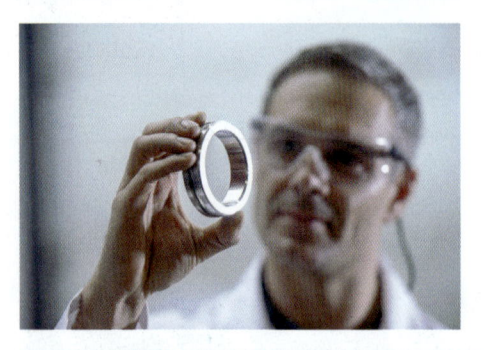

▲ Sometimes you need objects to be so clean that you need to use sound to clean them.

▲ When a changing current flows through a wire in the magnetic field in a loudspeaker the cone moves in and out.

Key Words

compression, rarefaction, pressure wave, microphone, loudspeaker, ultrasound

How do you clean an object without touching it?

How does sound transfer energy?

Sound transfers energy. The vibration that makes the sound makes the air molecules vibrate to and fro in the direction of motion of the sound waves. This produces **compressions** and **rarefactions**. These are regions of high and low air pressure, so sound is a **pressure wave**.

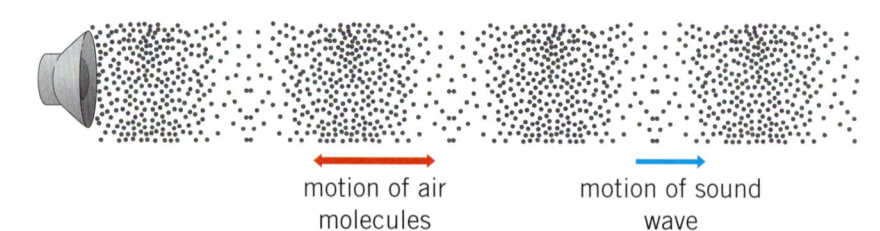

▲ Air molecules move backwards and forwards.

A Define compression and rarefaction.

When the regions of high and low pressure interact with particles in a solid or a liquid they exert a force on them.

This means that the walls of your classroom are a little bit warmer at the end of the lesson than at the start. The sound waves have interacted with the particles in the wall and made them vibrate a little more. The wall heats up.

Sound waves transfer energy in the direction of the sound wave. If the sound wave has a bigger amplitude or frequency it transfers more energy.

Making and detecting sound waves

You can make sound with a **microphone**, and detect it with a **loudspeaker**.

- A microphone converts changes in air pressure to a changing potential difference.
- A loudspeaker converts a changing potential difference to changes in air pressure.

When a singer sings into a microphone the sound wave hits a flexible plate called a diaphragm. The diaphragm vibrates, like your eardrum. It produces a changing potential difference.

Big Idea: Waves 4

Loudspeakers convert the changing potential difference back into sound when they vibrate.

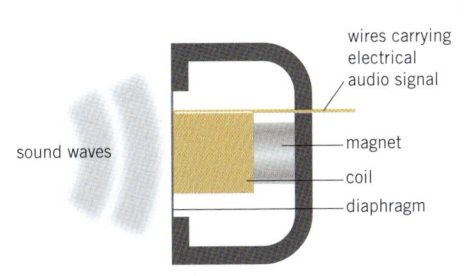

▲ A microphone detects sound in a similar way to your ear.

▲ The oscilloscope screen displays the changing potential difference that the microphone produces from the changing air pressure from the vibration of the girl's vocal chords.

What is ultrasound?

You can only hear frequencies up to 20 000 Hz. **Ultrasound** is sound with a frequency above 20 000 Hz.

B State the frequency of ultrasound.

How do we use ultrasound?

When sound or ultrasound interacts with solids or liquids it makes the particles in those materials vibrate. This means that you can use ultrasound to shake dust or dirt from objects. Scientists use ultrasonic cleaning to clean parts of their equipment that need to be very clean.

Physiotherapists also use ultrasound. Your body is mainly made of water, and when ultrasound interacts with liquids it can make the molecules move faster. The liquid gets warmer.

C State a use of ultrasound.

Wave energy and electricity

You can use the energy in water waves to generate electricity. Waves push air through a turbine and generator to produce electricity.

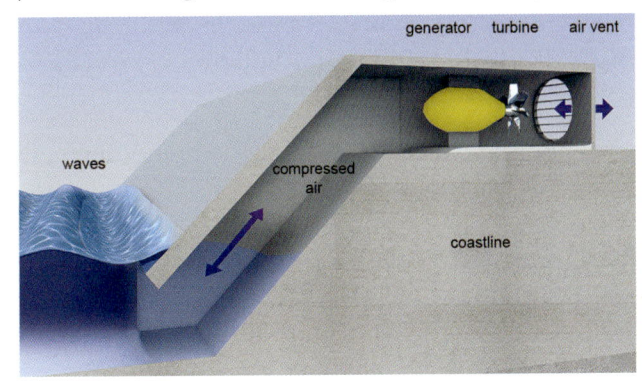

◀ You can use the energy transferred by water waves to generate electricity.

Link

You can learn more about how a loudspeaker works in 2.4.2 Using electromagnets.

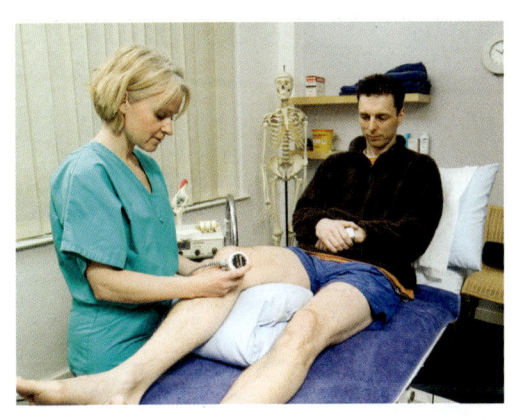

▲ The ultrasound warms muscles and ligaments, which helps them to heal faster.

Summary Questions

1 Copy and complete the sentences below:

The particles in a sound wave move _____ and _____. The direction of vibration is the _____ direction as that of the wave. When a sound wave interacts with particles it makes them vibrate or move _____. This can make the temperature _____. A wave with a higher _____ or higher _____ has more energy.

(7 marks)

2 Describe how a microphone works.

(3 marks)

3 Suggest why you need to use ultrasound and not sound to clean objects or for physiotherapy.

(3 marks)

Topic 4.3 Wave effects

4.3.2 Radiation and energy

Learning objectives

After this section you will be able to:
- describe the electromagnetic spectrum
- explain the effect of radiation on living cells
- explain, in terms of frequency, the difference in damage done by electromagnetic waves.

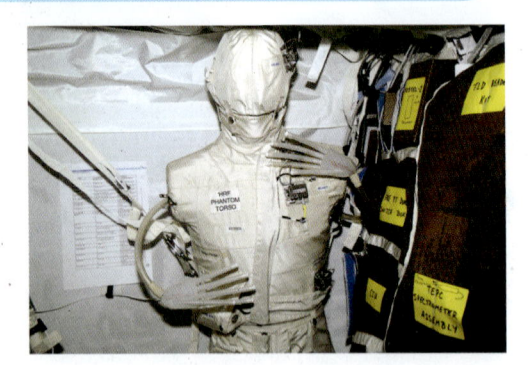

▲ NASA made a phantom torso to find out about radiation in space.

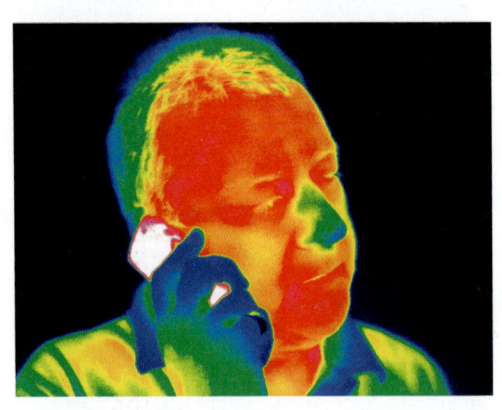

▲ An image produced by a thermal imaging camera of someone using a mobile phone.

Key Words

visible light, electromagnetic spectrum, ionisation, radio waves, microwaves, infrared (IR), ultraviolet (UV), X-rays, gamma rays

Do the astronauts on the International Space Station need to wear sunscreen?

To find out, NASA made a fake human torso with artificial skin, and put it on the space station for four months. They found that there was an increase in the radiation absorbed by the skin compared to Earth, but this did not pose a risk to astronauts.

The electromagnetic spectrum

The Sun emits a continuous spectrum of radiation. **Visible light** is just one part of this **electromagnetic spectrum**.

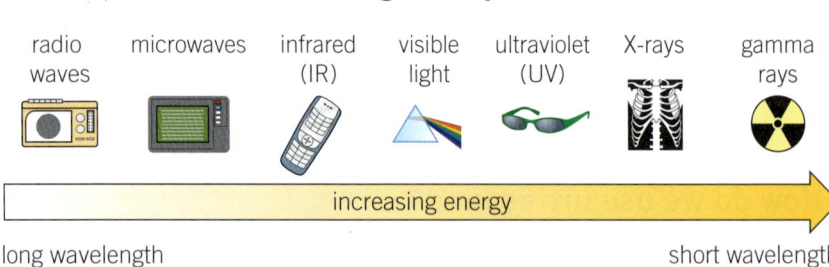

radio waves | microwaves | infrared (IR) | visible light | ultraviolet (UV) | X-rays | gamma rays

increasing energy →

long wavelength over 10 000 m

short wavelength 0.000 000 000 000 01 m

← increasing wavelength

increasing frequency →

▲ The electromagnetic spectrum is made up of waves with different properties.

A State the waves of the electromagnetic spectrum.

The electromagnetic spectrum is continuous, but we separate it into different bands of frequencies. Visible light has a range of frequencies. You have seen this when you split white light with a prism. Our eyes can detect visible light, but not the other waves of the electromagnetic spectrum.

The energy of a wave depends on its frequency. The higher the frequency the more energy the wave transfers.

Radiation and the human body

The Sun emits all the waves of the electromagnetic spectrum, but only some get through the atmosphere. The different waves have different effects on the body.

4.3 Wave effects

Waves with a low frequency and energy have a heating effect, but waves with a higher energy can knock electrons out of atoms in living cells. This is called **ionisation**. If the atoms are in your DNA then this can cause a mutation. The cell can replicate which can produce cancer.

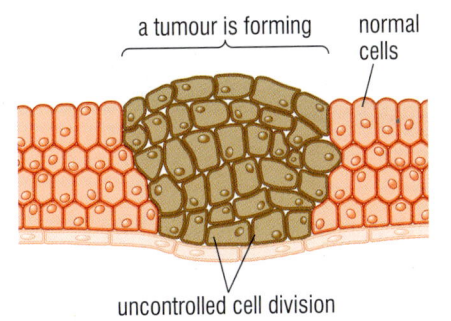

▲ Normal cells can divide to produce cancer.

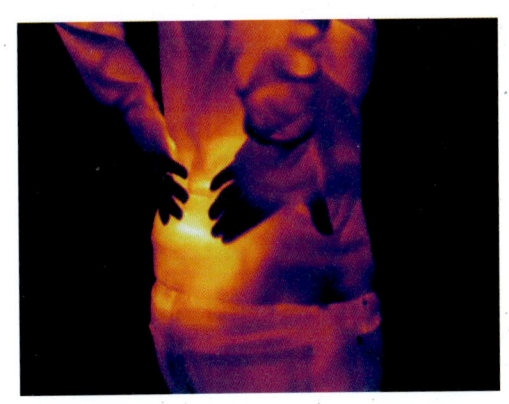

▲ A thermal image of a woman with back pain.

The type of cancer that you can develop depends on the type of radiation. Ultraviolet radiation is not very penetrating but can cause skin cancer.

Wave	Does it get through the atmosphere?	Is it absorbed by the body?	Effect on the body
radio waves	most gets through	all goes through you	heating
microwaves	hardly any gets through	most goes through you	heating
infrared (IR)	some gets through	most absorbed by your skin	heating
visible light	all gets through	a little absorbed by your skin	heating
ultraviolet (UV)	some gets through	nearly all absorbed by your skin	ionising
X-rays	hardly any gets through	most goes through you	ionising
gamma	hardly any gets through	most goes through you	ionising

X-rays and **gamma rays** are much more penetrating, and could cause cancer in any part of the body. Luckily the atmosphere blocks X-rays and gamma rays from the Sun.

Other sources of radiation

Not all the radiation that we are exposed to comes from the Sun. Here are some uses of the waves of the electromagnetic spectrum.

wave	radio waves	microwaves	infrared	visible light	ultraviolet	X-rays	gamma rays
use	TV signals	mobile phones	heating, cooking	photography	detecting forgeries	seeing broken bones	killing cancer cells

When we are using any device that emits electromagnetic radiation we need to assess the risks and benefits. Gamma rays cause so much damage to cells that we can use it in radiotherapy to kill cancer cells. This gives the rest of the body a dose of radiation, which is a risk because it could cause more damage.

Remember those waves!
Make up a mnemonic so that you can remember the waves of the electromagnetic spectrum.

Summary Questions

1. Copy and complete these sentences:
   The electromagnetic spectrum consists of these waves: gamma rays, _____, _____, _____, _____, _____, and _____. This list is in order of increasing _____. Electromagnetic radiation can have a _____ effect on the body or can _____ atoms, which can cause _____.
   (10 marks)

2. Describe the difference between the effect of light on the body and the effect of ultraviolet on the body.
   (6 marks)

3. Suggest and explain which wave of the Sun's spectrum is most dangerous to humans.
   (2 marks)

● Topic 4.3 Wave effects

4.4.1 Modelling waves

Learning objectives

After this section you will be able to:
- compare transverse and longitudinal waves
- use wave models to explain observations of wave behaviour
- describe what happens when waves superpose.

▲ We have drilled 12 km (7.5 miles) below the surface of the Earth.

Key Words

transverse wave, wave, longitudinal wave, transmission, superpose

▲ You can make a transverse wave on a slinky.

How do we know what is inside the Earth, when the biggest distance we have drilled down is not much more than the height of Everest?

Transverse or longitudinal?

You can send pulses down a slinky spring. You can make the pulses in two ways.

You can move your hand at right angles to the spring. This produces a **transverse wave** on the slinky. In a transverse wave the oscillation is at 90° to the direction of the **wave**.

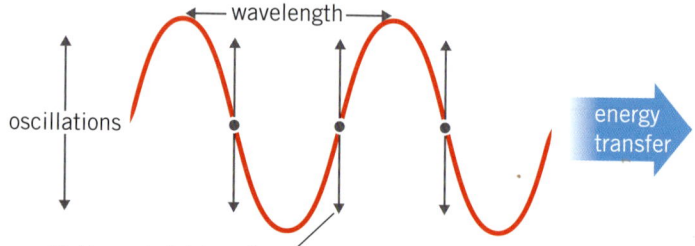

▲ In a transverse wave the oscillation is at 90° to the direction of the wave.

You can also push and pull the spring. This produces a **longitudinal wave** on the slinky. The oscillation is parallel to the direction of the wave – it is in the same direction as the spring itself.

A Write down the direction of oscillation in a transverse wave.

You have already modelled light using rays. There are other models you can use.

Modelling waves – the slinky

You can use a slinky to model longitudinal waves and transverse waves depending how you make the wave. You can change the speed of the wave by changing the material of the slinky, or using a rope.

This physical model shows that:
- the wave moves but the slinky does not
- *reflection*: you can reflect a pulse from a fixed end
- **transmission**: the pulse moves along the spring
- *absorption*: the amplitude decreases as the wave moves because energy is transferred by friction, heating up the ground a bit.

4.4 Wave properties

Modelling waves – ripples
In the wave model light behaves like ripples on water. If we see something happening to the water, we can use the idea to explain what happens with electromagnetic waves or sound.

- the wave moves but the water does not
- *frequency and wavelength*: as you move your hand more quickly the waves travel at the same speed but the wavelength decreases as the frequency increases
- *reflection*: you can reflect a wavefront from a barrier
- *refraction*: waves slow down when they go from deep to shallow water, and change direction. This explains why light is refracted when it goes from one medium to another with a different density.

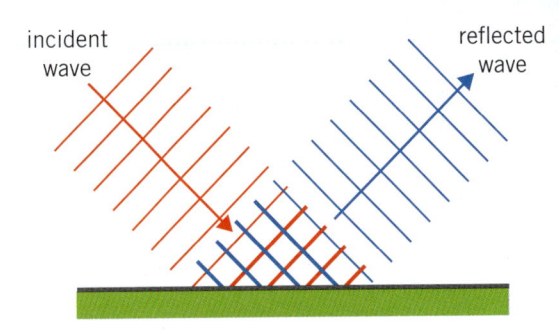

▲ A wave reflects off a barrier.

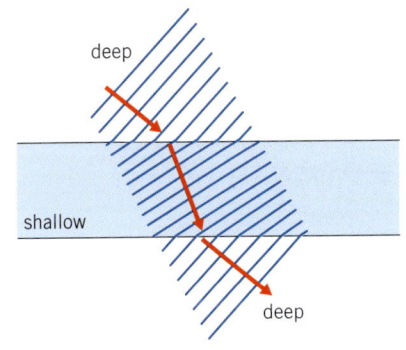

▲ Waves are refracted when they slow down.

Adding waves
When waves are put together they **superpose**. This means that they add up or they cancel out.

If the waves are in step they will add up. You get more than you had before. If they are not in step then they cancel out and you get less than you had before.

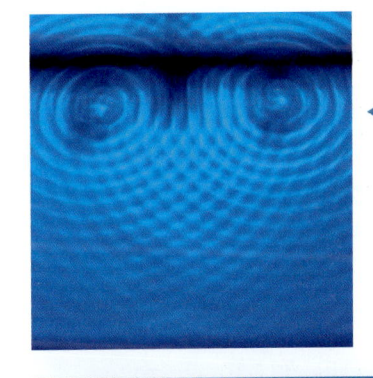

◀ Water waves in a ripple tank add up and cancel out to make an interference pattern.

B Write down two things that happen when waves combine.

Different types of wave
All waves transfer energy without transferring matter. They are reflected, and can be refracted, transmitted, or absorbed when they travel through media. They can all superpose.

They have different speeds, and travel in different media.

Wave	Type	Speed	Media
electro-magnetic	transverse	300 000 km/s in air	any, including a vacuum
sound/ultrasound	longitudinal	300 m/s in air, 3 km/s in rock	any, but not a vacuum
earthquake	transverse	2 km/s in rock	solid rock
earthquake	longitudinal	same as sound	solid and liquid rock

Scientists have worked out that the centre of the Earth has a solid inner core and liquid outer core by detecting earthquake waves on the other side of the Earth to the earthquake's centre. They measured:

- which types of wave arrived
- the times of travel of the waves.

Summary Questions

1 In a transverse wave the vibration is at _____ to the direction of travel. You use springs or _____ to model waves like light or sound being reflected or _____ (change direction).
(3 marks)

2 Compare light and sound waves.
(6 marks)

3 Suggest how you can use a wave model to explain how noise-cancelling earphones work.
(6 marks)

● Topic 4.4 Wave properties

4 Waves: Summary

Key Points

Wave effects
- When a wave travels through a substance, particles move to and fro.
- Energy is transferred in the direction of movement of the wave.
- Waves with a higher frequency or larger amplitude transfer more energy.
- You can use high-frequency sound waves to agitate a liquid for cleaning objects, or to massage muscles for physiotherapy. You can also use waves to generate electricity.
- A microphone turns the pressure wave of sound hitting it into an electrical signal (a changing potential difference).
- Light and other electromagnetic radiation can damage living cells. Low-frequency radiation, like microwaves and infrared, have a heating effect on human tissue. High-frequency radiation, like ultraviolet and X-rays, can cause cancer. Lower-frequency radiation can cause skin cancer.

Wave properties
- A wave is a vibration that transports energy from place to place without transporting matter.
- In a transverse wave the vibration is perpendicular (at 90°) to the direction of travel of the wave.
- When waves combine (superpose) they can add up or cancel out.
- Slinkys and water waves are physical models that you can use to demonstrate wave properties such as reflection, refraction, transmission, absorption, and superposition.
- Waves differ in the medium that they can or cannot travel through, in their speed, and in how they interact with matter.
- Sound is longitudinal, needs a medium to travel through, and travels at 330 m/s in air. Light is transverse, does not need a medium to travel through, and travels at 300 000 km/s in air.

BIG Write

The Big Exhibition

Your hospital wants to put on an exhibition that shows how they use X-rays. They want to make big display boards to highlight how the risks and benefits to using X-rays.

You have been asked to come up with designs for the boards. You must decide:

- how to introduce the scientific ideas about radiation to the general public
- how to explain about risks and benefits
- how to make the boards attractive so that people will stop to read them.

Produce designs for at least three boards for the exhibition.

Key Words

compression, rarefaction, pressure wave, microphone, loudspeaker, ultrasound, visible light, electromagnetic spectrum, ionisation, radio waves, microwaves, infrared (IR), ultraviolet (UV), X-rays, gamma rays, transverse wave, wave, longitudinal wave, transmission, superpose

End-of-Big Idea questions

1. Radiation can affect human tissue.
   a. Name two types of radiation that have a heating effect on human tissue. *(2 marks)*
   b. Name two types of radiation that have an ionising effect on human tissue. *(2 marks)*
   (4 marks)

2.
   a. Describe what happens when a wave hits a barrier. *(1 mark)*
   b. Describe what happens when waves superpose. *(2 marks)*
   c. Describe two models of light that you have used. *(2 marks)*
   (5 marks)

3. Waves can be transverse or longitudinal.
   a. Explain why a Mexican wave is transverse. *(1 mark)*
   b. Explain why sound is a longitudinal wave. *(1 mark)*
   (2 marks)

4. A student has collected data about different types of plastic block. He measured the mass and the angle of refraction of a ray of light going into the block. Each block is the same size.

   Here are his results:

Mass of block (g)	Angle of refraction (°)
250	27
220	32
275	24
300	21

   a. State **one** variable that the student must keep the same during this investigation. *(1 mark)*
   b. State the name of the independent variable. *(1 mark)*
   c. State the name of the dependent variable. *(1 mark)*
   d. Describe the relationship between the mass and the angle of refraction. *(1 mark)*
   e. Describe **one** way that the student could improve the way that the results are presented in the table. *(1 mark)*
   (5 marks)

5. You can detect sound with your ear or a microphone.
   a. Describe two similarities between the ear and the microphone. *(2 marks)*
   b. Explain why exposure to sound does not increase your risk of cancer, but exposure to radiation might increase the risk. *(4 marks)*
   (6 marks)

6. Light slows down from 300 000 km/s to 200 000 km/s in glass and to 226 000 km/s in water. A ray of light enters each medium with an angle of incidence of 40°. State and explain whether the angle of refraction would be bigger or smaller in water than in glass. **(2 marks)**

7. Apply ideas about light, sound, and materials to describe and explain what happens to the material in the room during and after a science lesson. **(6 marks)**

5 Matter

What is stuff made of? In this Big Idea you will learn about the elements that make up everything in the Universe. You will explore ways of classifying elements, and find out about the patterns in their physical and chemical properties.

You already know

- Everything is made up of tiny particles.
- All materials are made up of one or more elements.
- The elements are listed in the Periodic Table.
- Metals are on the left of the Periodic Table, and non-metals are on the right.
- Physical properties are features of a substance that can be observed without changing the substance itself.
- Chemical properties describe how substances react with other substances.

Q What is the name of the change of state in which liquid water becomes ice?

BIG Questions

- What are atoms and elements?
- What are the patterns in the properties of elements?
- How can we use the Periodic Table to predict element properties?

Picture Puzzler
Key Words

Can you solve this Picture Puzzler?

The first letter of each of these images spells out a science word that you will come across in this book.

Picture Puzzler
Close Up

Can you tell what this zoomed-in picture is?

Clue: The tiny particles that all matter is made from.

Making connections

In **Book 1, 5.1 The particle model** you learnt about the tiny particles that make up matter.

In **Book 1, 6.1 Metals and non-metals** you learnt about elements, and how they can be classified as metals and non-metals.

In **6.4 Types of reaction** you will learn more about different types of chemical reactions.

5.3.1 Elements

Learning objectives

After this section you will be able to:
- state what an element is
- recall the chemical symbols of 16 elements
- use observations from experiments to explain why a substance must be an element.

How many elements do you think make up the materials in your phone?

What are elements?

As you know, **elements** are substances that contain only one type of atom. Every material, and everything in the Universe, is made up of one or more elements. It is not possible to break down an element into other substances.

There are 98 naturally occurring elements. A smartphone contains around 60 of these elements. The Periodic Table below shows which ones.

Key Words

element, chemical symbol

Golden smartphones

The mass of gold in a typical smartphone is 0.025 g. Calculate the number of phones that contain a total of 1 g of gold. The price of gold is approximately £30 per gram. Calculate the number of phones that, when recycled, contain a total of £1000 worth of gold.

H																	He
Li 41	Be 63											B 41	C	N	O	F	Ne
Na	Mg 94											Al 44	Si	P	S	Cl	Ar
K	Ca	Sc 65	Ti 63	V 63	Cr 76	Mn 96	Fe 57	Co 54	Ni 62	Cu 70	Zn 38	Ga 38	Ge 44	As 38	Se 47	Br	Kr
Rb	Sr 78	Y 95	Zr 66	Nb 42	Mo 70	Tc	Ru 63	Rh 96	Pd 39	Ag 44	Cd 38	In 60	Sn 36	Sb 57	Te 38	I	Xe
Cs	Ba 63	*	Hf 38	Ta 41	W 53	Re 90	Os 38	Ir 69	Pt 66	Au 40	Hg 45	Tl 100	Pb 100	Bi 46	Po	At	Rn
Fr	Ra	**	Rf	Db	Sg	Bh	Hs	Mt	Ds	Rg	Cn	Nh	Fl	Mc	Lv	Ts	Og

*Lanthanides	La 75	Ce 60	Pr 41	Nd 41	Pm	Sm 38	Eu 100	Gd 63	Tb 63	Dy 100	Ho 63	Er 63	Tm 88	Yb 88	Lu 63
*Actinides	Ac	Th 35	Pa	U 63	Np	Pu	Am	Cm	Bk	Cf	Es	Fm	Md	No	Lr

Big Idea: Matter 5

Most of the elements in your phone do not exist as elements alone. They exist either as mixtures or are joined to other elements in compounds.

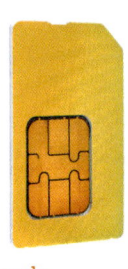

▲ Gold is used in SIM cards.

▲ Phone batteries rely on lithium.

▲ Touchscreens include a substance made from the elements indium, tin, and oxygen.

A Name three elements in a smartphone.

What are chemical symbols?

Every element has its own **chemical symbol**. This is the one- or two-letter code for the element. Scientists all over the world use the same chemical symbols, no matter what language they speak or write in.

When you write a chemical symbol, make sure the first letter is a capital letter. The second letter is lowercase. For example, the chemical symbol for magnesium is Mg, not MG, mg, or mG.

The table shows the chemical symbols for some elements.

Name of element	Chemical symbol
aluminium	Al
bromine	Br
carbon	C
chlorine	Cl
copper	Cu
gold	Au
hydrogen	H
iodine	I
iron	Fe

Name of element	Chemical symbol
magnesium	Mg
nitrogen	N
oxygen	O
potassium	K
sodium	Na
sulfur	S
tungsten	W
zinc	Zn

For some elements, the chemical symbol is the first letter of its English name. For others, the chemical symbol is the first and second, or first and third, letters of its name.

The chemical symbols of some elements come from their Latin names, for example *aurum* for gold and *ferrum* for iron. The chemical symbol of tungsten comes from its German name, Wolfram.

B Write down the chemical symbols of the elements hydrogen, aluminium, magnesium, and sodium.

Summary Questions

1. Write down the names and chemical symbols of six elements that are in a smartphone.

   (6 marks)

2. A teacher melts a substance and passes electricity through it. The substance breaks down to form two different substances – a brown liquid and a silver-coloured liquid. Explain why the substance cannot be an element.

   (2 marks)

3. Suggest two advantages of using the same chemical symbols for the elements in every language.

   (2 marks)

● Topic 5.3 Elements

5.3.2 Atoms

Learning objectives

After this section you will be able to:
- state what atoms are
- represent atoms using particle diagrams.

Look at the picture below. What do you think it shows?

▲ A silicon chip. This photograph was taken with a normal camera.

The picture shows the surface of a silicon crystal. Silicon is an element. Every computer, calculator, and mobile phone has silicon crystals inside. The crystals are called silicon chips. They contain millions of tiny electronic parts. These make the computers, calculators, and phones work.

Atoms

The picture below shows atoms of silicon. As you know, an **atom** is the smallest part of an element that can exist.

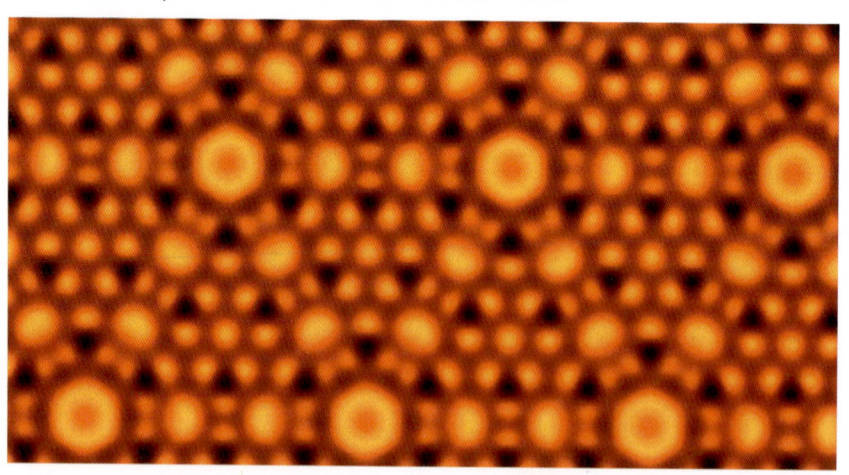

The picture above was not taken with a normal camera. It was taken with a special type of microscope that can detect things as small as an atom. You cannot see atoms with your eye, or even with an ordinary microscope.

A State what an atom is.

How many types of atom are there?

Every element is made up of one type of atom. As you know, all the atoms of an element are the same as each other. The atoms of one element are different to the atoms of all other elements.

Key word

atom

There are about 100 elements that exist naturally, so there are about 100 types of atom.

All silicon atoms are the same. But silicon atoms are different to gold atoms. For example, gold atoms are bigger.

Gold atoms are also heavier than silicon atoms. This explains the data in the table below.

Element	Mass of 1 cm³ of the element (g)
gold	19.3
silicon	2.33

B Describe two differences between gold and silicon atoms.

Just one atom?

One atom on its own does not have the properties of the element. A gold atom is not yellow. It is not shiny. It is not in the solid, liquid, or gas state.

◀ The atoms in this piece of gold are all the same.

The properties of an element are the properties of very many atoms joined together. The piece of gold in the picture has a mass of 1000 g. It is made up of about 3 000 000 000 000 000 000 000 000 atoms. Together, these atoms make the gold yellow and shiny.

The atoms are touching each other in rows. They vibrate on the spot. The gold in the picture is in the solid state. If you heat gold to 1063 °C its atoms start moving around. The gold is melting. One atom of gold cannot melt. Only a group of many atoms can melt.

Going for gold?

A gold ring has a mass of 10 g. Choose data from the paragraphs above to estimate the number of atoms in the ring.

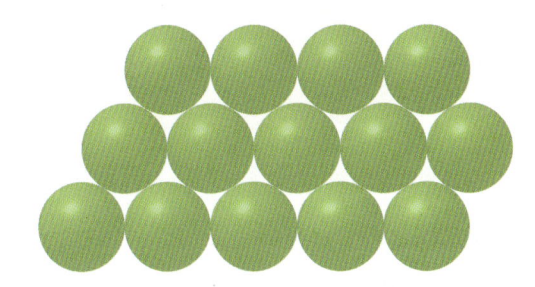

▲ This diagram represents gold atoms in solid gold.

Fantastic Fact!

The 2012 Olympic gold medals are only 1% gold by mass. There are 170 times more silver atoms than gold atoms in a gold medal.

Summary Questions

1. Copy and complete the sentences below.

   The smallest part of an element that can exist is called an _____. All the atoms of an element are the _____. The atoms of one element are _____ to the atoms of all other elements.

   (3 marks)

2. An Olympic bronze medal is made up of three elements – copper, zinc, and tin. State the number of types of atom in the medal. Explain your answer.

   (2 marks)

3. Create and illustrate a visual summary to summarise and organise the information on this spread.

   (6 marks)

Topic 5.3 Elements

5.3.3 Compounds

Learning objectives

After this section you will be able to:
- state what a compound is
- represent molecules, elements, mixtures, and compounds using particle diagrams
- use particle diagrams to classify a substance as an element, mixture, or compound.

▲ This particle diagram shows that a hydrogen molecule consists of two hydrogen atoms.

▲ An oxygen molecule consists of two oxygen atoms.

▲ A water molecule has one oxygen atom joined to two hydrogen atoms.

Key Words

compound, molecule

Link

You can learn more about boiling points in Book 1, 5.1.4 Boiling.

How much water have you used today?

Water is vital for survival. But what is water? As you know, water is made up of atoms of two elements, hydrogen and oxygen. This means that water is a **compound**. A compound is a pure substance made up of atoms of two or more elements. The atoms are strongly joined together.

Most of the things that you use are made from compounds, mixtures of compounds, or mixtures of elements. Very few things are made from pure elements. The properties of a compound are different to the properties of the elements it is made up of.

A State what a compound is.

Why is water different to its elements?

Hydrogen is a gas at room temperature. Mixed with air, and ignited with a spark, it explodes. Hydrogen atoms go round in pairs. These are **molecules** of hydrogen. A molecule is a group of two or more atoms strongly joined together. Most non-metals, and compounds of non-metals, exist as small or giant molecules.

Oxygen is a gas at room temperature. You cannot see or smell it. Oxygen exists as molecules. Each molecule is made up of two oxygen atoms. In the air, oxygen molecules mix with atoms and molecules of other substances.

Water exists as molecules. The molecules are made up of atoms of two elements, hydrogen and oxygen. This means that water is a compound.

Water molecules are different to hydrogen molecules and oxygen molecules. This is why water has different properties to hydrogen and oxygen. For example, water has a higher boiling point than hydrogen.

Weak forces hold molecules close to each other in liquid hydrogen. Stronger forces hold molecules close together in liquid water. It takes more energy to separate water molecules from each other than to separate hydrogen molecules from each other. This explains why water has a higher boiling point than hydrogen.

B State which has the higher boiling point, water or hydrogen.

What is salt?

Do you add salt to your food? Salt is a compound. Its scientific name is sodium chloride. It contains atoms of two elements, sodium and chlorine.

- Sodium is a shiny metal. It is solid at 20 °C. It reacts vigorously with water.
- Chlorine is a smelly green poisonous gas at 20 °C.

So why doesn't salt smell? Or poison you? Or fizz in your mouth?

In salt, the atoms of sodium and chlorine are not just mixed up. They are joined together to make one substance – sodium chloride. This compound has different properties to the elements in it.

C Describe one difference in properties between sodium chloride and sodium.

Organising ideas
Make a table showing properties of sodium, chlorine, and sodium chloride. Use the table to help you plan and then write some paragraphs comparing the properties of the three substances. Explain why the properties of the two elements (sodium and chlorine) are different from the properties of the compound (sodium chloride).

Fantastic Fact!
Tooth enamel is a compound of calcium (a shiny metal that fizzes in water), phosphorus (a poisonous solid that catches fire easily), and oxygen (a gas that helps things burn).

Summary Questions

1. Copy the sentences below, choosing the correct bold words.

   A compound is a substance made up of atoms of **one/two** or more elements. The properties of a compound are **the same as/different to** the properties of its elements. A molecule is a group of **two/three** or more atoms **weakly/strongly** joined together.

   (4 marks)

2. Look at the particle diagram below. Does it represent an element, a compound, or a mixture of elements? Explain how you decided. *(2 marks)*

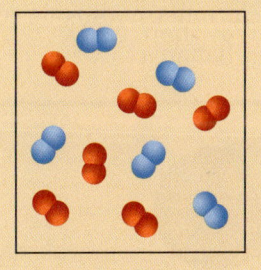

3. Suggest an explanation for this boiling-point data:
   oxygen = −183 °C; water = 100 °C
   (3 marks)

4. Write a paragraph to compare the properties of hydrogen, oxygen, and water. Explain why the properties of the two elements are different from the properties of the compound they make.

   (6 marks)

● Topic 5.3 Elements

5.3.4 Chemical formulae

Learning objectives

After this section you will be able to:
- use particle diagrams to classify a substance as an element, mixture or compound, and as molecules or atoms
- name compounds using their chemical formulae
- use chemical formulae to name the elements present and determine their relative proportions
- represent atoms, molecules, elements, mixtures and compounds using particle diagrams.

Key Words

chemical formula, hydroxide, nitrate, sulfate, carbonate

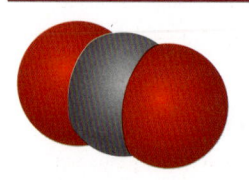

◂ A carbon dioxide molecule has one carbon atom and two oxygen atoms.

A carbon monoxide ▸ molecule has one carbon atom and one oxygen atom.

What's water?

Water contains 2 g of hydrogen for every 16 g of oxygen. Nitrogen dioxide contains 14 g of nitrogen for every 32 g of oxygen. Which compound has the higher proportion of oxygen? Show your working.

Are the windows closed? If so, there is probably more carbon dioxide in the room now than there was 10 minutes ago. Every cell in your body makes carbon dioxide, which you breath out. Carbon dioxide is a compound. It is made up of two elements – carbon and oxygen.

Carbon monoxide is another compound. It also consists of atoms of carbon and oxygen. But carbon monoxide is poisonous. It can be deadly if you breathe it in.

Why are carbon compounds different?

You already know that the properties of a compound depend on the elements in it. The relative numbers of atoms of each element also make a difference.

Carbon dioxide always has 12 g of carbon for every 32 g of oxygen. The amounts of carbon and oxygen in carbon monoxide are different. Carbon monoxide has 12 g of carbon for every 16 g of oxygen.

A State the number and types of atoms that make up one carbon dioxide molecule. Use the diagrams on the left to help you.

How do we name compounds?

Compounds made up of oxygen and another element have two-word names. The second word is *oxide*.

Elements in compound	Name of compound
aluminium and oxygen	aluminium oxide
zinc and oxygen	zinc oxide

Some elements form more than one type of oxide.

Molecule of compound made up of…	Name of compound
1 carbon atom and 1 oxygen atom	carbon **mon**oxide
1 carbon atom and 2 oxygen atoms	carbon **di**oxide
1 sulfur atom and 2 oxygen atoms	sulfur **di**oxide
1 sulfur atom and 3 oxygen atoms	sulfur **tri**oxide

The compound of sodium and chlorine is called sodium chloride. Chlori**n**e becomes chlori**d**e. In any compound of a metal with a non-metal, the end of the name of the non-metal becomes **-ide**.

◀ A sulfur dioxide molecule has one sulfur atom and two oxygen atoms. You can represent it with either a 2-D or 3-D diagram.

A sulfur trioxide molecule has one ▶ sulfur atom and three oxygen atoms. You can represent it with either a 2-D or 3-D diagram.

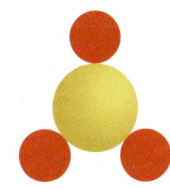

B Name the compound of sodium and chlorine.

What is a chemical formula?

A **chemical formula** shows the elements present in a compound. It also shows the relative number of atoms of each element that are in the compound - 'relative number' means how many of one type of atom there are compared to another. For example:

- The chemical formula of carbon dioxide is CO_2. This shows that there is one carbon atom for every two oxygen atoms.
- The chemical formula of carbon monoxide is CO. This shows that there is one carbon atom for every oxygen atom.

When you are writing chemical formulae, the numbers should be:

- to the right of their chemical symbol, just below the line
- smaller than the chemical symbols.

Many compounds are made up of atoms of more than two elements. These include groups of compounds called hydroxides, nitrates, sulfates, and carbonates. For example:

- A **hydroxide** includes hydrogen and oxygen atoms. The formula of sodium hydroxide is NaOH.
- A **nitrate** includes nitrogen and oxygen atoms. The formula of sodium nitrate is $NaNO_3$. The formula shows that for every one atom of sodium, there is one nitrogen atom and three oxygen atoms.
- A **sulfate** includes sulfur and oxygen atoms. The formula of copper sulfate is $CuSO_4$.
- A **carbonate** includes carbon and oxygen atoms. The formula of calcium carbonate is $CaCO_3$.

C Write down the names of the three elements that make up copper sulfate.

Summary Questions

1 Copy and complete the sentences below.
The formula of carbon dioxide is _____. This shows that a molecule of carbon dioxide is made up of _____ carbon atom and _____ atoms of _____. (4 marks)

2 Name the compounds with these formulae:
a NO   d KOH
b NO_2 e $ZnSO_4$
c HCl   f $CuCO_3$
(6 marks)

3 The formulae below represent compounds that exist as molecules. Name the elements in each compound, and write down the number of atoms of each element in the molecule.
a H_2O b N_2O_4 c CH_4 (6 marks)

4 Draw a diagram to represent the particles described in each of the question parts below. Use one circle to represent one atom.
a One oxygen molecule, made up of two oxygen atoms.
b One argon atom.
c Four nitrogen molecules, each made up of two nitrogen atoms.
d One carbon dioxide molecule, made up of one carbon atom joined to two oxygen atoms.
e A mixture of all the atoms and molecules in parts **a** to **d**.
(5 marks)

5 The formula of sodium hydroxide is NaOH and the formula of potassium hydroxide is KOH. Predict the formula of lithium hydroxide. Explain how you made your prediction. (2 marks)

● Topic 5.3 Elements

5.3.5 Polymers

Learning objectives

After this section you will be able to:
- describe the structure of a polymer
- represent polymers using particle diagrams
- explain how polymer properties depend on their molecules.

▲ Wool is a natural polymer used in clothing.

▲ Starch is a natural polymer found in potatoes and rice.

▲ Rubber is a natural polymer used to make tyres.

Foul Fact

Lobsters, cockroaches, and ants make a polymer – chitin – to form their exoskeletons.

Do you know what umbrellas, beach balls, and carrier bags have in common?

They are made from **polymers**. A polymer is a substance with very long molecules. A polymer molecule has identical groups of atoms, repeated many times.

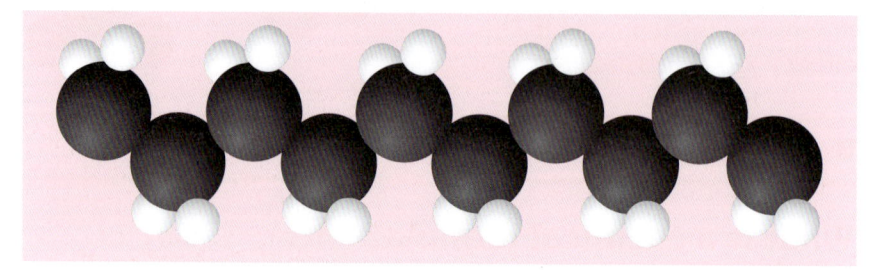

▲ This is part of a molecule of a polymer called poly(ethene). One molecule has thousands of –C_2H_4– units, joined in a long chain. The black spheres represent carbon atoms. The white spheres represent hydrogen atoms.

A State what a polymer is.

How do polymer properties depend on their molecules?

The properties of a polymer depend on its molecules. Polymer molecules are relatively big and heavy. This means that they melt at higher temperatures than substances with smaller molecules.

The table shows the melting temperatures of substances with big and small molecules.

Substance	Number of atoms in one molecule	Melting temperature (°C)
methane, CH_4	5	–182
poly(ethene)	thousands	between 105 and 180

B Explain why methane melts at a lower temperature than poly(ethene).

Why are natural polymers useful?

Plants and animals make **natural polymers**, including wool, cotton, starch, and rubber.

Sheep make wool. Wool fibres trap air between them. This means that wool traps heat, making it useful for jumpers and socks.

Big Idea: Matter 5

Rubber trees produce rubber. Rubber molecules are long and bendy, so they can slide over each other. This means that rubber is flexible. It is also waterproof and durable. These properties make it suitable for tyres.

C Give an example of a polymer, and one of its uses.

Why are synthetic polymers useful?
Synthetic polymers do not occur naturally. They are made in chemical reactions. There are hundreds of synthetic polymers including plastics such as poly(ethene) and PVC. Scientists work hard to develop new polymers. Each polymer has its own properties.

Poly(ethene)
Poly(ethene) is the scientific name for polythene. There are two types of poly(ethene).

- The molecules in low-density poly(ethene) (LDPE) slide over each other. This makes it flexible. LDPE is also strong. LDPE is used for carrier bags.
- High-density poly(ethene) (HDPE) is also strong and flexible. It is harder than LDPE. Its surfaces can be very smooth. HDPE is used in artificial knee joints. Artificial joints also include metal, such as titanium.

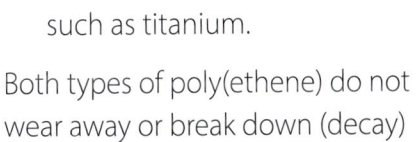

▲ Poly(ethene) bags can be dangerous to wildlife.

Both types of poly(ethene) do not wear away or break down (decay) naturally. This property is very important for artificial knee joints. But the same property makes it hard to get rid of carrier bags.

D State why low-density poly(ethene) makes good carrier bags.

Plotting polymers
Every polymer has its own properties. Plot the density data in the table below on a bar chart. Show your chart to a partner. Ask them to check your scale, labels, and accuracy.

Polymer	Density (g/cm³)
low-density poly(ethene)	0.92
high-density poly(ethene)	0.96
poly(propene)	0.90
poly(vinyl chloride)	1.30
soft rubber	1.10

Key Words
polymer, natural polymer, synthetic polymer

Summary Questions

1 Copy and complete the sentences below.

A polymer has _____ molecules. Each molecule has identical groups of _____, repeated many times. There are two types of polymer: _____ polymers and _____ polymers. Synthetic polymers include poly(ethene) and _____. Both types of poly(ethene) are _____ because their molecules slide over one another.

(6 marks)

2 The list gives some properties of poly(styrene). Choose properties from the list that explain why polystyrene is suitable for:

a packaging

b disposable cups.

Properties: low density; does not conduct electricity; poor conductor of heat; white colour.

(2 marks)

3 Look at the particle diagrams for substances A and B below. Suggest which substance has the higher melting point. Justify your answer.

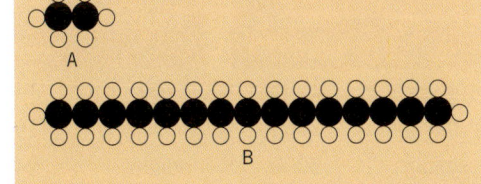

A

B

(2 marks)

● Topic 5.3 Elements

5.4.1 The Periodic Table

Learning objectives

After this section you will be able to:

- state what the groups and periods of the Periodic Table tell you about the elements
- use data to describe a trend in physical properties
- use patterns in data for physical properties to estimate a missing value for an element.

▲ Palladium is used in catalytic converters in cars, surgical instruments, and some flutes.

Key Words

physical properties, Periodic Table, group, period, trend

Palladium is on the left of the stepped line on the Periodic Table. This shows that it is a metal. What can you predict about its properties?

Like most metals, palladium is shiny. It is a good conductor of heat and electricity. These are **physical properties**. They describe features of the material that you can observe without changing the substance.

The **Periodic Table** shows all the elements. It groups together elements with similar properties. If you know the position of palladium (Pd) in the Periodic Table, you can make even better predictions about its properties.

What are groups?

In the Periodic Table, the vertical columns are called **groups**. The elements in a group have similar properties. Going down a group, there are patterns in properties.

1	2											3	4	5	6	7	0
					H												He
Li	Be											B	C	N	O	F	Ne
Na	Mg											Al	Si	P	S	Cl	Ar
K	Ca	Sc	Ti	V	Cr	Mn	Fe	Co	Ni	Cu	Zn	Ga	Ge	As	Se	Br	Kr
Rb	Sr	Y	Zr	Nb	Mo	Tc	Ru	Rh	Pd	Ag	Cd	In	Sn	Sb	Te	I	Xe
Cs	Ba	La	Hf	Ta	W	Re	Os	Ir	Pt	Au	Hg	Tl	Pb	Bi	Po	At	Rn
Fr	Ra																

▲ Metals are on the left of the stepped line, and non-metals are on the right. The numbers show some groups of the Periodic Table.

A State the name given to the vertical columns in the Periodic Table.

The tables below show data for elements near palladium in the Periodic Table. Each table shows the elements in one group.

Sophie studies the data. She makes this prediction:

Element	Melting point (°C)
iron	1535
ruthenium	2500
osmium	3000

Element	Melting point (°C)
cobalt	1492
rhodium	1970
iridium	2440

Element	Melting point (°C)
nickel	1453
palladium	
platinum	1769

For the groups headed by iron and cobalt, melting point increases from top to bottom. The nickel group is likely to show the same pattern. So I predict that the melting point of palladium is between 1453 °C and 1769 °C.

A data book gives the melting point of palladium as 1550 °C. Sophie's prediction is correct.

Big Idea: Matter 5

What are periods?

The horizontal rows of the Periodic Table are called **periods**. Going across a period, there are patterns in the properties of the elements.

The bar charts show the melting points of the Period 2 and Period 3 elements.

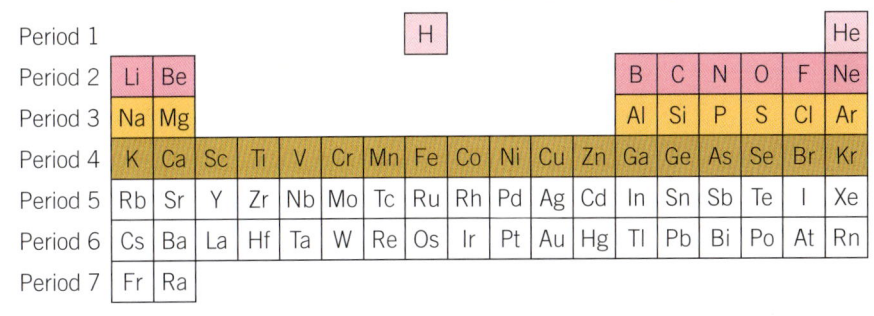

▲ Some periods of the Periodic Table.

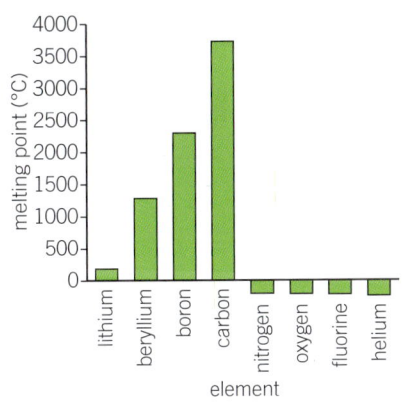

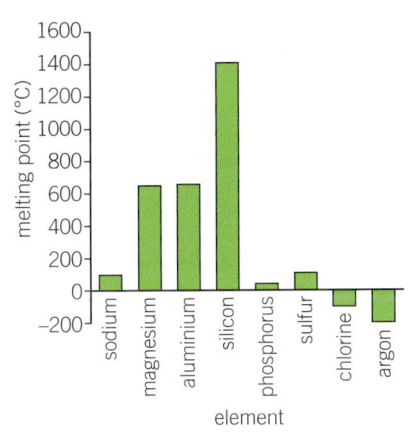

▲ The melting points of Period 2 elements.

▲ The melting points of Period 3 elements.

Adam describes the patterns, or **trends**, shown on the bar charts.

For Period 2, the melting point increases from left to right for the first four elements. The melting points of the other elements are low. The pattern is similar for Period 3.

B State the name given to the horizontal rows in the Periodic Table.

Predictable patterns?

The tables show the sizes of atoms of the Period 2 and Period 3 elements. Draw bar charts to display these data. Describe the trends in atomic radius for the two periods. Then write a sentence to compare the trends.

Period 2

Element	Atomic radius (nm)
lithium	0.123
beryllium	0.089
boron	0.082
carbon	0.070
nitrogen	0.065
oxygen	0.066
fluorine	0.064

Period 3

Element	Atomic radius (nm)
sodium	0.157
magnesium	0.136
aluminium	0.125
silicon	0.117
phosphorus	0.110
sulfur	0.104
chlorine	0.990

Fantastic Fact

The Periodic Table has this name because there is a repeating pattern of properties, like the repeating pattern of menstrual periods.

Summary Questions

1 Copy the sentences below, choosing the correct bold words.

The vertical columns of the Periodic Table are **groups/periods**. The horizontal rows are **groups/periods**. There are patterns in element properties **down/across** groups and **down/across** periods. Metals are on the **left/right** of the stepped line of the Periodic Table and non-metals are on the **left/right**.

(6 marks)

2 The tables give density data. Draw two bar charts to display the data. Use your bar charts, and the Periodic Table, to predict the density of palladium.

Element	Density (g/cm³)
cobalt	8.9
rhodium	12.4
iridium	22.5

Element	Density (g/cm³)
nickel	8.9
palladium	
platinum	21.4

(3 marks)

3 Draw a big outline of the Periodic Table. Add labels to summarise the information on this spread.

(6 marks)

● Topic 5.4 Periodic Table

5.4.2 The elements of Group 1

Learning objectives

After this section you will be able to:
- state the properties and reactivity of the Group 1 elements
- use data and observations to describe trends and predict properties of Group 1 elements
- describe the reactions of any Group 1 element.

◀ Sodium is a good conductor of heat. It is a coolant in nuclear power stations.

Key Words

Group 1, alkali metals, chemical properties

Which conclusion?

The bar chart shows densities for Group 1 elements. Sam says there is no trend. Ben says there is a trend – overall, density increases down the group. Use the bar chart to work out an even better description of the trend.

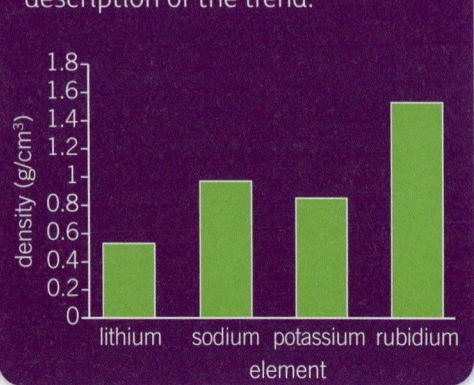

What do the pictures have in common?

▲ A mobile-phone battery.
▲ Engine-lubricating grease.
▲ Red fireworks.

They all rely on compounds of lithium. Lithium is an element in **Group 1**, on the left of the Periodic Table. The Group 1 elements are also called the **alkali metals**.

Are Group 1 elements like other metals?

The Group 1 elements are to the left of the stepped line. This shows that they are metals. In many ways, Group 1 elements are like other metals:

- They are good conductors of electricity and heat.
- They are shiny when freshly cut.

In some ways, Group 1 elements are different to other metals. The table shows that Group 1 elements have lower melting points than other metals.

Element	Is the element in Group 1?	Melting point (°C)
lithium	yes	180
sodium	yes	98
potassium	yes	64
rubidium	yes	39
copper	no	1083
platinum	no	1796

▲ The Group 1 elements.

A State one way in which Group 1 elements differ from other metals.

Are there trends in Group 1 properties?

The Group 1 elements show patterns in physical and **chemical properties**.

Physical properties

The data on the opposite page show that melting point decreases from top to bottom of Group 1. The data below show that boiling point also decreases from top to bottom of Group 1.

Element	Boiling point (°C)
lithium	1330
sodium	890
potassium	774
rubidium	688

B Describe the trend in boiling point as you move down Group 1.

Chemical properties

Chemical properties describe how substances react with other substances. The Group 1 elements are very reactive.

All the Group 1 elements have exciting reactions with water. The reactions make hydrogen gas. The gas moves the reacting element around on the water. The reactions also make alkaline solutions, so universal indicator turns purple.

lithium + water → lithium hydroxide + hydrogen

There is a pattern in the reactions. They all produce hydrogen and a metal hydroxide. The reactions get more vigorous going down the group.

▲ Lithium, at the top of Group 1, reacts quite vigorously with water.

▲ The reaction of potassium with water is very vigorous.

C Name the gas produced when Group 1 elements react with water.

Big Idea: Matter 5

Summary Questions

1 Write five correct sentences from the sentence starters and enders.

Sentence starters	Sentence enders
From top to bottom of Group 1…	…have low densities.
From bottom to top of Group 1…	…are reactive.
All Group 1 elements…	…are called alkali metals.
	…boiling point decreases.
	…react with water to make hydrogen and an alkaline solution.
	…the vigour of the reaction with water increases.

(5 marks)

2 The table gives hardness values for some Group 1 elements. The bigger the value, the harder the element.

Element	Mohs hardness
lithium	0.6
sodium	0.5
potassium	
rubidium	0.3
caesium	0.2

a Plot the hardness values on a bar chart. (6 marks)
b Describe the trend in hardness values. (2 marks)
c Predict the hardness of potassium. Explain your prediction. (2 marks)

3 Predict and describe in detail what happens when a scientist adds rubidium to water. Name the products of the reaction. Justify your prediction. (6 marks)

4 Describe in detail trends in the physical and chemical properties of the Group 1 elements. (6 marks)

● Topic 5.4 Periodic Table

5.4.3 The elements of Group 7

Learning objectives
After this section you will be able to:
- state the properties and reactivity of the Group 7 elements
- use data and observations to describe trends and predict properties of Group 7 elements
- describe the reactions of any Group 7 element.

Foul Fact
Five thousand soldiers died from chlorine poisoning in World War 1.

▲ Chlorine is pale green. Bromine is dark red in the liquid state, and orange in the gas state. In the solid state iodine crystals are grey-black. Iodine vapour is purple.

Key Words
Group 7, halogen

Better bar charts
Plot a bar chart for the Group 7 boiling-point data opposite. Swap bar charts with a partner. Can you suggest improvements?

Have you ever smelt chlorine in tap water? Chlorine and its compounds do a vital job. Tiny amounts destroy deadly bacteria, making water safe to drink and swim in.

A State one use of chlorine.

Are Group 7 elements like other non-metals?
Chlorine is in **Group 7** of the Periodic Table. The other elements of the group are fluorine, bromine, iodine, and astatine. The Group 7 elements are also called **halogens**.

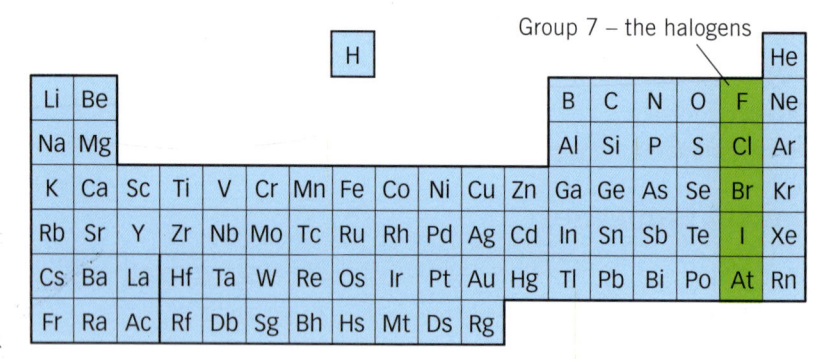

▲ Group 7 is towards the right of the Periodic Table.

The halogens have low melting points, like most non-metals. They do not conduct electricity. Iodine is a brittle solid at room temperature.

B Name the elements in Group 7.

Are there patterns in Group 7 properties?
Physical properties
The table shows melting- and boiling-point data.

Element	Melting point (°C)	Boiling point (°C)	State at room temperature
fluorine	−220	−188	gas
chlorine	−101	−35	gas
bromine	−7	59	liquid
iodine	114	184	solid

In Group 7, melting point increases from top to bottom. This is different to Group 1, where melting point decreases from top to bottom.

C Describe the pattern in boiling points for the Group 7 elements.

The colours of the elements get darker from top to bottom.

Chemical properties
The Group 7 elements are reactive. Their reactions are similar. For example, all the Group 7 elements react with iron. The word equations summarise the reactions.

iron + chlorine → iron chloride

iron + bromine → iron bromide

iron + iodine → iron iodide

There is a trend in reactivity. The reaction of chlorine with iron is very vigorous. There is a bright flame. The reactions get less vigorous going down the group. This is different to Group 1, in which reactions get more vigorous from top to bottom.

D Describe how the reactions of the Group 7 elements with iron change going down the group.

What are displacement reactions?
Angus adds chlorine solution to potassium bromide solution. He records his observations.

	Appearance
chlorine solution (before reaction)	pale green
potassium bromide solution (before reaction)	colourless
mixture after reaction	orange

◀ Chlorine solution reacting with potassium bromide solution.

The orange substance is bromine. It is a product of the reaction. In the reaction, chlorine displaces bromine from potassium bromide. Elements nearer the top of Group 7 displace elements lower in the group from their compounds. Examples of displacement reactions are:

chlorine + potassium bromide → potassium chloride + bromine

bromine + potassium iodide → potassium bromide + iodine

The displacement reactions of halogens are similar to the displacement reactions of metals. In both, a more reactive element takes the place of a less reactive element in its compounds.

Big Idea: Matter 5

◀ Iron reacts vigorously with chlorine.

Summary Questions

1 Copy and complete the sentences below.

The Group 7 elements are also called the _____. The melting and boiling points _____ from top to bottom. The reactions get _____ vigorous from top to bottom.

(3 marks)

2 Predict which of the reactions below will happen. Explain your choices.

a fluorine + potassium chloride → potassium fluoride + chlorine

b iodine + potassium chloride → potassium iodide + chlorine

c bromine + sodium iodide → sodium bromide + iodine

d chlorine + sodium bromide → sodium chloride + bromine

(3 marks)

3 Predict the product of the reaction of iron with fluorine. What would a scientist see if she did the reaction? Justify your predictions.

(4 marks)

4 A student adds a halogen solution to potassium chloride solution. There is no reaction. Predict the position of the halogen in the Periodic Table, compared to the position of chlorine. Justify your prediction.

(3 marks)

● Topic 5.4 Periodic Table

5.4.4 The elements of Group 0

Learning objectives

After this section you will be able to:
- state the properties and reactivity of the Group 0 elements
- use data and observations to describe trends and predict properties of Group 0 elements
- describe the reactions of any Group 0 element.

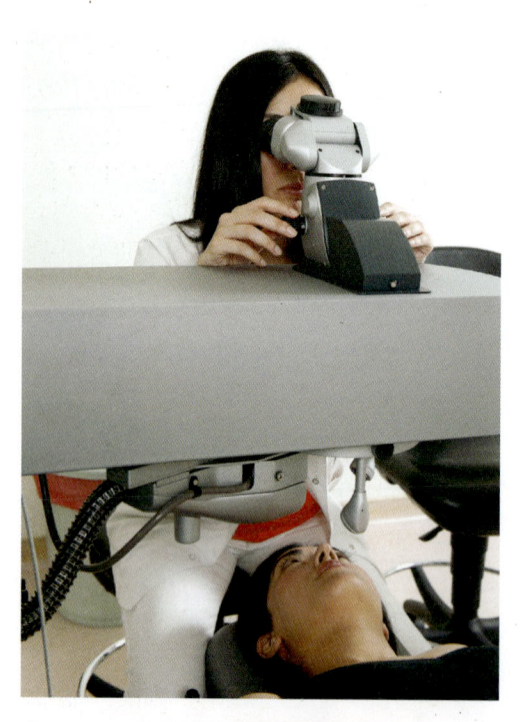

What do double glazing, bar-code scanners, and helium balloons have in common?

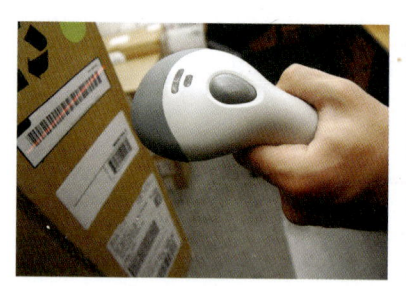

They all make use of elements in the same group of the Periodic Table, **Group 0**. Group 0 includes helium, neon, argon, krypton, xenon, and radon. The elements of Group 0 are also called the **noble gases**.

A Name the six noble gases.

Are there patterns in Group 0 properties?

Physical properties

The noble gases have very low melting and boiling points, like many other non-metals. They are colourless gases at room temperature. The table shows their boiling points.

Element	Boiling point (°C)
helium	−269
neon	−246
argon	−186
krypton	−152
xenon	−108

B Describe the pattern in boiling points for the Group 0 elements

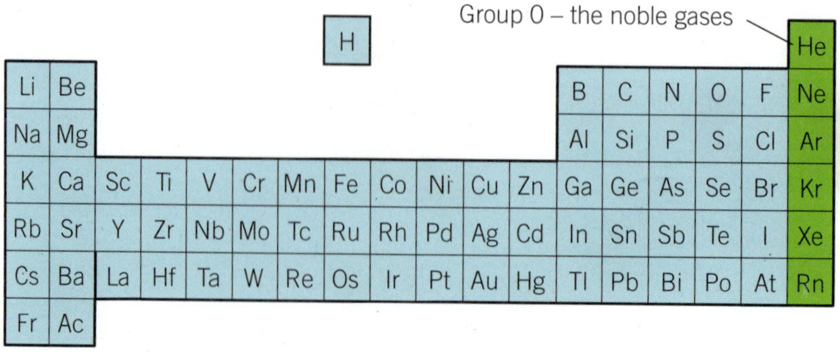

▲ Eye surgeons use krypton lasers to repair tears in the retina at the back of the eye.

▲ Group 0 is on the right of the Periodic Table.

Key Words

Group 0, noble gases, unreactive

The noble gases glow brightly when high-voltage electricity passes through them. This property explains why noble gases are used in advertising signs. The letters contain neon gas.

▲ This sign contains neon gas.

▲ Helium has a lower density than the air. This is why it is used in helium balloons.

▲ Argon is a better insulator than air, so it is used in the gap between the two panes of glass in double glazing.

Chemical properties

The noble gases take part in very few reactions. Scientists say they are **unreactive**. From top to bottom of the group, the noble gases get slightly more reactive.

- As far as we know, helium and neon never take part in chemical reactions.
- By the year 2000, a group of Finnish scientists had made the compound argon fluorohydride, ArHF, but it only existed at temperatures below −265 °C.
- Krypton reacts with the most reactive element there is, fluorine, to make krypton difluoride, KrF_2.
- Xenon, like the other Group 0 elements, is very unreactive. However, it does form compounds with fluorine and oxygen.

C State the meaning of the word unreactive.

Where do noble gases come from?

All the noble gases exist in the atmosphere, mixed with other gases. Companies use fractional distillation to separate them from the air. Helium is also found mixed with natural gas under the ground or under the sea. It is expensive to separate helium from the mixture.

Using Group 0

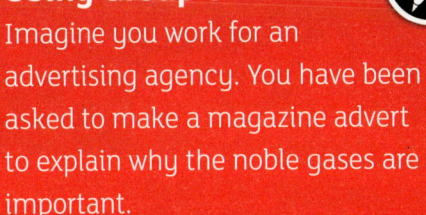

Imagine you work for an advertising agency. You have been asked to make a magazine advert to explain why the noble gases are important.

First, discuss with a partner what the advert will include. Make notes to summarise your ideas. Then create your advert. Make sure it is eye-catching and persuasive.

Summary Questions

1. Each sentence below has one mistake. Copy the sentences, correcting the mistakes.

   The noble gases are all in Group 1 of the Periodic Table. The element at the top of the group is neon. The noble gases are metals. They have vigorous reactions. From bottom to top of the group, boiling point increases.

   (5 marks)

2. The table shows the melting points of the noble gases. Describe the pattern, and predict the melting point of argon.

Element	Melting point (°C)
helium	−270
neon	−249
argon	
krypton	−157
xenon	−112

   (2 marks)

3. Compare the trends in boiling point for the Group 7 and Group 0 elements. You will need to use data from this and the previous spread. *(4 marks)*

● Topic 5.4 Periodic Table

5 Matter: Summary

Key Points

Elements
- All materials are made up of one or more elements.
- Elements are substances that cannot be broken down.
- Every element has its own chemical symbol.
- An atom is the smallest part of an element that can exist.
- Every element is made up of one type of atom. All the atoms of an element are the same. The atoms of different elements are different.
- The properties of a substance are the properties of many atoms.
- A compound is a substance made up of atoms of two or more elements, strongly joined together. Its properties are different to those of its elements.
- A molecule is a group of two or more atoms that are strongly joined together.
- A chemical formula shows the relative number of atoms of each element in a compound.

Periodic Table
- You can use the arrangement of elements in the Periodic Table to explain and predict patterns in physical and chemical properties.
- In the Periodic Table, the horizontal rows are periods and the vertical columns are groups.
- Going across periods and down groups, there are patterns in the elements' properties.
- Group 1 elements have low melting and boiling points, and low densities. They are reactive.
- Group 1 elements react vigorously with water to make hydroxides and hydrogen. The reactions get more vigorous from top to bottom of the group.
- Going down Group 7, melting and boiling points increase. The colours of the elements get darker. The elements are reactive. The reactions get less vigorous from top to bottom of the group.
- Group 0 elements are called the noble gases. They are unreactive.

Key Words

physical properties, Periodic Table, group, period, trend, Group 1, alkali metals, chemical properties, Group 7, halogen, Group 0, noble gases, unreactive

Maths challenge

The elements of Group 3
The table opposite shows some properties of the Group 3 elements.

Task
Display the data on two bar charts. Then write a few sentences to describe the patterns in properties.

Tips
- For both bar charts, write the names of the elements on the x-axis.
- Each bar chart needs a different label and a different scale for the y-axis.
- Make sure the y-axis scales are even.

Element	Density (g/cm³)	Boiling point (°C)
boron	2.3	3930
aluminium	2.7	2470
gallium	5.9	2400
indium	7.3	2000
thallium	11.8	1460

End-of-Big Idea questions

1. 🧪 Carbon dioxide is a compound made up of two elements.
   a. State what is meant by the word element. *(1 mark)*
   b. State the number of types of atom in the element carbon. *(1 mark)*
   c. One of the elements in carbon dioxide is carbon. Name the other element. *(1 mark)*
   d. State the number of types of atom in carbon dioxide. *(1 mark)*
   e. Copy and complete the sentences below. The formula of carbon dioxide is CO_2. There is _____ atom of carbon for every two atoms of _____. *(2 marks)*

   (6 marks)

2. 🧪🧪 The diagram below shows a molecule of sulfur dioxide. Each sphere represents one atom. Different-coloured spheres represent atoms of different elements.

   a. State the total number of atoms in the molecule. *(1 mark)*
   b. State the number of different types of atom in the molecule. *(1 mark)*
   c. State whether sulfur dioxide is an element or a compound. Explain your decision. *(2 marks)*
   d. Copy and complete the table below. *(2 marks)*

Name of element	Number of atoms of this element in one sulfur dioxide molecule
sulfur	
	2

   e. Write the formula of sulfur dioxide. *(2 marks)*

   (8 marks)

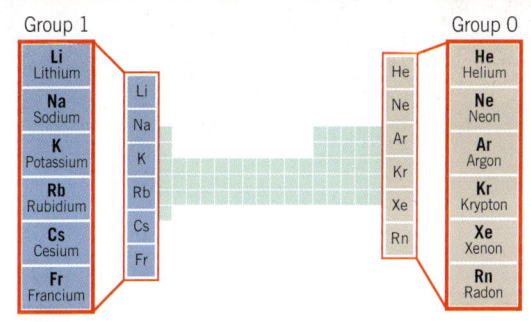

3. 🧪🧪🧪 The following table shows data for six elements. The diagram shows their positions in the Periodic Table.

Name of element	Chemical symbol	Melting point (°C)
lithium	Li	180
sodium	Na	98
potassium	K	64
neon	Ne	−249
argon	Ar	−189
krypton	Kr	−157

   Compare the melting point patterns for the Group 1 and Group 0 elements.

   (6 marks)

4. 🧪🧪🧪 The outline periodic table shows the positions of five elements. Each element is represented by a letter of the alphabet. The letters are not the same as the chemical symbols for the elements.

   Match the elements represented by the letters in the Periodic Table to the statements below.
   a. A shiny element that conducts electricity and reacts vigorously with water. *(1 mark)*
   b. An unreactive gas at room temperature. *(1 mark)*
   c. A reactive non-metal with a low boiling point. *(1 mark)*
   d. An element that could be used for electrical cables. *(1 mark)*
   e. An element that could be pumped into a container used to store important documents. *(1 mark)*

   (5 marks)

6 Reactions

Chemical reactions are vital to life. We depend on chemical reactions – including the products they make and the energy they transfer – for everything we do. In this Big Idea you will learn what happens to atoms in chemical reactions. You will find out how chemical reactions transfer energy, and why chemical reactions are important.

Q Is boiling an example of a chemical reaction?

You already know

- In chemical reactions, substances react to make new substances, called products.
- Chemical reactions are not easily reversible.
- In a chemical reaction, you might see flames, notice substances getting cooler or hotter, smell products as they are made, or hear sounds as the reaction occurs.
- You can show chemical reactions in word equations.
- Some metals burn in air. On burning, they transfer energy to the surroundings as heat and light.

BIG Questions

- What happens to the atoms in chemical reactions?
- How does mass change in chemical reactions?
- Why do chemical reactions transfer energy?

Picture Puzzler
Key Words

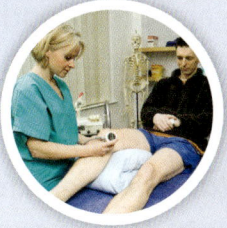

Can you solve this Picture Puzzler?
The first letter of each of these images spells out a science word that you will come across in this book.

Picture Puzzler
Close Up

Can you tell what this zoomed-in picture is?
Clue: There is one of these in the exhaust system of most cars.

Making connections

In **Book 1, 6.2 Metals and non-metals** you learnt about atoms, and about the burning reactions of some metals.

In **7.3 Climate** you will learn how the products of burning reactions impact on the environment.

6.3.1 Atoms in chemical reactions

Learning objectives

After this section you will be able to:
- describe the model of chemical change and conservation of mass
- write word equations from information about chemical reactions
- use particle diagrams to show what happens in a chemical reaction.

▲ At the high temperatures of a car engine, nitrogen and oxygen react together to make nitrogen monoxide.

Link

You learnt how to write word equations in Book 1, 6.2.2 Chemical reactions of metals and non-metals.

At the high temperatures of a car engine, nitrogen and oxygen from the air react together to make a new substance, nitrogen monoxide. In this chemical reaction, two elements join together to make a compound. As for all chemical reactions, the change is not easily reversible. Once nitrogen monoxide has been formed, it is very difficult to split it up into its elements.

Like all **chemical reactions**, the reaction involves a transfer of energy between the reacting substances and the surroundings.

Word equations

You can write a word equation to represent the reaction of nitrogen with oxygen:

$$\text{nitrogen} + \text{oxygen} \rightarrow \text{nitrogen monoxide}$$

As you know, in any word equation:
- the starting substances, the **reactants**, are on the left of the arrow
- the substances that are made, the **products**, are on the right of the arrow
- the arrow means *reacts to make*.

A Write a word equation for the reaction of nitrogen with oxygen to make nitrogen monoxide.

Rearranging atoms

In every chemical reaction atoms are rearranged to make new substances. The atoms are joined together in one way before the reaction and in a different way after the reaction. All the atoms that are present before the reaction are still present after the reaction. The total number of atoms does not change. The only difference is that they are joined to each other in different arrangements.

In the air, nitrogen exists as molecules. Each molecule is made up of two nitrogen atoms, so its formula is N_2.

◄ You can represent a nitrogen molecule, N_2, like this.

Oxygen gas also exists as molecules. Each molecule is made up of two oxygen atoms, so its formula is O_2.

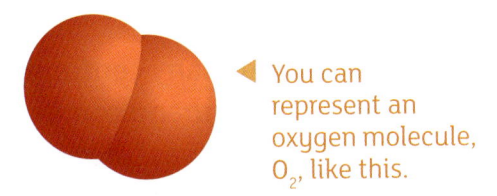

◀ You can represent an oxygen molecule, O_2, like this.

In the chemical reaction of nitrogen with oxygen, nitrogen and oxygen molecules split up. The nitrogen and oxygen atoms are rearranged. They join together differently to form nitrogen monoxide molecules, NO. Each nitrogen monoxide molecule is made up of one nitrogen atom joined to one oxygen atom.

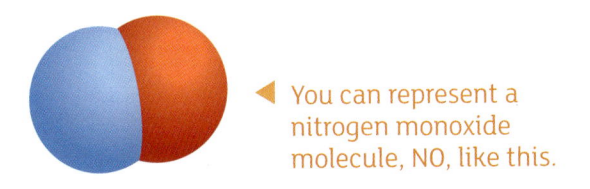

◀ You can represent a nitrogen monoxide molecule, NO, like this.

The diagram below summarises how the atoms are arranged in the reaction of nitrogen with oxygen. There are the same number of atoms of each element before and after the reaction. The number of atoms is **conserved**.

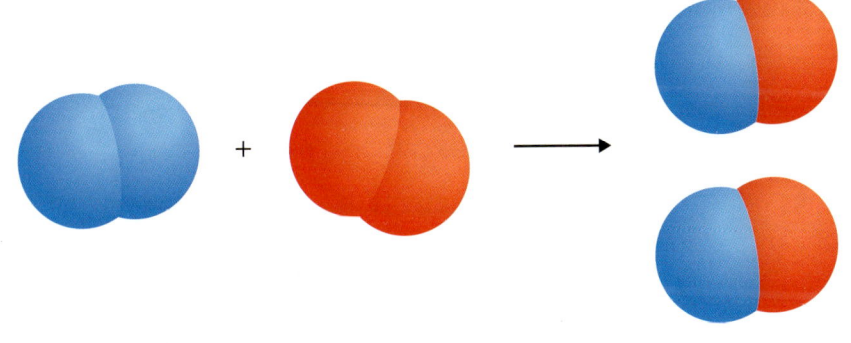

▲ This particle diagram shows what happens when nitrogen reacts with oxygen.

B Look carefully at the particle diagram above. Write down the number of nitrogen atoms in the reactants and in the products. Then write down the number of oxygen atoms in the reactants and in the products.

Big Idea: Reactions 6

Key Words

chemical reaction, reactants, products, conserved

Link

You can learn about acids and bases in 6.1.2 Acids and alkalis.

Summary Questions

1. Copy and complete the sentences below choosing the correct bold words.

   In a chemical reaction, atoms are **created/rearranged**. The atoms are joined together in **the same/different** arrangements after the reaction. The total number of each type of atom is **greater/less/the same** after the reaction.

   (3 marks)

2. The chemical reaction of hydrogen with oxygen makes water. In the reaction, two hydrogen molecules, H_2, and one oxygen molecule, O_2, split up. These atoms join together in a different arrangement to make two water molecules, H_2O. Draw a particle diagram to show what happens in this reaction.

   (3 marks)

3. In the air, nitrogen monoxide, NO, reacts with oxygen, O_2, to make nitrogen dioxide, NO_2. Draw a particle diagram to show what happens in this reaction. You will need to work out the number of each type of molecule in the reactants and products.

   (3 marks)

● Topic 6.3 Types of reaction

6.3.2 Combustion

Learning objectives

After this section you will be able to:

- state the energy transfers involved in combustion
- write word equations for combustion reactions
- use particle diagrams to describe what happens in combustion reactions
- predict the products of the combustion of a given reactant.

▲ This apparatus makes methane from waste.

▲ This vehicle burns waste cooking oil.

▲ North Sea oil and methane gas are fossil fuels.

How do you heat your home? Many central-heating systems burn methane gas. Methane comes from under the ground, or under the sea. It was formed from tiny plants and animals that lived millions of years ago.

If you live in Poundbury, Dorset, your methane might come from another source. Waste from chocolate and cereal factories produces methane in just a few weeks.

What are fuels?

Methane is a **fuel**. A fuel is a substance that stores energy in a chemical store. When a fuel burns, it transfers energy to the surroundings as heat. Fuels include petrol, diesel, coal, ethanol, hydrogen, and waste cooking oil.

A State the meaning of the word fuel.

What are combustion reactions?

Fuels burn in chemical reactions. Burning is also called **combustion**. In a combustion reaction, a substance reacts with oxygen, and energy is transferred to the surroundings as heat and light.

The fuel methane is a compound of carbon and hydrogen. Its chemical formula is CH_4. When it burns, it reacts with oxygen from the air. The reaction makes two products, carbon dioxide and water:

methane + oxygen → carbon dioxide + water

The particle diagram below represents this reaction. It shows that one molecule of methane reacts with two molecules of oxygen to make one molecule of carbon dioxide and two molecules of water.

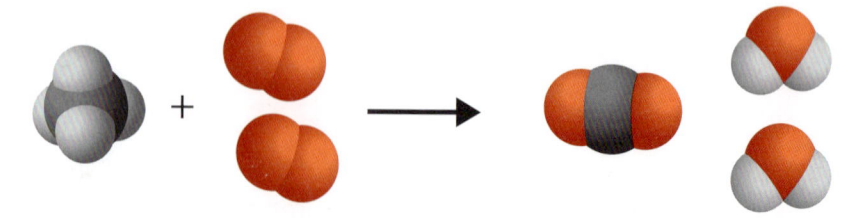

Petrol is a mixture of compounds. Most of its compounds consist of atoms of hydrogen and carbon. Petrol makes mainly carbon dioxide and water when it burns in car engines.

Key Words

fuel, combustion, fossil fuel, non-renewable, renewable

B Name the two elements that methane is made up of.

Petrol, diesel, coal, and methane from under the ground or sea are **fossil fuels**. They are **non-renewable**. This means that they cannot be replaced once they have been used. They will run out one day.

Future fuels?

For thousands of years, people have used cow dung as a fuel for cooking and heating. Now, scientists are finding ways of using other waste substances, such as cooking oil and chicken faeces, to fuel homes and vehicles. These fuels are **renewable**, since they can be made over a short timescale.

In Brazil, India, and several European countries, drivers fill car fuel tanks with ethanol. The ethanol is made from crops such as sugar cane, so it is a renewable fuel. The crops remove carbon dioxide from the atmosphere as they grow.

Scientists and engineers are also developing new types of cars that burn hydrogen in their engines. In this combustion reaction, hydrogen joins with oxygen from the air. There is one product, water.

$$\text{hydrogen} + \text{oxygen} \rightarrow \text{water}$$

Some people think that hydrogen should be used to fuel more cars. This is because its only combustion product is harmless water. The combustion reactions of methane, petrol, diesel, ethanol, cooking oil, and chicken faeces produce mainly carbon dioxide and water.

Carbon dioxide is a greenhouse gas. Extra carbon dioxide in the atmosphere causes climate change.

But where does the hydrogen to fuel cars come from? Companies make hydrogen from methane, or water. Sometimes, the processes they use to make the hydrogen also produce greenhouse gases.

C Name the two reactants when hydrogen burns in air.

Fuels for the future
Should we fuel cars with petrol and diesel or find other fuels, such as hydrogen or waste cooking oil? Start by making notes about the pros and cons of different fuels. Include information about their products of combustion and whether or not the fuels are renewable. Then write a few paragraphs to explain your decision.

Summary Questions

1 Copy the sentences below, choosing the correct bold words.
  a A fuel is a substance that stores energy in a **gravitational**/**chemical** store. (1 mark)
  b Fuels burn to transfer **useless**/**useful** energy. (1 mark)
  c Combustion is another word for **burning**/**melting**. (1 mark)
  d In a combustion reaction, a substance reacts with **nitrogen**/**oxygen** from the air. (1 mark)

2 Cooking oil contains compounds of carbon, hydrogen, and oxygen. Predict two products of its combustion. (2 marks)

3 Propane and butane are fuels. Like methane, they are both compounds of carbon and hydrogen. Like methane, when propane burns it is reacting with oxygen to make carbon dioxide and water. Butane reacts with oxygen in a similar way to methane and propane.
  a Predict the two products formed when butane reacts with oxygen. (2 marks)
  b Write the reaction as a word equation. (1 mark)
  c Devise a general rule that describes how compounds made up of carbon and hydrogen react with oxygen. (2 marks)

4 Nathan says that burning any fuel contributes to climate change. Riana thinks Nathan is wrong. Use cartoon pictures and speech bubbles to show them having a conversation about burning fuels. (6 marks)

• Topic 6.3 Types of reaction

6.3.3 Thermal decomposition

Learning objectives

After this section you will be able to:
- state what thermal decomposition is
- write word equations for decomposition reactions
- use particle diagrams to describe what happens in decomposition reactions
- predict the products of the decomposition of a given reactant.

▲ Copper carbonate.

Key Words

decomposition, thermal decomposition

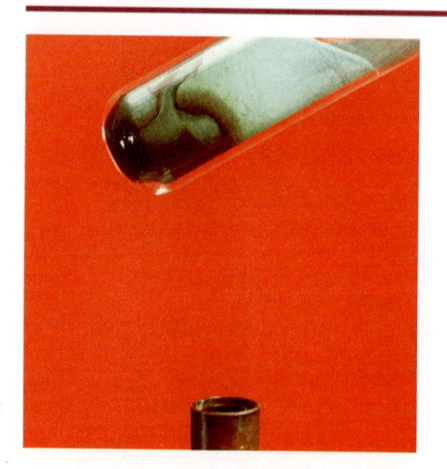

▲ Copper carbonate decomposes on heating to form copper oxide and carbon dioxide.

What made this man's hair so blond?

He put hydrogen peroxide in his hair. Hydrogen peroxide is a compound. It has atoms of two elements, hydrogen and oxygen. Its formula is H_2O_2.

You cannot bleach hair with old hydrogen peroxide. This is because hydrogen peroxide molecules break up. When this happens there are two products – water and oxygen.

$$\text{hydrogen peroxide} \rightarrow \text{water} + \text{oxygen}$$

This particle diagram represents the reaction. It shows that two hydrogen peroxide molecules break up to make two water molecules and one oxygen molecule. The total number of atoms of each element is the same in the reactants and products.

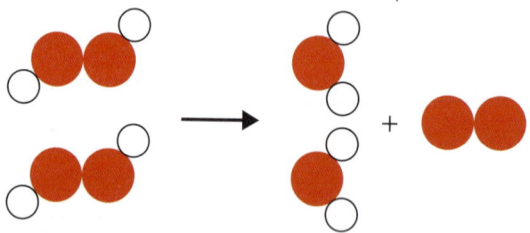

The reaction shown above is a **decomposition** reaction. In decomposition reactions, a single compound breaks down into simpler compounds or elements.

A State what a decomposition reaction is.

Thermal decomposition reactions

Copper carbonate is a green compound. It is made up of atoms of three elements – copper, carbon, and oxygen.

If you heat copper carbonate, it breaks down. The reaction makes copper oxide and carbon dioxide. Copper oxide is black. It remains in the test tube. Carbon dioxide forms as a gas.

$$\text{copper carbonate} \rightarrow \text{copper oxide} + \text{carbon dioxide}$$

Big Idea: Reactions 6

You can show that the gas is carbon dioxide by bubbling it through limewater in the apparatus shown. The limewater goes cloudy.

Other types of carbonate decompose on heating:

lead carbonate → lead oxide + carbon dioxide

zinc carbonate → zinc oxide + carbon dioxide

When a single substance breaks down on heating to make more than one product, the reaction is a **thermal decomposition** reaction. You can say that each product is simpler than the starting substance, because it has atoms of a smaller number of different elements.

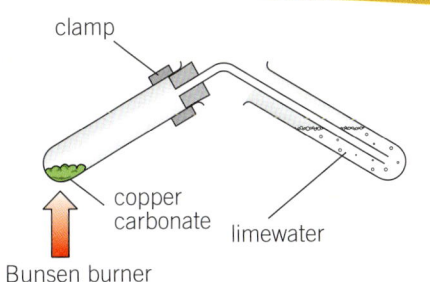

▲ Apparatus to test the gas produced when copper carbonate is heated.

B Name the products of the thermal decomposition reaction of lead carbonate.

Other thermal decomposition reactions

The elements of Group 2 of the Periodic Table form nitrates. The table shows some of their formulae.

Compound	Formula
magnesium nitrate	$Mg(NO_3)_2$
calcium nitrate	$Ca(NO_3)_2$
strontium nitrate	$Sr(NO_3)_2$

On heating, magnesium nitrate decomposes to make three products – magnesium oxide, nitrogen dioxide, and oxygen. This word equation summarises the reaction:

magnesium nitrate → magnesium oxide + nitrogen dioxide + oxygen

The nitrates of the other Group 2 elements also decompose on heating. You need to heat calcium nitrate more strongly than magnesium nitrate to make it break down. You need to heat strontium nitrate even more strongly.

◄ Magnesium nitrate decomposes to make brown nitrogen dioxide gas, as well as other products.

C Name the products of the thermal decomposition reaction of magnesium nitrate.

Summary Questions

1. Copy and complete the sentences below.

   In a decomposition reaction, a single _____ breaks down to make _____ compounds and elements. Copper carbonate decomposes to make _____ oxide and _____ dioxide gas. Hydrogen peroxide decomposes to make water and _____ gas. (5 marks)

2. Choose the reactions below that are decomposition reactions, and the reactions that are combustion reactions. Explain each choice. (4 marks)

   a calcium + oxygen → calcium oxide

   b zinc carbonate → zinc oxide + carbon dioxide

   c hydrogen peroxide → water + oxygen

   d methane + oxygen → carbon dioxide + water

3. Predict the products of the thermal decomposition reaction of strontium nitrate and show the reaction as a word equation. (6 marks)

4. Devise a general rule to predict the products of the thermal decomposition reactions of the nitrates of the Group 2 elements. (3 marks)

● Topic 6.3 Types of reaction

6.3.4 Conservation of mass

Learning objectives

After this section you will be able to:
- state what is meant by conservation of mass
- explain observations about mass in a chemical or physical change
- calculate masses of reactants and products
- balance symbol equations.

What happens to wood in campfires? Wood is a mixture of many substances. On burning, the substances react with oxygen. The reactions make many products, including ash and carbon dioxide. The total mass of wood is equal to the mass of ash and all the other products.

In any chemical reaction, atoms are rearranged and join together differently. The number and mass of each type of atom does not change. This explains why the total mass of the reactants is equal to the total mass of the products. This is called **conservation of mass**. Mass is also conserved in **physical changes**, such as dissolving and melting. A physical change is one that changes the physical properties of a substance, but does not make new substances.

A State what conservation of mass means.

Calculating masses

Yon-Hee has some magnesium. She finds its mass. She burns the magnesium, and finds the mass of the product.

mass of magnesium = 0.24 g

mass of product = 0.40 g

Yon-Hee wonders why the mass appears to have increased. The word equation for the reaction helps her to work out the answer.

magnesium + oxygen → magnesium oxide

Magnesium has reacted with oxygen from the air. The oxygen has its own mass. The total mass of magnesium and oxygen at the start of the reaction is equal to the mass of magnesium oxide made in the reaction.

Yon-Hee calculates the mass of oxygen that reacted:

total mass of reactants = total mass of products

0.24 g + mass of oxygen = 0.40 g

mass of oxygen = 0.40 g − 0.24 g

mass of oxygen = 0.16 g

▲ On burning, wood makes many products, including ash (which is a mixture of substances) and carbon dioxide.

◀ Burning magnesium.

Mass matters
Look at Yon-Hee's calculation. Predict the masses of reactants and products if she started with 0.48 g of magnesium.

Big Idea: Reactions 6

Writing balanced equations

Word equations show reactants and products in reactions.

Balanced symbol equations also show:

- the formulae of reactants and products
- how the atoms are rearranged
- the relative amounts of reactants and products.

A balanced symbol equation is a bit like a particle diagram for a reaction. It shows the atoms in the reactants and products, and how they are rearranged.

Follow the steps shown in the examples below to write balanced symbol equations for chemical reactions.

Burning carbon

- First, write a word equation:

  carbon + oxygen → carbon dioxide

- Write chemical symbols or formulae for each reactant and product. You cannot guess these.

  $C + O_2 \rightarrow CO_2$

- Now balance the equation. There must be the same number of atoms of each element on each side of the equation. The equation shows one atom of carbon on each side of the arrow, and two atoms of oxygen. It is balanced.

B State what balanced symbol equations show.

Burning magnesium

- Write a word equation and add formulae:

  magnesium + oxygen → magnesium oxide

  $Mg + O_2 \rightarrow MgO$

- Balance the amounts of oxygen. There are two atoms on the left of the arrow, and one on the right. Add a big 2 to the left of the MgO. Do not add or change any little numbers:

  $Mg + O_2 \rightarrow 2MgO$

The big 2 applies to both Mg and O in magnesium oxide.

- Now balance the amounts of magnesium. There is one atom on the left of the arrow, and two on the right. Add a big 2 to the left of the Mg. The equation is balanced.

  $2Mg + O_2 \rightarrow 2MgO$

Key Words

conservation of mass, physical change, balanced symbol equation

Summary Questions

1. 🧪 Copy and complete the sentences below.

   In chemical reactions, the total number of _____ does not change. This means that the total mass of reactants _____ the total mass of products. This is called _____ of mass.

   (3 marks)

2. 🧪🧪 Miss Keefe heats 8.6 g of solid magnesium nitrate. The mass of the solid product is 2.32 g. Explain why the mass of solid decreases in the reaction.

   (2 marks)

3. 🧪🧪🧪 Kezi heats 12.5 g of zinc carbonate. It decomposes to make 8.1 g of zinc oxide. Calculate the mass of carbon dioxide made.

   (2 marks)

4. 🧪🧪🧪 Nitrogen, N_2, reacts with oxygen, O_2, to make nitrogen monoxide, NO. Write a balanced equation for the reaction. If you need help, look back at the particle diagram from the reaction on 6.3.1.

   (3 marks)

5. 🧪🧪🧪 Hydrogen peroxide, H_2O_2, decomposes to make water, H_2O, and oxygen, O_2. Write a balanced symbol equation for the reaction. If you need help, look back at the particle diagram for the reaction on 6.3.3.

   (6 marks)

- Topic 6.3 Types of reaction

6.4.1 Exothermic and endothermic

Learning objectives

After this section you will be able to:
- describe exothermic and endothermic changes
- use experimental observations to distinguish exothermic and endothermic reactions.

Have you ever used a cold pack on an injury? How did the pack get cold?

One type of cold pack includes two substances. An outer bag contains liquid water. An inner bag contains solid ammonium nitrate. When you break the inner bag, the water and ammonium nitrate mix. The solid dissolves in the water, and the mixture cools. The injured body part transfers energy to the mixture, so the injury cools down and feels better. The mixture slowly returns to the temperature of the surroundings.

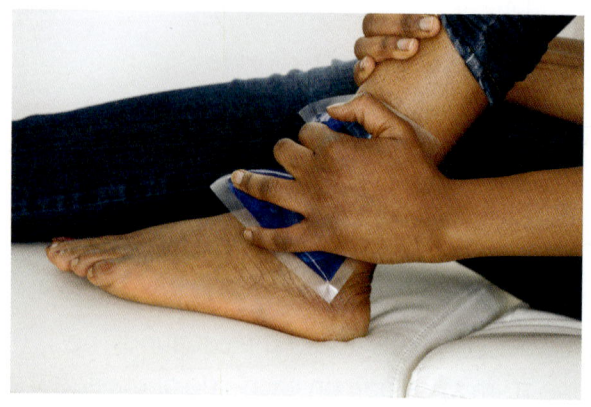

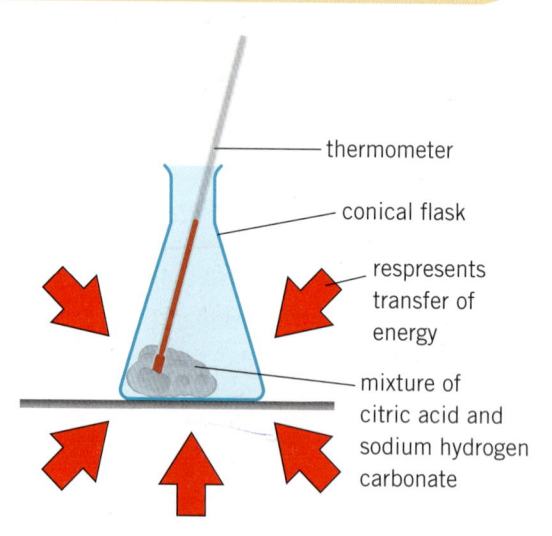

▲ The reaction of citric acid with sodium hydrogen carbonate is endothermic.

◀ A cold pack on a sports injury.

What is an endothermic change?

The process in the cold pack is an **endothermic change**. In this type of change, energy is transferred *from* the surroundings *to* substances that are reacting, changing state, or dissolving. Endothermic changes include:

- some chemical reactions
- melting and boiling
- dissolving some substances in water.

Tom has some citric acid crystals. Their temperature is 20 °C. He adds sodium hydrogen carbonate powder. There is a chemical reaction. The reacting mixture feels cold. Its temperature goes down to 10 °C. The temperature decrease shows that it is an **endothermic reaction**.

Once the reaction is complete, Tom leaves his mixture of products in the lab. After a while its temperature returns to 20 °C.

A State what an endothermic reaction is.

Foul Fact!

You can get frostbite from cold packs if you don't use them properly. Never leave them on your skin for longer than the pack says.

What is an exothermic change?

Some changes are exothermic. In this type of change, energy is transferred *to* the surroundings *from* substances that are reacting, changing state, or dissolving. **Exothermic changes** include:

- chemical reactions, for example, combustion
- freezing and condensing
- dissolving some substances in water.

◀ Burning reactions transfer energy to the surroundings. They are exothermic.

Zoe has some dilute sulfuric acid. She also has some sodium hydroxide solution. The temperature of both solutions is 20 °C. Zoe mixes them. There is a chemical reaction. She measures the temperature again. It is 30 °C. The temperature increase shows that it is an **exothermic reaction**.

Once the reaction is complete, Zoe leaves the mixture of products in the lab. After a while its temperature returns to 20 °C.

Literacy
Here's an easy way to remember the difference between exothermic and endothermic reactions:
Exothermic reactions transfer energy out. You go out through an **ex**it.
Endothermic reactions transfer energy in. You go in through an **en**trance.

Big Idea: Reactions 6

Key Words
endothermic change, endothermic reaction, exothermic change, exothermic reaction

Summary Questions

1. Copy the sentences below, choosing the correct bold words.
   All chemical reactions involve **colour/energy** transfers. If the temperature increases, the change is **exothermic/endothermic**. If the temperature decreases, the change is **exothermic/endothermic**. Boiling and melting are **exothermic/endothermic** changes. *(4 marks)*

2. The table shows the temperature changes when some substances dissolve in water. Write down the names of the substances that dissolve exothermically. Explain your choices. *(3 marks)*

Name of substance	Temperature before dissolving (°C)	Temperature after dissolving (°C)
potassium chloride	20	10
calcium chloride	20	35
sodium hydrogen carbonate	20	15
sodium carbonate	20	24

3. Use data from the table in question 2 to select two substances that could be used, along with water, for a hand warmer, and two that could be used for a cool pack. Justify your choices. *(4 marks)*

4. Write a paragraph to compare exothermic and endothermic changes. Include examples to illustrate your answer. *(6 marks)*

● Topic 6.4 Chemical energy

6.4.2 Energy level diagrams

Learning objectives

After this section you will be able to:
- identify whether an energy level diagram is showing an exothermic or endothermic reaction
- use energy level diagrams to explain energy changes in changes of state and chemical reactions.

An ice cube melts as energy is transferred from the drink it is in to the ice cube. Why is melting endothermic?

In ice, forces of attraction hold water molecules in a pattern. When energy is transferred to the ice, these forces are disrupted. The water molecules move out of their arrangement, and the ice melts.

A State whether melting ice is an endothermic or exothermic process.

Energy level diagrams for changes of state

The **energy level diagrams** below represent changes of state. Both diagrams show that liquid water stores more energy than the same amount of ice. The first diagram shows that ice takes in energy from the surroundings as it melts. The second shows that water gives out energy to the surroundings as it freezes. Freezing is exothermic.

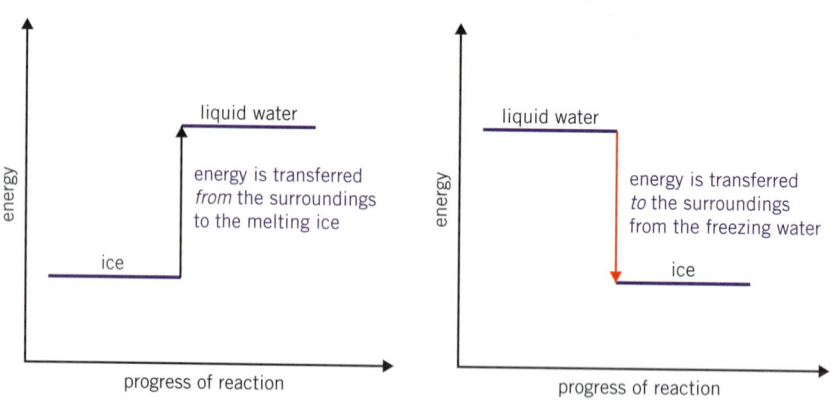

▲ Melting is endothermic.

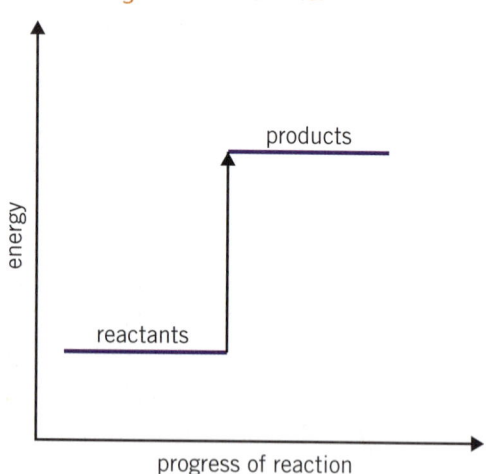

▲ Energy level diagrams for melting and freezing.

B State whether melting ice gives out energy to the surroundings or takes in energy from the surroundings.

Energy level diagrams for chemical reactions

You can also use energy level diagrams to show energy changes in chemical reactions. The diagrams at the top of the next page represent the combustion reactions of two fuels, hydrogen and diesel. They are drawn to the same scale.

The energy level diagrams show that the combustion reactions are exothermic. This means that, in both reactions, the energy stored in the reactants (fuel and oxygen) is greater than the energy stored in the products.

▲ An energy level diagram for an endothermic reaction.

Key Words

energy level diagram

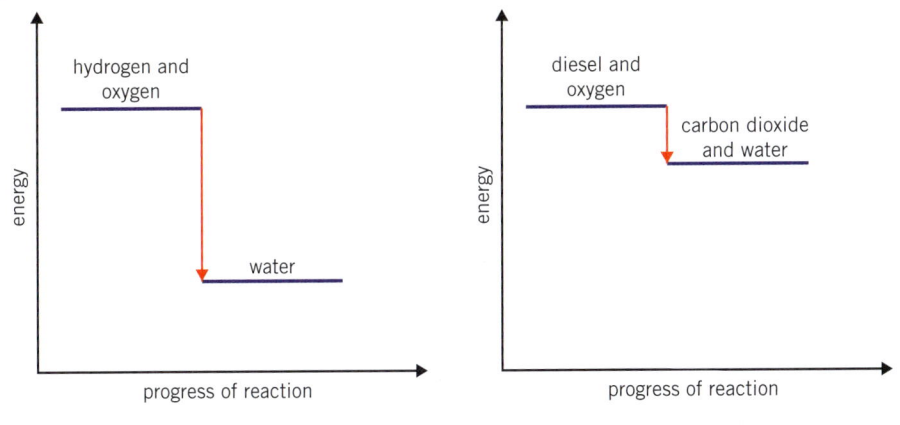

● Big Idea: Reactions 6

▲ Energy level diagrams for the combustion reactions of hydrogen (left) and diesel (right).

Together, the diagrams show that burning 1 kg of hydrogen transfers much more energy to the surroundings than burning 1 kg of diesel.

Energy changes for exothermic reactions have negative values. For example, the energy change for the combustion of 1 kg of hydrogen is −142 MJ/kg, and the energy change for the combustion of 1 kg of diesel is −45 MJ/kg.

C State whether the reactants or products have more energy in an exothermic reaction.

The energy level diagram opposite represents an endothermic reaction. The products store more energy than the reactants. During the reaction, energy is transferred from the surroundings to the reacting mixture. Energy changes for endothermic reactions have positive values.

Maths
The table gives data about three fuels that can be used to heat a house. Write a paragraph to compare the data. Then suggest other factors to consider when choosing a heating fuel.

Fuel	Energy transferred to surroundings during the combustion of 1 kg of the fuel (MJ/kg)
coal	33
methane (natural gas)	56
wood	21

Summary Questions

1 Copy and complete the sentences below.
An energy level diagram shows how energy is _____ in a chemical reaction. If the total energy of the reactants is greater than the total energy of the products, the reaction is _____. If the total energy of the products is greater, the reaction is _____.
(3 marks)

2 The energy level diagram below shows the relative energies of a substance in two different states. Does the arrow represent boiling or condensing? Explain your answer. *(3 marks)*

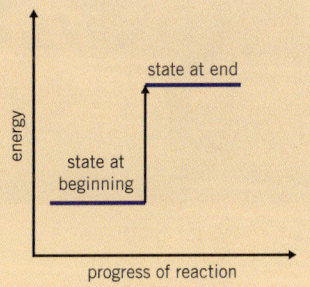

3 Sketch an energy level diagram and use words to explain why freezing is exothermic.
(3 marks)

4 The energy level diagram below shows the energy change when a substance dissolves in water. Suggest whether the process could be better used in a hand warmer or in a cold injury pack. Justify your decision. *(3 marks)*

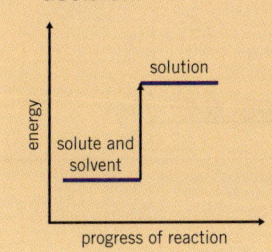

● Topic 6.4 Chemical energy

6.4.3 Bond energies

Learning objectives

After this section you will be able to:
- state what happens to chemical bonds during exothermic and endothermic reactions
- use ideas about bond energies to explain energy changes in chemical reactions.

▲ Testing exhaust emissions.

Key Words

chemical bond, catalytic converter, catalyst

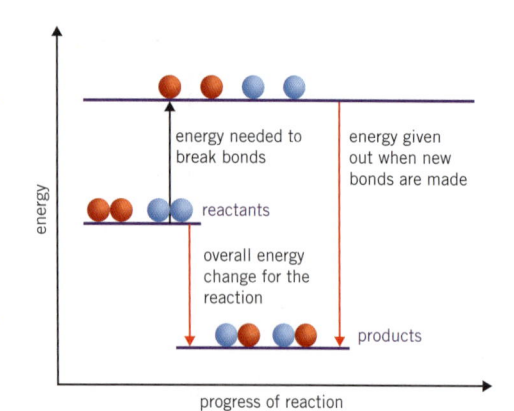

▲ Energy transfers in bond breaking and making.

Every year, UK cars must pass an exhaust emissions test. Why?

There are strict limits on the amounts of exhaust pollutants because they damage both human health and the environment. One of these pollutants is nitrogen monoxide, NO.

At normal temperatures, nitrogen and oxygen in the air do not react together. But, as you know, in a hot car engine the elements react rapidly. The product is nitrogen monoxide.

$$N_2 + O_2 \rightarrow 2NO$$

Bond breaking, bond making

The reaction of nitrogen with oxygen needs energy to get it started. Heat from the car engine supplies this energy. The energy breaks bonds in nitrogen and oxygen molecules. Bond breaking is endothermic.

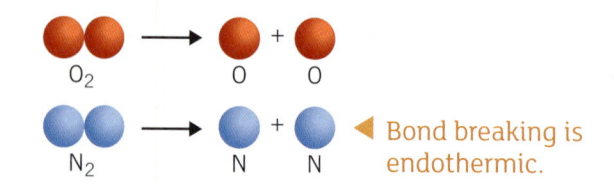

◄ Bond breaking is endothermic.

New bonds then form between nitrogen and oxygen atoms. This makes nitrogen monoxide molecules. When new bonds form, energy is transferred to the surroundings. Bond making is exothermic.

◄ Bond making is exothermic.

A State whether bond making is endothermic or exothermic.

The energy level diagram shows that, in the reaction of nitrogen with oxygen, the energy transferred *from* the surroundings to break bonds is less than the energy transferred *to* the surroundings when new bonds form. Overall, energy is transferred to the surroundings in this reaction, so the reaction is exothermic.

Big Idea: Reactions 6

Exothermic or endothermic?

The difference between the energy transferred in bond making and bond breaking determines whether a reaction is exothermic or endothermic:

- A reaction is exothermic if the energy needed to break bonds in the reactants is *less than* the energy released to the surroundings on making new bonds in the products.
- A reaction is endothermic if the energy needed to break bonds in the reactants is *more than* the energy released to the surroundings on making new bonds in the products.

▲ Inside a catalytic converter.

Bond energies

In a molecule, strong forces hold the atoms together. These forces are **chemical bonds**. Some bonds are stronger than others. The energy needed to break a bond is its bond energy. The table gives some bond energies.

You can use bond energy values to predict whether a chemical reaction will be exothermic or endothermic. Look at the equation for the reaction of hydrogen with chlorine.

The energy required to break bonds in H_2 and Cl_2 is (436 + 243) = 679 kJ/mol.

$$H_2 + Cl_2 \rightarrow 2HCl$$

The energy released to the surroundings on making bonds in HCl is (2 × 432) = 864 kJ/mol.

Since less energy is needed to break bonds than is released on making new bonds, the reaction is exothermic.

Bond	Bond energy (kJ/mol)
H–H	436
Cl–Cl	243
H–Cl	432

B Explain why the reaction of hydrogen with chlorine is exothermic.

What is a catalyst?

A car exhaust system includes a **catalytic converter**. Here, harmful exhaust substances take part in chemical reactions to make less harmful substances.

A catalytic converter includes metals such as platinum and rhodium. The metals act as **catalysts**. They speed up chemical reactions but are unchanged at the end.

C State what a catalyst is.

Summary Questions

1 Copy the sentence below, choosing the correct bold word.

A reaction is exothermic if the energy required for bond breaking is **less than/more than** the energy released on bond making.

(1 mark)

2 Sketch an energy level diagram to represent the reaction of hydrogen with chlorine to make hydrogen chloride.

(3 marks)

3 Use data in the table to predict whether the reaction $H_2 + F_2 \rightarrow 2HF$ is exothermic or endothermic.

(4 marks)

Bond	Bond energy (kJ/mol)
H–H	436
F–F	158
H–F	562

● Topic 6.4 Chemical energy

6 Reactions: Summary

Key Points

Types of reaction
- A physical change changes the physical properties of a substance, but does not form any new substance.
- In a chemical reaction, one or more new substances are formed.
- In a chemical reaction, atoms are rearranged and joined together differently to make new substances. The total number of atoms is conserved.
- In a chemical reaction, the total mass of reactants is equal to the total mass of products. This is conservation of mass.
- Word equations represent reactions simply. They show reactants on the left and products on the right. The arrow means reacts to make.
- In a balanced symbol equation, chemical formulae represent the reactants and products. The equation shows how atoms are rearranged. It gives the relative amounts of reactants and products.
- Chemical reactions can make useful products and transfer energy.
- Combustion is a type of reaction in which oxygen reacts with another reactant. Energy is transferred to the surroundings as heat and light.
- A fuel stores energy in a chemical store which it can release as heat.
- In a thermal decomposition reaction, a compound breaks down when it is heated. The products are elements and simpler compounds.

Chemical energy
- Exothermic changes transfer energy to the surroundings. They give out energy, usually as heat or light.
- Endothermic changes transfer energy from the surroundings. They take in energy, usually as heat.
- A chemical bond is a force that holds atoms together in molecules.
- A catalyst is a substance that speeds up a chemical reaction but is unchanged at the end.

Key Words
chemical reaction, reactants, products, conserved, fuel, combustion, fossil fuel, non-renewable, renewable, decomposition, thermal decomposition, conservation of mass, physical change, balanced symbol equation, endothermic change, endothermic reaction, exothermic change, exothermic reaction, energy level diagram, chemical bond, catalytic converter, catalyst

BIG Write

Tune in
Radio 99 makes exciting discussion programmes. And you will be on next week! A listener has sent in this text: 'Rusting, explosions, making drugs... They are all chemical reactions. Chemistry should be banned.'

Task
Plan what to say to convince listeners that chemical reactions are very important, and that chemistry must not be banned.

Tips
- Give examples of useful chemical reactions, and ask listeners to imagine a world without chemistry. What would they miss?

End-of-Big Idea questions

1. Izzy heats some magnesium in a Bunsen burner. It burns with a bright flame. A white ash forms.
   a. Describe **two** observations that show this is a chemical reaction. *(2 marks)*
   b. State what happens to the atoms in a chemical reaction. *(1 mark)*
   (3 marks)

2. Marcus plans an investigation to find out which fuel makes water hotter, ethanol or propanol. He burns each fuel in turn to heat water. He measures how hot the water gets.
   a. State whether the combustion reactions are exothermic or endothermic. Explain your decision. *(2 marks)*
   b. Name the independent variable in the investigation. *(1 mark)*
   c. Name **two** variables that Marcus must keep the same. *(2 marks)*
   d. Explain why he must keep these variables the same. *(1 mark)*
   (6 marks)

3. On heating, a white substance that is solid at room temperature makes three products – a brown gas, a colourless gas that relights a glowing splint, and a white solid. The mass of white solid remaining at the end is less than the mass of white solid at the start. The reaction must be a thermal decomposition reaction. Explain why.
   (2 marks)

4. Sze-Kie heats some calcium carbonate in a test tube. There is a chemical reaction:

   calcium carbonate → calcium oxide + carbon dioxide
   a. State what type of reaction the word equation shows. *(1 mark)*
   b. Name the product(s) of the reaction. *(1 mark)*
   (2 marks)

5. In the reaction shown by the word equation in question 4, Sze-Kie started with 100 g of calcium carbonate. At the end of the reaction, there was 56 g of calcium oxide in the test tube. Calculate the mass of carbon dioxide made. Show your working. *(2 marks)*

6. The combustion of methane is a chemical reaction. Here are some ways of representing this reaction.

   Equation X
   methane + oxygen → carbon dioxide + water

   Equation Y
   $CH_4 + 2O_2 \rightarrow CO_2 + 2H_2O$

   Diagram Z

   Key: carbon atom, oxygen atom, hydrogen atom

   a. Explain how Equation X, Equation Y, and Diagram Z all show that burning methane is a chemical reaction. *(2 marks)*
   b. Compare the advantages and disadvantages of representing the reaction with Equation X, Equation Y, and Diagram Z. *(6 marks)*
   (8 marks)

7 Earth

Where do we get the materials we need? All the materials we use come from the Earth, the oceans, or the atmosphere. In this Big Idea you will learn how we extract metals from the Earth, and what we can do to prevent vital resources running out. You will also find out about the atmosphere, and consider the causes and effects of global warming.

You already know

- The Sun heats the surface of the Earth.
- Extra carbon dioxide in the atmosphere causes global warming.
- Climate change causes floods and droughts.
- Metals are joined with other elements in compounds.
- Rocks are mixtures of minerals.
- Metals are arranged in order of how readily they react with other substances in the reactivity series.

Q Write down three impacts of climate change.

BIG Questions

- What causes climate change?
- How do we obtain the materials we need?
- How can we conserve the Earth's resources?

Picture Puzzler
Key Words

Can you solve this Picture Puzzler?

The first letter of each of these images spells out a science word that you will come across in this book.

Picture Puzzler
Close Up

Can you tell what this zoomed-in picture is?

Clue: The metal extracted from this makes cars, ships, and dishwashers.

Making connections

In **Book 1**, **6.2 Metals and non-metals** you learnt about the reactivity series and metal oxides.

In **5.4 Periodic Table** you learnt about elements and compounds.

7.3.1 Global warming

Learning objectives

After this section you will be able to:
- state how an increase in greenhouse gases has increased the temperature on Earth
- name two greenhouse gases
- state the names and percentages of the gases that make up the Earth's atmosphere
- describe and explain what is meant by global warming.

You take a deep breath of fresh air. What gases are entering your lungs?

What is the atmosphere?

The air around us is called the **atmosphere**. The atmosphere is a mixture of gases that surrounds the Earth. It is mainly two elements, nitrogen and oxygen. There are smaller amounts of other substances, including carbon dioxide and argon.

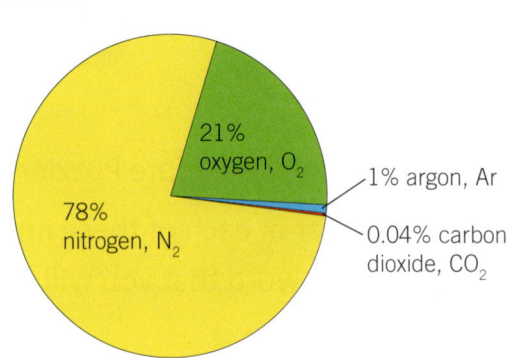

▲ The most common substances in the Earth's atmosphere, by volume.

- 78% nitrogen, N_2
- 21% oxygen, O_2
- 1% argon, Ar
- 0.04% carbon dioxide, CO_2

A Look at the pie chart above. State the percentages of nitrogen, oxygen, argon, and carbon dioxide in the atmosphere.

How does the atmosphere keep us warm?

The Sun heats the Earth's surface. The warm surface of the Earth emits radiation. Some of this radiation goes back into space, and some is absorbed by gases in the atmosphere. This keeps the Earth warmer than it would be if all the radiation went back into space.

The transfer of energy from the Sun to the thermal energy store of gases in the Earth's atmosphere is the **greenhouse effect**. Different gases store different amounts of energy. Molecules of carbon dioxide and methane store large amounts of energy compared to molecules of nitrogen and oxygen.

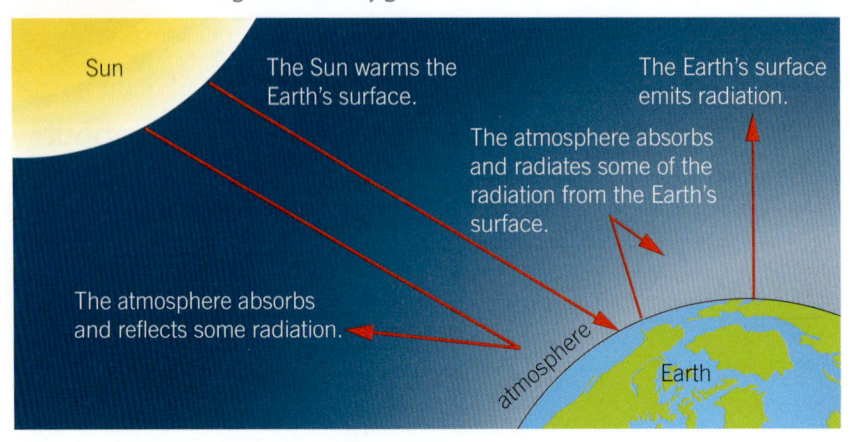

Bar charts
Draw a bar chart to show the percentages of oxygen, nitrogen, and argon in the air. When you have finished, discuss with a partner whether your chosen scale allows you to show on your bar chart the percentage of carbon dioxide in the air.

Foul Fact
A typical cow burps 280 kg of the greenhouse gas methane into the air every year.

- Sun
- The Sun warms the Earth's surface.
- The Earth's surface emits radiation.
- The atmosphere absorbs and radiates some of the radiation from the Earth's surface.
- The atmosphere absorbs and reflects some radiation.
- atmosphere
- Earth

This explains why carbon dioxide and methane are called **greenhouse gases**. Without carbon dioxide in the atmosphere, Earth would be too cold for life.

B Name two greenhouse gases.

What is global warming?

Ever since thermometers were first invented, scientists have been measuring and recording air temperatures. They have collected this data and calculated average worldwide temperatures for each year. The graph shows the global average air temperature at the Earth's surface since about 1867.

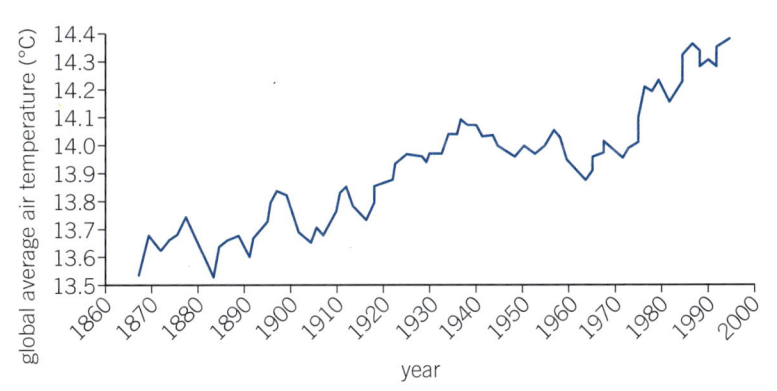

▲ The changing global average air temperature since the 1860s.

The graph above shows that temperatures have changed over time. This gradual increase in the air temperature at the surface of the Earth is called **global warming**.

In the 1950s scientists began to wonder whether extra carbon dioxide in the atmosphere was causing global warming. They set up an observatory on the slopes of a remote mountain in Hawaii to measure the concentration of carbon dioxide in the atmosphere. Scientists have collected data from the observatory ever since. The graph below displays some of their data. It shows that the concentration of carbon dioxide in the atmosphere has increased since 1960.

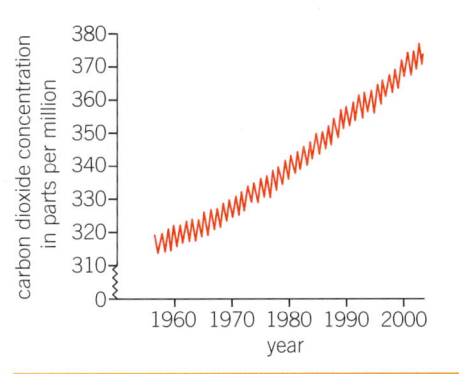

◄ The changing concentration of carbon dioxide in the atmosphere.

C Describe the meaning of global warming.

Key Words

atmosphere, greenhouse effect, greenhouse gas, global warming

Link

You can learn what causes changes in the concentration of carbon dioxide in 7.3.3 Climate change.

Summary Questions

1. Copy and complete the sentences below.

   The air that surrounds us is called the _____. The main gas in the atmosphere is _____. Two important greenhouse gases are _____ and _____ _____. The transfer of energy from the Sun to the thermal store of gases in the atmosphere is called the _____ _____. The gradual increase in the surface temperature of the Earth is called _____ _____.

   (6 marks)

2. Use your own knowledge to suggest two human activities that affect the amount of carbon dioxide in the atmosphere.

   (2 marks)

3. Compare the shapes of the two graphs on this page, starting from the year 1960. Suggest what they might show about a link between carbon dioxide concentration and temperature. Justify whether or not you can be sure that a change in one factor causes the change in the other.

   (3 marks)

● Topic 7.3 Climate

7.3.2 The carbon cycle

Learning objectives
After this section you will be able to:
- list the processes that recycle carbon naturally
- use the carbon cycle to show how carbon is recycled.

Link
You can learn more about how plants use carbon dioxide in 9.4.1 Photosynthesis.

▲ Burning fossil fuels adds carbon dioxide to the atmosphere.

A question of balance
With a partner, identify four ways that you could reduce the amount of carbon dioxide that you add to the atmosphere in your everyday life. Explain how each method reduces the concentration of carbon dioxide in the atmosphere.

Carbon dioxide molecules enter and leave the atmosphere all the time. But, until 1960, the overall amount of carbon dioxide did not change much. Its maximum concentration was never more than 0.03%. Why?

Carbon dioxide: into and out of the atmosphere
Two processes *add* carbon dioxide to the atmosphere:

- **Respiration** transfers energy from food in plants and animals. Carbon dioxide is a waste product of respiration.

    glucose + oxygen → carbon dioxide + water

- **Combustion.** Fuels such as wood, petrol, and methane produce carbon dioxide on burning.

    methane + oxygen → carbon dioxide + water (+ energy)

Petrol and methane are examples of **fossil fuels**. They were made from the remains of organisms that died millions of years ago. Burning any fossil fuel releases carbon dioxide, and adds it to the atmosphere.

A Name two processes that add carbon dioxide to the atmosphere.

Two processes *remove* carbon dioxide from the atmosphere:

- **Photosynthesis.** Plants use carbon dioxide and water to make glucose.

    carbon dioxide + water —light→ glucose + oxygen

- Dissolving in the oceans.

B Name two processes that remove carbon dioxide from the atmosphere.

Until 1960, carbon dioxide was added to the atmosphere and removed from it at the same rate. This meant that its concentration did not change much.

However, as you saw in 7.3.1 Global warming, the concentration of carbon dioxide in the atmosphere has increased greatly since 1960. You can find out about the reasons for this increase, and its consequences, in 7.3.3 Climate change.

What is the carbon cycle?

Carbon, as the element and in its compounds, is constantly recycled through natural processes in the atmosphere, in ecosystems, and in the Earth's crust. Human activities, including burning fossil fuels, also contribute to carbon recycling. The **carbon cycle** summarises these processes.

The diagram of the carbon cycle below also shows **carbon sinks**. Carbon sinks absorb and store carbon and its compounds. Carbon sinks include:

- the ocean
- the soil
- areas of vegetation, such as forests.

C Name three carbon sinks.

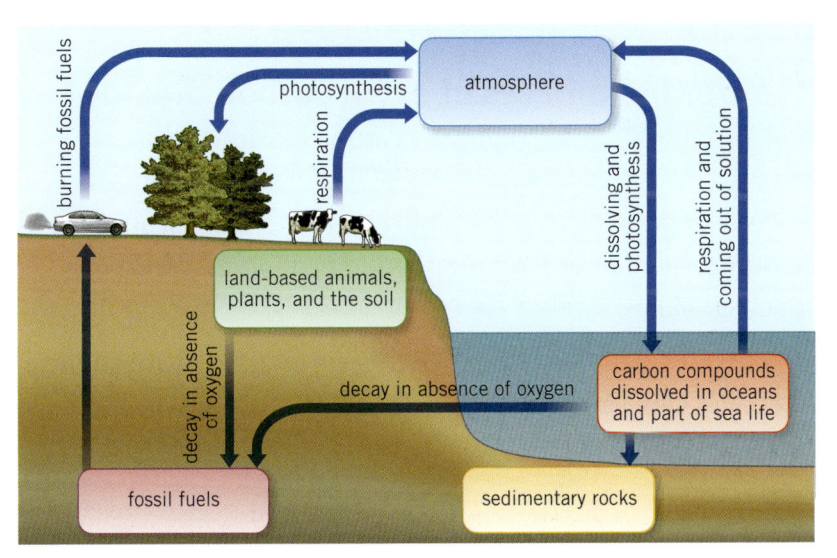

▲ The carbon cycle.

◄ This yew tree in Scotland has stored carbon compounds in its trunk for over 3000 years.

Key Words

respiration, combustion, fossil fuel, photosynthesis, carbon cycle, carbon sink

Fantastic Fact

Some of the oldest living carbon sinks are a group of olive trees in Lebanon, called The Sisters. They are between 6000 and 8000 years old.

Summary Questions

1. Copy and complete the sentences below, choosing the correct bold words.

   Carbon dioxide enters the atmosphere by **photosynthesis/ respiration** and **dissolving/ combustion**. It leaves the atmosphere by **photosynthesis/ respiration** and **dissolving/ combustion**. Forests are carbon **sinks/cycles**. Other carbon sinks include the ocean and the **soil/Earth's core**.

   (6 marks)

2. Describe a route that a carbon atom might take around the carbon cycle. Name two carbon sinks the atom passes through, and give the names of the processes by which it moves around the cycle. Draw a diagram to summarise the route of your carbon atom.

   (5 marks)

3. Create a carbon-cycle board game, in which players throw a dice to follow different routes around the carbon cycle.

   (6 marks)

● Topic 7.3 Climate

7.3.3 Climate change

Learning objectives

After this section you will be able to:
- state one cause of global warming that scientists have evidence for
- describe how human activities affect the carbon cycle
- describe how global warming can impact on climate and local weather patterns.

What links the pictures?

The pictures show human activities that add extra carbon dioxide to the atmosphere. These activities include:
- burning fossil fuels to generate electricity, heat homes, and fuel cars
- burning or cutting down forests to make space for crops or cattle
- farming animals such as cows.

A List three ways that human activities increase the concentration of carbon dioxide in the atmosphere.

What are the impacts of extra carbon dioxide?

Almost all scientists agree that extra carbon dioxide in the atmosphere causes global warming. Global warming changes local weather patterns. In some areas rainfall increases, leading to flooding. Other areas suffer droughts and heatwaves, which may cause crop failures.

Long-term changes to weather patterns are called **climate change**. As a result of climate change, glaciers and polar ice are melting. Melting ice makes sea levels rise. This causes flooding on low-lying coasts.

Climate change may lead to the extinction of some plant and animal species. It makes it harder for humans to grow enough food.

▲ Climate change leads to floods.

▲ Climate change leads to crop failures.

B State what climate change is.

Are humans causing climate change?

The graphs in 7.3.1 Global warming show that the patterns of temperature increase and carbon dioxide increase are similar. The graph on the next page shows changes in atmospheric carbon dioxide levels over the past 400 000 years.

Big Idea: Earth 7

Key Word

climate change

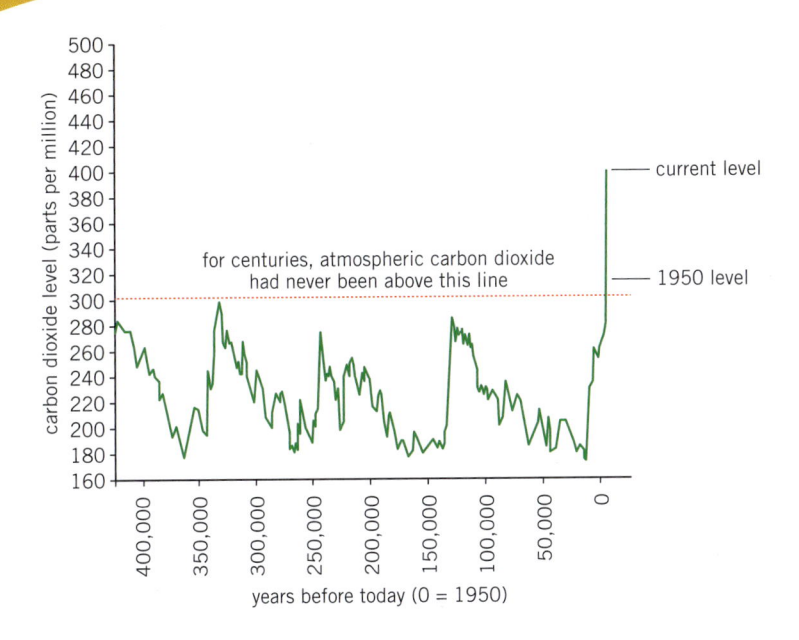

[Graph: carbon dioxide level (parts per million) vs years before today (0 = 1950), showing fluctuations between ~180 and ~300 ppm over 400,000 years, with a sharp spike to current level ~400 ppm. Labels: "current level", "1950 level", "for centuries, atmospheric carbon dioxide had never been above this line"]

The graphs on their own cannot show that human activities cause climate change. However, 97% of climate scientists now agree with the Intergovernmental Panel on Climate Change (IPCC), which took evidence from 2500 scientists and concluded that global warming caused by human activity is 'very likely' to be causing changes in climate.

Huge amounts of evidence support the view of the IPCC. For example, lab experiments show that carbon dioxide and methane molecules trap heat. Carbon dioxide levels have risen hugely since 1950 compared to the 400 000 years before. Data also show that sea levels rose 17 cm in the last century, and that the 20 warmest years on record have occurred since 1981.

A few people disagree with the IPCC. They say that natural events – such as small changes in the Earth's orbit – are more important than human activity in causing climate change. They also point out that greenhouse gases are released in volcanic eruptions and other natural processes.

C Describe three pieces of evidence that global warming caused by human activity is causing changes in climate.

Can we prevent climate change?

There are many ways of reducing emissions of greenhouse gases caused by human activities. These include:

- generating electricity from solar panels and other renewable sources instead of burning fossil fuels
- using cars less
- buying and wasting less.

Summary Questions

1. Copy and complete the sentences below.
   Humans add carbon dioxide to the atmosphere by burning _____ fuels. Extra carbon dioxide in the atmosphere causes global _____. This causes _____ change.
   (3 marks)

2. Describe two impacts on local weather patterns caused by humans burning increasing amounts of fossil fuels.
   (2 marks)

3. A government suggests reducing carbon emissions from cars by allowing people to drive their cars on three days a week only. Evaluate the implications of this idea.
   (3 marks)

4. Compare human and natural causes of global warming. Use the graph on this page to suggest which has had the greater impact since 1960.
   (4 marks)

5. Evaluate the claim that human activity is causing climate change.
   (6 marks)

Topic 7.3 Climate

7.4.1 Extracting metals

Learning objectives

After this section you will be able to:
- state what an ore is
- recall the methods of extracting metals
- describe how the Earth's resources are extracted
- justify the choice of extraction method for a metal, given data about reactivity
- suggest factors to consider when extracting metals.

What materials can you see in the picture? Where do the materials come from?

The materials that make everything we use originally came from **natural resources** in the Earth's crust, atmosphere, or oceans. Natural resources act as raw materials for making millions of products.

What is an ore?

Many of the materials we use are metals. Most metals are found joined with other elements in compounds. A few metals, such as gold, are found on their own. Naturally occurring metals, and their compounds, are called **minerals**.

Aluminium hydroxide is a mineral. It is mixed with other minerals in bauxite rock. Bauxite is an example of an **ore**. An ore is a naturally occurring rock that contains enough of a mineral to make it worth getting the mineral – and then the metal it includes – out of the rock.

A State the meaning of the word ore.

How are metals extracted?

Bauxite itself is not useful. But the aluminium it contains has many uses. Aluminium companies make money by extracting aluminium from bauxite. The **extraction** of a metal is the separation of the metal from its compounds.

The method chosen for the extraction of a metal depends on the reactivity of the metal.

Which metals are extracted by heating with carbon?

Iron is the main metal in steel. Steel makes ships, cars, trains, and washing machines.

There are two main stages in extracting iron from its ore. These are:

1. Separate iron oxide from the compounds it is mixed with.
2. Use chemical reactions to extract iron from iron oxide.

The chemical reactions involve heating iron oxide with charcoal. Charcoal is a form of carbon. It is cheap, and easy to get hold of.

▲ Bauxite is the most commonly mined aluminium ore.

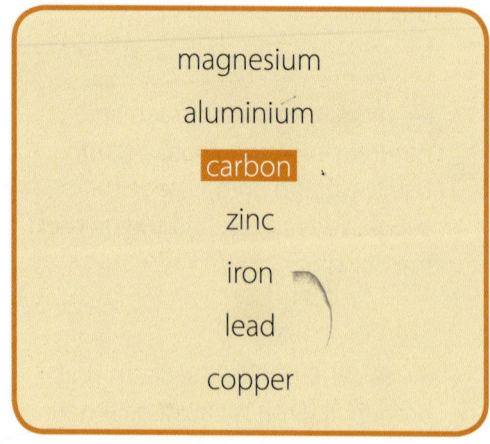

magnesium
aluminium
carbon
zinc
iron
lead
copper

▲ Part of the reactivity series, including carbon.

B Describe two stages in extracting iron from its ore.

Carbon is a non-metal. But we can place it in the reactivity series, between aluminium and zinc.

Any metal that is below carbon in the reactivity series can be displaced from its compounds by carbon. For example, you can heat carbon powder with copper oxide powder. Carbon displaces copper from copper oxide:

carbon + copper oxide → copper + carbon dioxide
$C(s) + 2CuO(s) → 2Cu(s) + CO_2(g)$

You can also heat carbon with lead oxide:

carbon + lead oxide → lead + carbon dioxide
$C(s) + 2PbO(s) → 2Pb(s) + CO_2(g)$

C Carbon displaces copper from copper oxide. Write a word equation for this reaction.

Why are some metals extracted by electrolysis?

The more reactive a metal is, the more difficult it is to separate it from its compounds. If a metal is above carbon in the reactivity series, carbon will not displace the metal from its oxide.

Since aluminium is above carbon, it is extracted from its ore by **electrolysis**. This involves passing an electric current though liquid aluminium oxide. The electricity splits up the compound into its elements, aluminium and oxygen.

Extracting a metal by electrolysis is expensive. Its mineral must be heated to a high temperature so that it melts. Huge amounts of electricity are needed to split up the compound. Generating the electricity may produce greenhouse gases such as carbon dioxide.

One company overcomes some of these problems by electrolysing aluminium oxide in Iceland. The electricity there is generated cheaply from renewable sources such as water and steam.

Potassium, sodium, and lithium are very reactive metals. They are also extracted from their minerals by electrolysis.

Ore waste
Iron ore from different places contains different amounts of iron. Companies extract iron from ores containing different percentages of iron. Calculate the masses of waste from 1 tonne (1000 kg) of each of these ores: an ore that is 16% iron and an ore that is 50% iron.

Big Idea: Earth 7

Key Words
natural resources, mineral, ore, extraction, electrolysis

Fantastic Fact
We use awesome amounts of ore. In 2010 world iron ore production was 2400 million tonnes. China dug out 900 million tonnes of this.

Summary Questions

1 Copy the sentences below, choosing the correct bold words.
An ore is a **substance/rock** that it is worth extracting metal from. Most metals exist in the Earth's crust as **compounds/elements**. These are **joined to/mixed with** other substances in ores.
(3 marks)

2 Use the reactivity series to suggest whether magnesium is extracted from its minerals by heating with carbon, or by electrolysis. Justify your answer.
(2 marks)

3 Describe how iron ore is converted into iron, which is useful for making ships and cars.
(2 marks)

4 A company has discovered a new source of iron ore. Suggest factors to take into account when deciding whether or not to extract metal from this ore.
(4 marks)

5 Suggest two ways that the waste products from the extraction of iron could be reduced.
(2 marks)

● Topic 7.4 Earth resources

7.4.2 Recycling

Learning objectives

After this section you will be able to:
- state why certain natural resources will run out
- explain why recycling some materials is particularly important
- describe how Earth's resources are recycled.

▲ Many materials can be recycled.

Key Word

recycling

▲ If we continue to use tin as we do now, tin ore might run out by 2030.

What do you recycle?

You can recycle many types of material, including metals, paper, and plastics. But is it worth the effort?

Where do resources come from?

As you know, materials that make everything we use come originally from the Earth's crust, atmosphere, or oceans. These resources will not last forever, and the faster we extract them, the sooner they will run out.

The table shows an estimate of when the materials we get four elements from might run out.

Element	Uses of element	When the source of the element will run out (estimated year)
phosphorus	making fertilisers	between 2060 and 2110
gold	jewellery, electrical connections	2040
tin	food containers, solder	2030
aluminium	aeroplanes, overhead power cables, kitchen foil	2500

A State where all the materials we use originally come from.

What is recycling?

Recycling means collecting and processing materials that have been used so that the materials can be used again. Examples of recycling include:

- recycling paper to make new paper
- recycling plastic bottles to make fleeces
- recycling aluminium cans to make aluminium sheets to make more cans.

How is aluminium recycled?

Alex puts out an aluminium can for recycling. A lorry takes it to a factory. At the factory, machines shred the can and remove its decoration.

A furnace melts the aluminium shreds. The liquid cools and freezes in a mould. This is an aluminium ingot.

▲ An aluminium ingot.

The ingot is heated to 600 °C to soften it. Huge rollers roll it into thin sheets. The sheets are made into new cans.

B Describe what recycling is.

Advantages and disadvantages

There are many advantages of recycling. For example:

- Recycling means resources will last longer.
- Recycling uses less energy than using new materials. Around 255 MJ of energy is needed to extract 1 kg of aluminium from its ore. Only 15 MJ is needed to make 1 kg of recycled aluminium.
- Recycling reduces waste and pollution. Extracting aluminium from its ore creates huge amounts of dangerous 'red mud' waste.

C List three advantages of recycling.

Recycle and remake
Calculate how many kilograms of recycled aluminium you could make using the same amount of energy it takes to extract 1 kg of aluminium from its ore.

There are some disadvantages to recycling. Some people think that separating rubbish is a nuisance. The lorries that collect recycling use fuel and create pollution.

D State two disadvantages of recycling.

Can you recycle everything?
Some materials are easier to recycle than others. Companies that recycle plastic waste need to separate different sorts of plastic from each other. This is often done by hand, and takes a long time.

▶ This girl is wearing a fleece made from recycled bottles.

7.4 Earth resources

Bottled fleeces
A company states that it needs 25 two-litre plastic bottles to make one fleece. Estimate the number of bottles needed to make a fleece for everyone in your school.

Link
You can learn more about metal ores in 7.4.1 Extracting metals.

Summary Questions

1. Write down the two statements below that are examples of recycling:
   - collecting old glass bottles, melting the glass, and making new bottles
   - using a plastic bag from the supermarket to wrap your packed lunch in
   - collecting and melting poly(propene) bottle tops, and using them to make poly(propene) rope.

   (2 marks)

2. Describe how aluminium is recycled.

   (4 marks)

3. Give three reasons to explain why it is important to recycle aluminium.

   (3 marks)

4. Suggest changes you could make to limit your consumption of natural resources.

   (3 marks)

● Topic 7.4 Earth resources

7 Earth: Summary

Key Points

Climate
- Everything we use comes from the Earth's crust, atmosphere, or oceans.
- The atmosphere is the mixture of gases around the Earth. It is mainly nitrogen and oxygen, with smaller amounts of argon and carbon dioxide.
- Carbon sinks absorb and store carbon. They include areas of vegetation, the oceans, and the soil.
- The carbon cycle shows how carbon compounds are recycled, and how they enter and leave carbon sinks.
- The concentration of carbon dioxide in the atmosphere is increasing because of deforestation and burning fossil fuels.
- Extra carbon dioxide in the atmosphere causes global warming, which leads to climate change.

Earth resources
- Zinc and metals below carbon in the reactivity series are extracted by heating their oxides with carbon.
- Aluminium and metals above carbon in the reactivity series are extracted from their minerals by electrolysis.
- Recycling involves collecting and processing materials that have been used, in order to make new objects.

Key Words

atmosphere, greenhouse effect, greenhouse gas, global warming, respiration, combustion, fossil fuel, photosynthesis, carbon cycle, carbon sink, climate change, natural resources, mineral, ore, extraction, electrolysis, recycling

Maths challenge

Ranking recycling
Imagine that you work for a recycling company and that your job is to design the website. Your boss has given you the data below.

Task
Design the homepage of the website. Include a chart or graph of the information in the table. In your chart, show the changes in the percentages of waste recycled in each country between 2001 and 2010.

Tips
Provide information about where our resources come from and how we can recycle them.

Country	% of waste recycled in 2001	% of waste recycled in 2010
Austria	57.3	62.8
Portugal	15.5	18.8
Iceland	17.3	23.4
Ireland	11.3	35.7
Norway	44.3	42.1
UK	12.4	38.8

Data: European Environment Agency

End-of-Big Idea questions

1 🧪 Write the missing labels on the pie chart.

argon 1%   carbon dioxide 0%

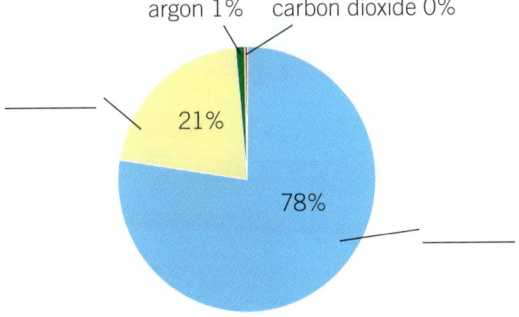

21%

78%

gases in the atmosphere of the Earth

(2 marks)

2 🧪🧪 The diagram shows the carbon cycle.

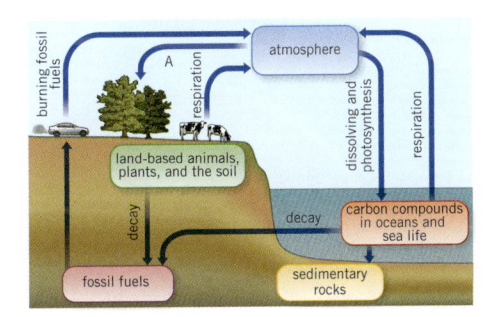

a Name **three** carbon sinks shown on the carbon cycle. *(3 marks)*
b Name the process represented by arrow A. *(1 mark)*
c Name **two** processes that add carbon dioxide to the atmosphere. *(2 marks)*
d Give **two** reasons to explain why the amount of carbon dioxide in the atmosphere has increased since the year 1800. *(2 marks)*

(8 marks)

3 🧪🧪 The table gives estimates of the energy for making aluminium in two ways.

Energy to make 1 kg of aluminium, in MJ	
...from recycled aluminium	...from bauxite ore
15	260

a Connor uses 67 aluminium cans a year. Each can has a mass of 14.9 g. Show how to work out that the total mass of aluminium in his cans is about 1 kg. *(2 marks)*
b Connor recycles all his cans. Lee also uses 67 cans, but recycles none of them. How much energy does Connor 'save' each year, compared to Lee? *(2 marks)*
c It takes 2.45 MJ of energy to generate enough electricity to power Connor's TV for one hour. For how long would the amount of energy Connor 'saved' power his TV? *(2 marks)*

(6 marks)

4 🧪🧪 Describe and explain three human activities that affect the carbon cycle.

(6 marks)

5 🧪🧪🧪 Noah says that human activity is causing global warming, climate change, and flooding. His friend Ibrahim says that global warming is caused by changes in the Earth's orbit. State who you think is correct, and justify your decision.

(4 marks)

6 🧪🧪🧪 Evaluate the implications of the following suggestions to reduce carbon emissions:

a All school students walking or cycling to school, rather than coming by car or on the bus. *(3 marks)*
b An advertising campaign to encourage people to wear warm clothing in winter instead of turning up the heating at home. *(3 marks)*
c Generating more electricity by solar panels and wind turbines, and less by burning fossil fuels in power stations. *(3 marks)*

(9 marks)

8 Organisms

What do we need to stay healthy? In this Big Idea you will learn about how we breathe, and then look at the damage that can be caused through smoking, drinking alcohol, and taking drugs. Finally, you will study what makes a balanced diet and how your body breaks down the food you eat to release energy and the other nutrients you need to live and grow.

You already know

- Diet, exercise, drugs, and lifestyle have an impact on the way the human body functions.
- Animals, including humans, cannot make their own food.
- The simple functions of different types of teeth.
- The digestive system in humans is made up of different parts, each with its own special function.
- Humans need the right amounts and right types of nutrition to be healthy.

Q Name the main types of teeth. What is their function?

BIG Questions

- How does your body exchange gases with the environment?
- How can drugs affect your body?
- How does the body break down the foods you eat?

Picture Puzzler
Key Words

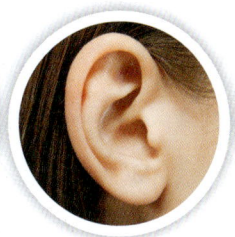

Can you solve this Picture Puzzler?

The first letter of each of these images spells out a science word that you will come across in this book.

Picture Puzzler
Close Up

Can you tell what this zoomed-in picture is?
Clue: It's made from flour.

Making connections

In **9.3 Respiration** you will find out how your body uses the oxygen you breathe in.

In your GCSE course you will learn about how oxygen is transported around the body in the circulatory system.

You will also learn in detail about how enzymes are used by the body to digest the foods you eat.

8.3.1 Gas exchange

Learning objectives

After this section you will be able to:

- describe the function of the gas exchange system
- explain how parts of the gas exchange system are adapted to their function
- explain why your breathing rate and volume can change.

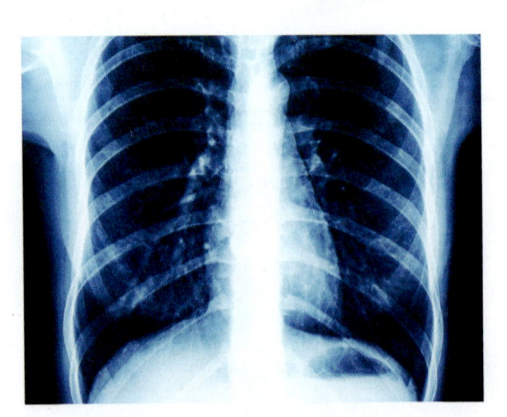

▲ You can see the lungs on a chest X-ray.

Link

You can learn more about why you breathe in 9.3.1 Aerobic respiration.

Key Words

gas exchange, lungs, ribs, respiratory system, trachea, bronchus, bronchiole, alveolus, breathing, inhale, respiration, exhale, condense

Fantastic Fact!

Your lungs are not the same size. The left lung is normally smaller than the right lung, which leaves space for your heart.

If you are travelling on a bus, the windows may sometimes steam up. This is because air contains lots of water vapour.

What happens when we breathe?

When you breathe, you take in oxygen and give out carbon dioxide. This is called **gas exchange**. It takes place inside your **lungs**. They are made of elastic tissue that can expand when you breathe in – this allows you to take in lots of oxygen. However, your lungs are delicate, so they are protected by your **ribs**, the hard and strong bones that make up your ribcage.

A Name the structure that protects your lungs.

The diagram below shows the main components of your **respiratory system** (gas exchange system). Follow the arrows with your finger to see how air travels through your mouth and nose and ends up in the blood around your lungs. The blood then takes the oxygen to all cells in your body.

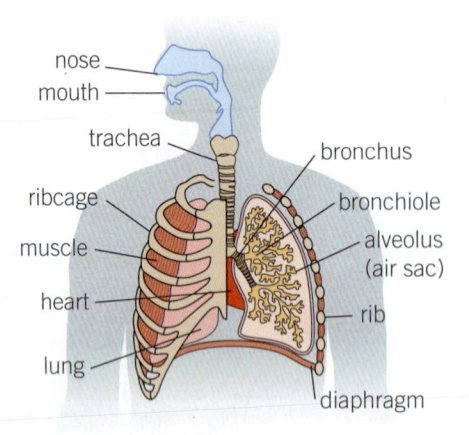

Air enters your body through your mouth and nose.
↓
Air moves down the **trachea** (windpipe) – a large tube.
↓
Air moves down a **bronchus** – a smaller tube.
↓
Air moves through a **bronchiole** – a tiny tube.
↓
Air moves into an **alveolus** – an air sac.
↓
Oxygen then diffuses into the blood.

There are millions of alveoli (plural of alveolus) in your lungs. They create a large surface area. They also have thin walls that are only one cell thick. This means that gas exchange can occur quickly and easily.

B State the scientific name for an air sac.

Big Idea: Organisms 8

Why do we breathe in and out?

Breathing is the movement of air in and out of the lungs. When we breathe in we **inhale** to take in oxygen. The oxygen is used in **respiration** to transfer energy. Respiration produces carbon dioxide, which needs to be removed from the body. When we breathe out we **exhale** to remove carbon dioxide.

The amount of oxygen required by your body cells determines how fast you need to breathe. You need more oxygen when you exercise. The harder you exercise, the faster your breathing rate and the greater the volume (depth) of breathing. This allows you to take in the oxygen you need to respire more, which transfers more energy to your muscle cells.

The pie charts below show how much of the different gases are present in inhaled and exhaled air. This is called the composition of the air.

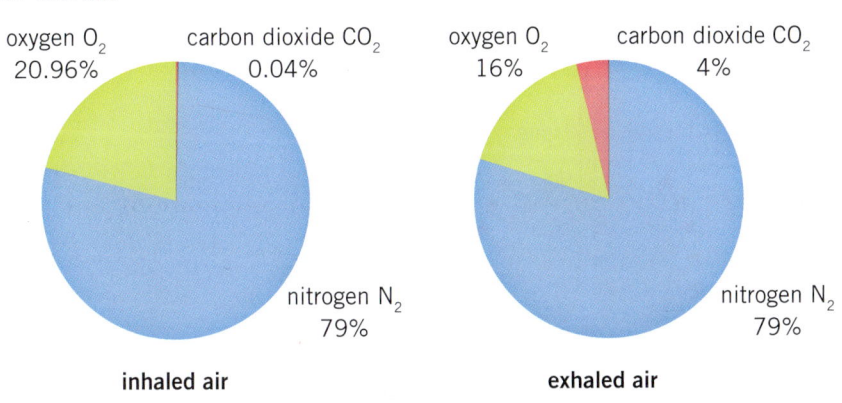

inhaled air: oxygen O_2 20.96%, carbon dioxide CO_2 0.04%, nitrogen N_2 79%

exhaled air: oxygen O_2 16%, carbon dioxide CO_2 4%, nitrogen N_2 79%

▲ These pie charts show the amount of each gas in inhaled and exhaled air.

c State which gas, present in air, is not used by the body.

▲ If you breathe onto a cold mirror, it steams up. This is because water vapour in the air you breathe out **condenses** on the cold surface.

Which chart?
The composition of inhaled and exhaled gases is shown in a pie chart. Why is this the best chart to use? Would another type of graph be better?

Link
You can find out more about condensing in Book 1, 5.1.5 More changes of state.

Summary Questions

1. Copy and complete the following table to show the differences between inhaled and exhaled air. Use the words **less**, **more**, **same**. Words can be used once, more than once, or not at all.

	inhaled	exhaled
oxygen		
carbon dioxide		
nitrogen		

(3 marks)

2. Draw a diagram of the gas exchange system and label how each structure is adapted to its function. (3 marks)

3. State and explain how a cyclist's breathing rate and volume are different between riding on the flat, compared to a hill climb. (3 marks)

4. Describe, step by step, the journey that carbon dioxide takes from the alveolus out of the body. (6 marks)

Topic 8.3 Breathing

8.3.2 Breathing

Learning objectives

After this section you will be able to:
- describe the processes of inhaling and exhaling
- explain what happens during breathing using the bell-jar model
- explain how exercise, smoking, and asthma affect the gas exchange system.

Even when you are sitting still, your ribcage is moving. This allows your lungs to fill with oxygen. This is essential for you to stay alive.

How do you breathe?

When you breathe, muscles in your chest tighten or **contract**.

A bell-jar model can show you what is happening inside your lungs when you breathe in and out. The jar represents your chest, the balloons represent your lungs, and the rubber sheet represents a muscle called the **diaphragm**.

Inhaling (breathing in)

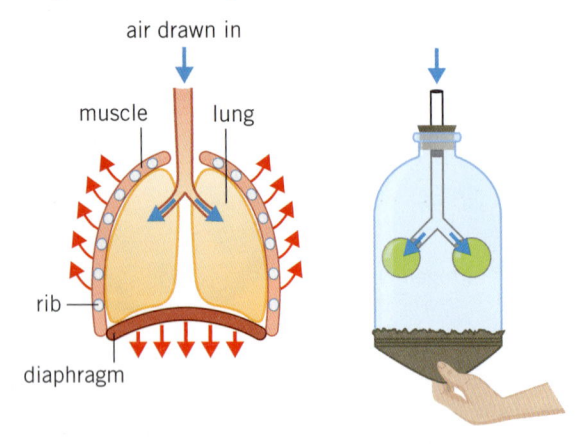

▲ Inhaling in the lungs and in the bell-jar model.

This is what happens in the body when we inhale:
- The muscles between your ribs contract – this pulls your ribcage up and out.
- The diaphragm contracts – it moves down.
- The volume inside your chest increases.
- The pressure inside your chest decreases – this draws air into your lungs.

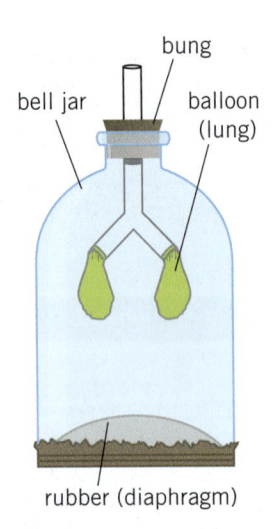

▲ A bell-jar model shows what happens inside the lungs when we breathe in and out.

A State what happens to your ribcage when you inhale.

To show inhaling, this is what happens in the bell-jar model:
- The rubber sheet is pulled down.
- The volume inside the jar increases.
- The pressure inside the jar decreases – air rushes into the jar.
- The balloons inflate.

Link

You can find out more about gas pressure in Book 1, 5.1.7 Gas pressure.

Key Words

contract, diaphragm, lung volume, asthma

Big Idea: Organisms 8

Exhaling (breathing out)
This is what happens in the body when we exhale:
- The muscles between your ribs relax – this pulls your ribcage down and in.
- The diaphragm relaxes – it moves up.
- The volume inside your chest decreases.
- The pressure inside your chest increases – this pushes air out of your lungs.

To show exhaling, this is what happens in the bell-jar model:
- The rubber sheet is pushed up.
- The volume inside the jar decreases.
- The pressure inside the jar increases – this makes air rush out of the jar and the balloons.
- The balloons deflate.

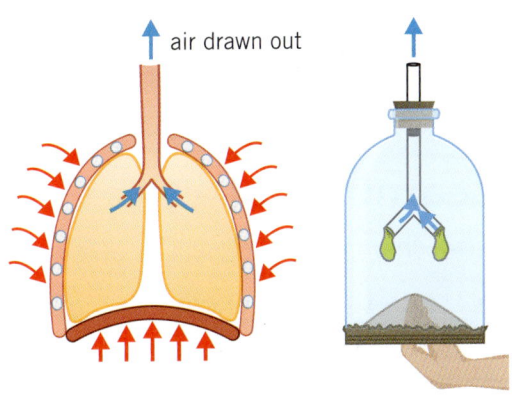

▲ Exhaling in the lungs and in the bell-jar model.

B State what happens to your diaphragm when you exhale.

How can we measure lung volume?
You can measure your **lung volume** using a plastic bottle.

As you breathe out into the plastic tube, air from your lungs takes the place of the water in the bottle. If you breathe out fully, the volume of water pushed out of the bottle is equal to how much air your lungs can hold.

Lung volume can be increased with regular exercise. A large lung volume means that more oxygen can enter your body. Smoking, diseases such as **asthma**, and old age can reduce lung volume.

C Name two factors that can reduce lung volume.

Lung volume
How big are your lungs? Calculate your own lung volume by breathing as hard as you can into a 3-litre bottle of water. Suggest why your doctor would not use this as an accurate measurement of your lung volume.

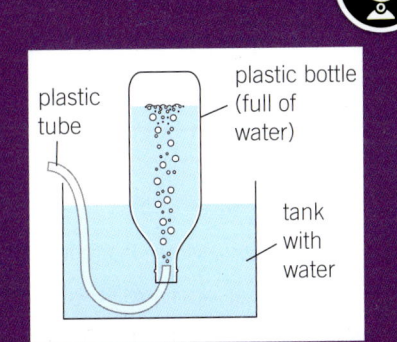

Summary Questions

1. Copy and complete the table using the following words:

   **up and out   down and in
   down   up   decreases
   increases**

	Inhaling	Exhaling
ribs move		
diaphragm moves		
chest volume		

   (3 marks)

2. Explain how changes in volume and pressure inside the chest move gases in and out of the lungs.

   (6 marks)

3. Imagine that you are an athletics coach at the Olympics. Describe how you would measure the lung volume of an athlete.

   (3 marks)

4. Describe how a bell-jar model can be used to represent inhalation. Include a diagram and suggest at least one problem with the model.

   (6 marks)

● Topic 8.3 Breathing

8.3.3 Drugs

Learning objectives

After this section you will be able to:

- state the difference between medicinal and recreational drugs
- describe the effects of drugs on health and behaviour.

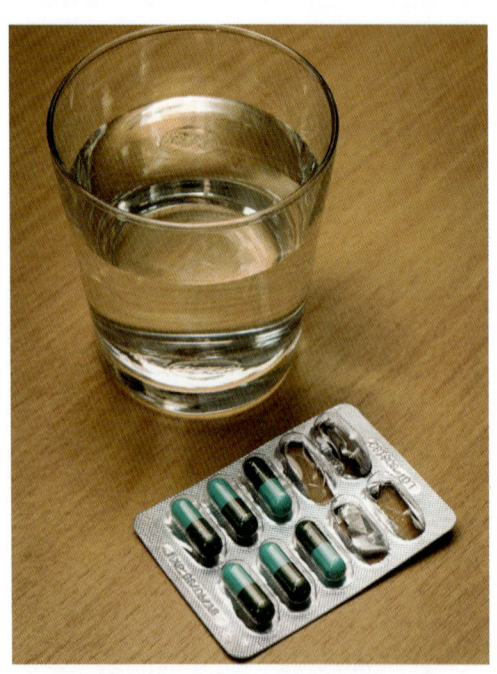

Some drugs can seriously damage your health, or even be deadly. Some can save your life, and are used widely in medicine. So what's the difference?

What are drugs?

Drugs are chemical substances that affect the way your body works. They alter the chemical reactions that take place inside your body. Sometimes these changes are helpful but in many cases they are harmful.

There are two types of drugs – **medicinal drugs** and **recreational drugs**.

A State what is meant by a drug.

What are medicinal drugs?

Medicinal drugs are used in medicine. They benefit your health in some way. They may be used to treat the symptoms of a condition – for example, paracetamol is taken to relieve pain. Other drugs can cure an illness. For example, antibiotics are often used to treat chest infections.

However, even medicinal drugs can cause harm if you do not take them in the right way. Some medicinal drugs also have unwanted side effects. When prescribing drugs, doctors have to weigh up the benefits of a person taking a drug over any possible risks.

▲ Antibiotic pills are used to treat bacterial infections.

B State what is meant by a medicinal drug.

What are recreational drugs?

Recreational drugs are drugs that people take for enjoyment, to help them relax, or to help them to stay awake. Recreational drugs normally have no health benefits and in many cases are harmful.

C State what is meant by a recreational drug.

Recreational drugs are not prescribed by a doctor. Many are illegal – this means that you are breaking the law if you take them. Even very small amounts of these drugs can damage your body. Examples of these drugs include heroin, cocaine, cannabis, and ecstasy.

Key Words

drug, medicinal drug, recreational drug, addiction, withdrawal symptoms

Big Idea: Organisms 8

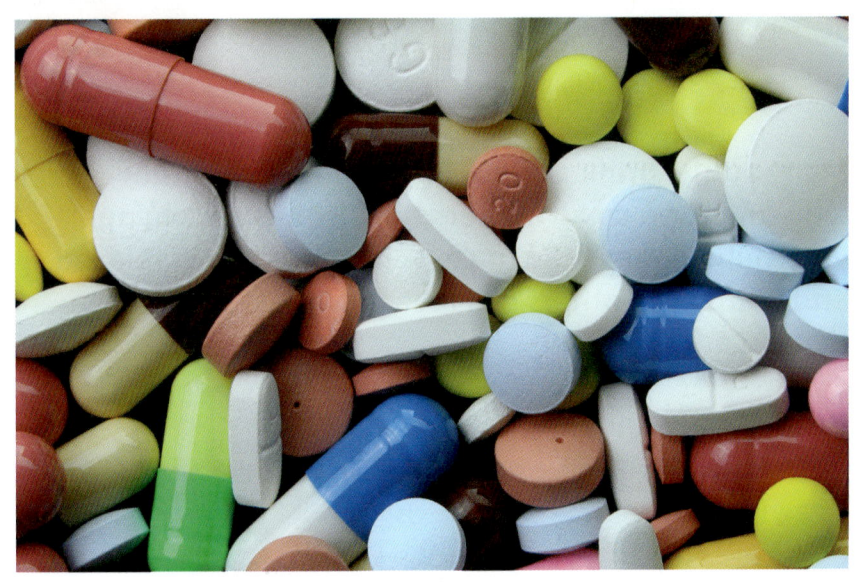

▲ Many recreational drugs are illegal.

▲ Caffeine is a recreational drug that speeds up your nervous system.

D Name three illegal drugs.

Some recreational drugs are legal to use. They can still be harmful. These include:
- alcohol – drinking alcohol affects your nervous system and damages your liver.
- tobacco – smoking significantly increases your risk of cancer, as well as lung and heart disease.

Drug addiction

If your body gets used to the changes caused by a drug, it may become dependent on the drug. This means that you need to keep taking the drug to feel normal. If this happens you have an **addiction**. If a person with an addiction tries to stop taking the drug, they may suffer **withdrawal symptoms**. These can be very unpleasant and make it even harder to give up the drug. Withdrawal symptoms include headaches, anxiety, and sweating.

E State what is meant by an addiction.

Drug factsheet
Produce a factsheet about one of the following drugs to share with other members of your class:
cannabis, cocaine, ecstasy, heroin.

Summary Questions

1. Copy and complete the sentences below.
   Drugs are _____ that affect the way your body works.
   _____ drugs are taken for enjoyment. _____ drugs benefit health.
   If you take drugs too often you may develop an _____. When addicted people stop taking drugs, they suffer _____ _____, which can make it harder to give up.
   (5 marks)

2. Describe three differences between medicinal drugs and recreational drugs.
   (3 marks)

3. Compare the effects of different types of drug on health and behaviour.
   (6 marks)

● Topic 8.3 Breathing

8.3.4 Alcohol

Learning objectives

After this section you will be able to:
- state what kind of drug ethanol is
- describe the effect of alcohol on health and behaviour
- describe the effect alcohol has on conception and pregnancy

Many adults drink alcohol but it can be harmful. Drinking even small amounts of alcohol can change your behaviour. It can make some people feel relaxed and happy but others can feel aggressive and depressed.

What is alcohol?

Alcohol contains the drug **ethanol**. When you drink alcohol, ethanol is absorbed into your bloodstream. It then travels to your brain, where it affects your nervous system. This chemical is called a **depressant** because it slows down your body's reactions.

A Name the drug found in alcoholic drinks.

If people drink a lot of alcohol regularly, they may need to drink greater and greater amounts to cause the same effect on their body. They may become addicted. People who have an addiction to alcohol are called **alcoholics**.

B State what is meant by the word alcoholic.

How much alcohol can you drink safely?

Different alcoholic drinks contain different amounts of alcohol. For example, spirits such as vodka and whisky contain more alcohol than beer.

To lower the risk of damage to your body from drinking alcohol, the government recommends that adults do not regularly drink more than 14 units of alcohol per week. One unit of alcohol is 10 ml of pure alcohol.

However, these are only guidelines because height, weight, and gender affect the way people react to alcohol.

C State the recommended maximum number of alcohol units per week for adults.

increasing alcohol intake	how a person would be affected
no alcohol	generally relaxed and happy
	drunk – person loses control of their muscles, making it difficult to walk and balance
	slurred speech
	blurred vision
	unconsciousness
excessive alcohol	death

▲ This diagram shows what happens to a person as they increase their alcohol intake.

Key Words

ethanol, depressant, alcoholic, unit of alcohol

Dangers of alcohol

Drinking large amounts of alcohol over a long time can cause stomach ulcers, heart disease, and brain and liver damage.

Your liver breaks down harmful chemicals (including ethanol) into harmless waste products, which are then excreted from your body. As a result of having to break down large amounts of ethanol the livers of heavy drinkers become scarred. This means their liver works less efficiently, taking longer to break down alcohol and other chemicals. This condition is called cirrhosis of the liver, and can result in death.

▲ Look at the difference in appearance of a diseased liver (left) and a healthy liver (right).

D Name three conditions that are more likely to occur if a person drinks a lot of alcohol for a long time.

Should pregnant women drink?

The Department of Health recommends that pregnant women do not drink any alcohol. Drinking alcohol increases the risk of miscarriage, stillbirth, premature birth, and low-birth-weight babies.

When a pregnant woman drinks alcohol, it diffuses into the baby's bloodstream. It can then damage the developing organs and nervous system. Foetal Alcohol Syndrome (FAS) affects the way a baby's brain develops. It can result in children with learning difficulties, facial problems, and poor immune systems.

Alcohol can also reduce fertility in both men and women. This means they are less likely to conceive (get pregnant). For example, alcohol reduces the amount of sperm that a man produces.

Big Idea: Organisms 8

pint of lager	alcopop	glass of wine	shot of vodka
3	1.5	2	1

units of alcohol

▲ Units of alcohol present in a range of drinks.

Units of alcohol

On drinks labels the alcohol content is given as a percentage of the whole drink. Wine that says 10% on its label contains 10% pure alcohol. Calculate the number of units of alcohol in a 200 ml glass of wine.
One unit = 10 ml of pure alcohol.

Summary Questions

1. Copy and complete the sentences below.
   Alcoholic drinks contain the drug _____. This is a _____, because it affects the _____ system, slowing down your body's reactions. Drinking alcohol can lead to brain and _____ damage.
   (4 marks)

2. Explain why it is important that pregnant women avoid alcohol.
   (3 marks)

3. Make a visual summary to show the effects of alcohol on behaviour, health, and life processes such as conception, growth, and development.
   (6 marks)

● Topic 8.3 Breathing

8.3.5 Smoking

Learning objectives

After this section you will be able to:
- describe the effects of tobacco smoke on health
- explain the effects of tobacco smoke on health.

Key Words

passive smoking, stimulant

▲ The chemicals in tobacco smoke can be deadly.

Most people know that smoking harms your health, yet many people still smoke. Even breathing in the smoke of someone else's cigarette can affect your health.

Why is smoking dangerous?

Smoking increases your chances of developing conditions such as breathing problems, cancer, heart attacks, and strokes. Smokers are much more likely to die prematurely than non-smokers. For example, male smokers are over 20% more likely to die from lung cancer than non-smokers.

A Name three conditions that a smoker is more likely to suffer from.

As well as affecting their own health, smokers endanger the health of others. By breathing in other people's smoke, your risk of developing circulatory and respiratory conditions increases. This is known as **passive smoking**.

Smoking in pregnancy greatly increases the risk of miscarriage. It can also increase the risk of low-birth-weight babies and affects the foetus's development. Parents who smoke after a baby is born increase the risk of sudden-infant-death syndrome (cot death) and respiratory illness, such as bronchitis and pneumonia.

B State what is meant by passive smoking.

Deadly smoke

Use the graph to answer the following questions:

1. Which smoking-related diseases cause the greatest number of deaths?
2. How many more deaths occurred due to lung disease than heart disease?
3. How many times more likely is a smoker to die from lung and throat cancer, compared to a stroke?

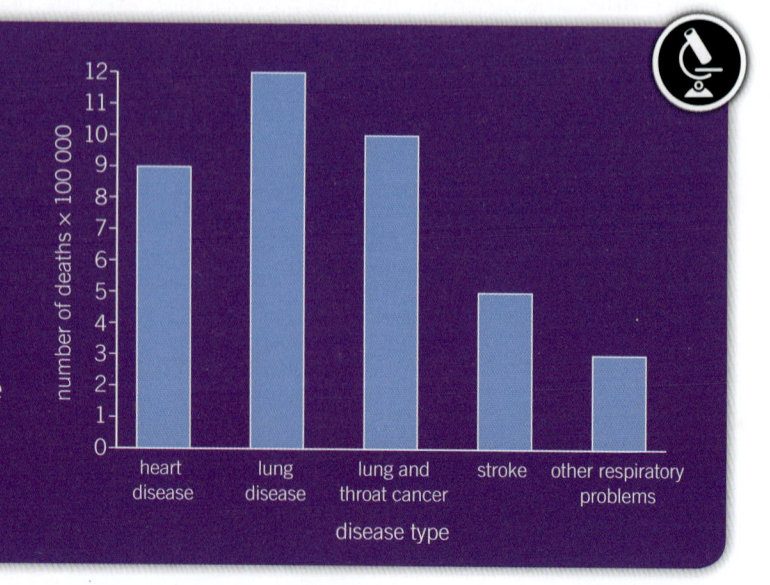

Big Idea: Organisms 8

What's in tobacco smoke?

Cigarettes contain tobacco. Tobacco smoke contains over 4000 chemicals, many of which are harmful. These include:

- tar – a sticky black material that collects in the lungs. It irritates and narrows the airways. Some of the chemicals it contains cause cancer.
- nicotine – an addictive drug that speeds up the nervous system. It is a **stimulant**, which makes the heart beat faster and narrows blood vessels.
- carbon monoxide – a poisonous gas that stops the blood from carrying as much oxygen as it should. It binds to the red blood cells in the place of oxygen.

C Name the addictive drug in tobacco smoke.

How does smoking cause disease?

Some examples of the way smoking causes disease are listed below:

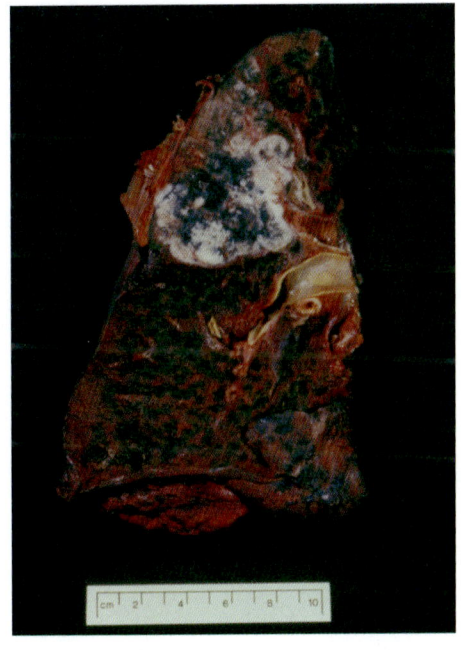

- Heart disease – smoking causes a person's arteries to become blocked. This prevents blood flowing properly, and can cause a heart attack or stroke.
- Emphysema (a lung disease) – chemicals in tobacco smoke affect the alveoli in your lungs. Their walls become weakened so they do not inflate properly when you inhale. They may also burst during coughing. This reduces the amount of oxygen that can pass into the blood, making the person breathless.
- Respiratory infections – the cells lining your windpipe produce mucus, which traps dirt and microorganisms. They also have cilia that sweep the mucus into your stomach, keeping your airways clean. Chemicals in tobacco smoke stop the cilia from moving. This allows mucus to flow into your lungs, making it harder to breathe and often causing infection. Smokers cough this mucus up, which can damage the lungs further.

▲ This diseased lung is full of tar. Healthy lungs should be pink.

Foul Fact

According to the World Health Organization, approximately one person dies every 6 seconds due to tobacco. Deaths caused by tobacco account for 10% of adult deaths.

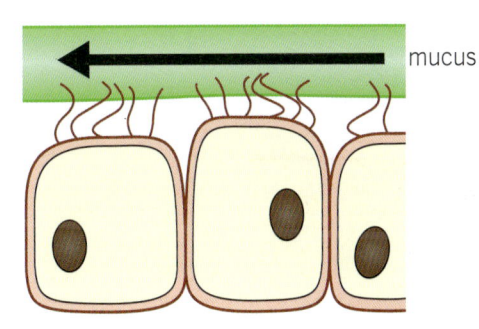

▲ Smoking makes it harder for ciliated cells to sweep mucus from your airways.

Summary Questions

1. Match the chemicals in tobacco smoke to their harmful effect.

tar	addictive and makes the heart beat faster
nicotine	reduces the amount of oxygen the blood can carry
carbon monoxide	contains chemicals that cause cancer

   (3 marks)

2. Suggest why smokers often cough a lot when they first wake in the morning.
   (2 marks)

3. Describe how tobacco smoke can cause problems during pregnancy.
   (2 marks)

4. Explain in detail three ways that smoking can damage your health.
   (6 marks)

Topic 8.3 Breathing

8.4.1 Nutrients

Learning objectives

After this section you will be able to:

- describe the components of a healthy diet and their functions in the body
- compare the nutritional content of different foods or diets
- describe the effects of deficiencies or excesses of different nutrients on a person's health.

Foul Fact

If you eat a lot of beetroots your urine turns pink. Eating a lot of asparagus turns your urine bright yellow!

▲ Carbohydrate-rich foods.

▲ Fat-rich foods.

We all know that sweets should only be eaten as a treat and you have probably heard many times that you should eat a balanced diet. But what does this mean, and why is it important?

Nutrients are important substances that your body needs to survive and stay healthy. There are different types of nutrients. We get most of them from food. The types of nutrient are:

1. **carbohydrates**, which provide energy
2. **lipids** (fats and oils), which provide energy
3. **proteins**, which are used for growth and repair
4. **vitamins**, which keep you healthy
5. **minerals**, which keep you healthy
6. water, which is needed in all cells and body fluids
7. **dietary fibre**, which provides bulk to food to keep it moving through the gut. Fibre is not a nutrient but it is important for a healthy diet.

To remain healthy you must eat a **balanced diet**. This means eating food containing the right nutrients in the correct amounts.

A State what is meant by a nutrient.

Carbohydrates

There are two types of carbohydrate:

- simple carbohydrates (sugars): these are found in foods such as sugar and fruit. They provide a quick source of energy.
- complex carbohydrates (starch): these are found in foods such as pasta and bread. They have to be broken down by the body, so the energy is released more slowly.

B State the function of carbohydrates.

Lipids

Lipids include fats and oils. They have three important jobs. They:

- provide you with a store of energy
- keep you warm, by providing a layer of insulation under your skin
- protect organs like your kidneys and heart from damage.

Big Idea: Organisms 8

Proteins

Proteins are needed to repair body tissues and to make new cells for growth. Your muscles, organs, and immune system are mostly made of proteins.

C State two functions of proteins.

Vitamins and minerals

Vitamins and minerals are essential substances for keeping you healthy but you only need tiny amounts. Vitamins are needed for you to grow, develop, and function normally. For example, vitamin A is needed for good eyesight. Vitamin D is needed with the mineral calcium to maintain healthy teeth and bones. Iron is a mineral which is important for making red blood cells.

Fruits and vegetables are a good source of vitamins and minerals.

D State why the body needs calcium and iron.

Water

Your cells are made up of about 70% water. To keep them healthy you need to constantly replace the water your body loses in sweat, tears, urine, faeces, and exhaling. You should drink over a litre of water every day. This can come from drinking water but tea, fruit juice, and squash all count.

Dietary fibre

Fibre is the parts of plants that the body cannot break down. It is an important part of your diet as it adds bulk to your food. This means it keeps food moving through the gut, and waste is pushed out of the body more easily, helping to prevent constipation.

▲ Fibre-rich foods.

Healthy eating
Design and film a healthy-eating TV advert on behalf of the government. The advert should aim to encourage young people to eat a balanced diet.

▲ Protein-rich foods.

Link
You can learn more about balanced diets in 8.4.3 Unhealthy diet.

Key Words
nutrient, carbohydrate, lipid, protein, vitamin, mineral, dietary fibre, balanced diet

Summary Questions

1 Match the nutrient to its role in the body. (6 marks)

carbohydrates	growth and repair
lipids	needed in small amounts to keep you healthy
protein	provide energy
vitamins and minerals	provide bulk to food
water	energy store and insulation
dietary fibre	needed in cells and bodily fluids

2 Describe the role of lipids in the body. (3 marks)

3 Suggest and explain the advice a doctor might give to a patient who has constipation. (3 marks)

4 Explain in detail what is meant by a balanced diet. Provide examples of what a balanced diet should contain. (6 marks)

Topic 8.4 Digestion

8.4.2 Food tests

Learning objectives

After this section you will be able to:
- describe how to test foods for starch, lipids, sugar, and protein
- describe the positive result for each food test.

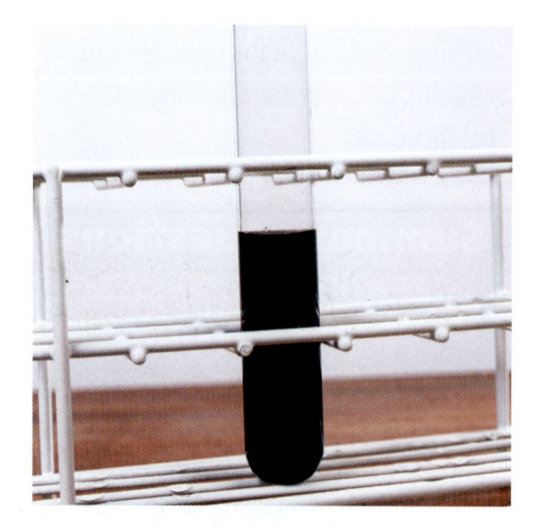

You may be able to guess by looking at some foods which nutrients they contain. For example, you may know that oily foods contain lipids. Scientists use food tests to find out which nutrients are in a food product.

How can you test foods?

A different chemical test exists for each type of nutrient. For most **food tests**, you will need a solution of the food. To prepare a food solution:

1. crush the food using a pestle and mortar
2. add a few drops of water, and mix well.

You should use a special type of water called distilled water – this is pure water that contains no other chemical substances.

How do you test for starch?

To test for starch you use iodine solution. Iodine solution is an orange-yellow liquid.

1. Add a few drops of iodine solution to the food solution.
2. If the solution turns a dark blue-black colour, the food contains starch.

▲ This food solution contains starch.

A State the colour change in iodine if a food contains starch.

Key Words

food test, hypothesis

How do you test for lipids?

To test for lipids in a solid piece of food you use a piece of filter paper.

1. Rub some of the food onto a piece of filter paper.
2. Hold the paper up to the light. If the paper has gone translucent, the food contains lipids.

B State how you would test a solid piece of food for lipids.

To test for lipids in a food solution you use ethanol. Ethanol is a colourless liquid.

Hypothesis

Scientists observe the world and come up with a **hypothesis** to explain what they observe. A hypothesis is an idea about things that always happen. A hypothesis can be tested in an investigation. You can use hypotheses to make a prediction.

Big Idea: Organisms 8

1. Add a few drops of ethanol to the food solution.
2. Shake the test tube and leave for one minute.
3. Pour the ethanol into a test tube of water.
4. If the solution turns cloudy, the food contains lipids.

How do you test for sugar?

To test for simple sugars such as glucose you use Benedict's solution. Benedict's solution is a blue liquid.

1. Add a few drops of Benedict's solution to the food solution.
2. Heat the test tube in a water bath.
3. If the solution turns orange-red, the food contains sugar.

▲ This food solution contains lipids.

▲ This food solution contains sugar.

C State the colour change in Benedict's solution if a food contains sugar.

How do you test for protein?

To test for protein you use copper sulfate solution and sodium hydroxide solution. Copper sulfate solution is a pale-blue liquid. Sodium hydroxide solution is a colourless liquid.

1. Add a few drops of copper sulfate solution to your food solution.
2. Add a few drops of sodium hydroxide solution.
3. If the solution turns purple, the food contains protein.

D State the colour change in a solution of copper sulfate and sodium hydroxide if a food contains protein.

◀ This food solution contains protein.

Summary Questions

1 Complete the table using the words below.

turns blue-black
turns orange-red
makes paper translucent
turns purple

Nutrient	Colour change if nutrient present
starch	
lipids	
sugar	
protein	

(4 marks)

2 Describe how to prepare a food solution of a breakfast cereal.

(3 marks)

3 Explain in detail how you would test a gingerbread-biscuit solution for the presence of starch, sugar, and protein.

(6 marks)

● Topic 8.4 Digestion

8.4.3 Unhealthy diet

Learning objectives

After this section you will be able to:

- recall how you get and use energy
- describe some health issues caused by an unbalanced diet
- calculate the energy requirements of different people.

▲ This food pyramid shows a healthy balanced diet. The largest part of your diet should be carbohydrate based. Lipids, oils, and sweets should only be eaten in very small quantities.

Link

You can learn more about energy in food in Book 1, 3.1.1 Food and fuels.

Key Words

malnourishment, starvation, obese, deficiency

You may have seen pictures of people who are either extremely overweight or underweight. Both of these conditions are caused by **malnourishment**. This means the people have eaten the wrong amount or the wrong types of food.

Where does your energy come from?

You need energy for everything you do, even to sleep. This energy comes from your food. The energy in food is measured in joules (J) or kilojoules (kJ) – 1 kilojoule is the same as 1000 joules.

If you look on a food label it will tell you how much energy is stored in that food.

A State the unit that energy in food is measured in.

Why is it unhealthy to be underweight?

Some people do not eat enough food. In extreme cases this is known as **starvation**. If the energy in the food you eat is less than the energy you use, you will lose body mass. This leads to you being underweight. Underweight people:

- often suffer from health problems, such as a poor immune system
- lack energy to do things, and are often tired
- are likely to suffer from a lack of vitamins or minerals.

B State three problems caused by being underweight.

Why is it unhealthy to be overweight?

Some people eat too much, or eat too many fatty foods. If the energy content in the food you eat is more than the energy you use, you gain body mass. This is stored as fat under the skin. If a person becomes extremely overweight, they are said to be **obese**.

Overweight people have an increased risk of:

- heart disease
- stroke
- diabetes
- some cancers.

Big Idea: Organisms 8

C State three diseases that obese people are more likely to suffer from.

What are vitamin and mineral deficiencies?

If a person does not have enough of a certain vitamin or mineral they are said to have a **deficiency**. This can damage a person's health. For example, a vitamin A deficiency can lead to 'night blindness'. This makes it difficult for you to see clearly in dim light. A vitamin D deficiency can lead to a condition called rickets, where your bones become weak.

D Name the condition caused by a vitamin A deficiency.

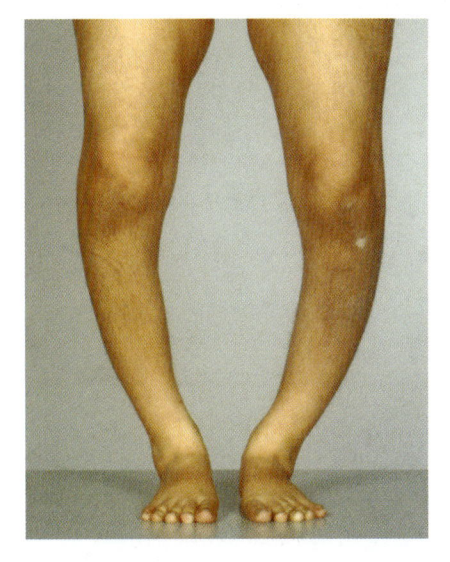

How much energy do you need?

Your body needs energy to function properly. The amount of energy you need depends on your age (as this affects your growth rate), your body size, and how active you are. The more exercise you do, the more energy your body requires.

Energy requirements

Use the graph below to estimate the energy that a female computer programmer needs each day. How did you arrive at your answer?

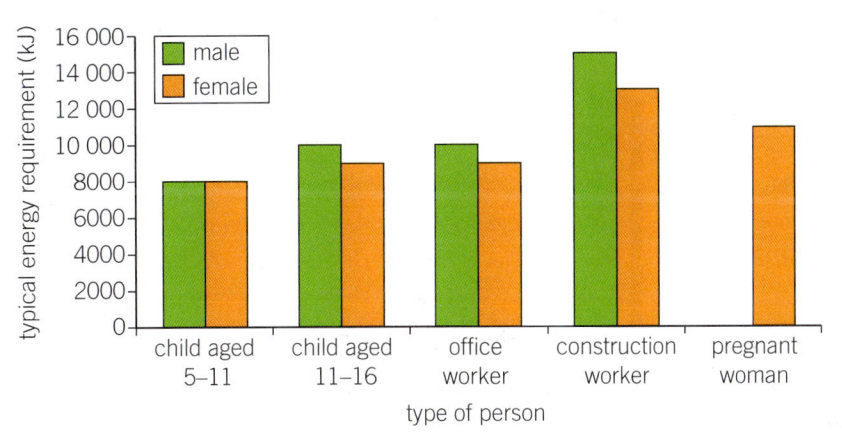

▲ This person is suffering from rickets.

Summary Questions

1. Copy and complete the sentences below.

   You gain the _____ you need to survive from food. Energy is measured in _____.

   If you take in more energy than you use you _____ body mass. If you become _____ your risk of _____ disease increases. An underweight person is often _____.

   (6 marks)

2. Use the graph on this page to answer the following questions.
   a. Calculate the extra energy a female office worker would need each day if she became pregnant. (2 marks)
   b. A male office worker starts a new job as a construction worker. Calculate the percentage increase in his daily energy needs. (4 marks)

3. Compare the health problems of being underweight with the health problems of being overweight.

   (6 marks)

▲ Daily energy requirements for different types of people.

● Topic 8.4 Digestion

8.4.4 Digestive system

Learning objectives
After this section you will be able to:
- state what happens during digestion
- describe the structure of the main parts of the digestive system
- describe how components of the digestive system are adapted to their function.

Link
You can learn more about molecules in 5.3.3 Compounds.

Fantastic fact
If you unravelled your small intestine it would be roughly four times taller than you – it is not very small!

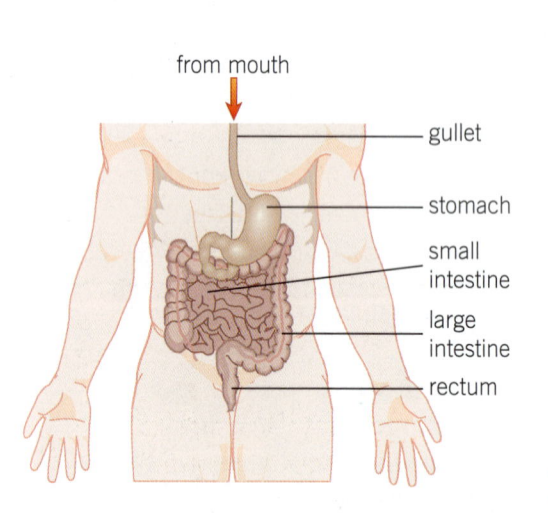

▲ Movement of food out of the digestive system.

You may sometimes notice your stomach rumbling. This is a hint that you need to eat. You know that the food contains nutrients. But how does your body get nutrients out of food?

What is the digestive system?
The **digestive system** is a group of organs that work together to break down food. The nutrients in most of the food you eat are large molecules, like lipids and proteins. During **digestion** these large molecules are broken down into small molecules of nutrients. These nutrients can then pass into the blood where they are used by the body.

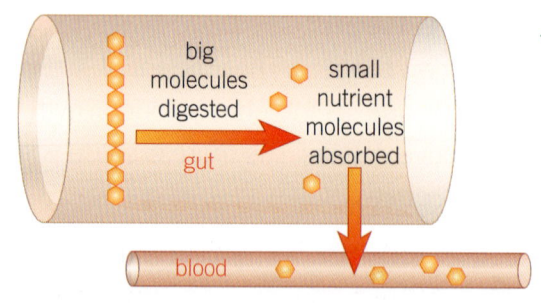

◀ During digestion large molecules are broken down into small molecules and pass into the bloodstream.

A State what happens during digestion.

Structures in the digestive system
The diagram opposite shows the main structures in your digestive system. It is often referred to as your gut.

Mouth	Food is chewed and mixed with saliva. Teeth help to break the food into smaller chunks.
Gullet	Food passes down this tube.
Stomach	Food is mixed with digestive juices and acids.
Small intestine	Digestive juices from the liver and pancreas are added and digestion is completed. Small molecules of nutrients pass through the intestine wall into the bloodstream.
Large intestine	Only food that cannot be digested gets this far. Water passes back into the body, leaving a solid waste of undigested food called faeces.
Rectum	Faeces are stored here until they leave the body.
Anus	This is a muscular ring through which faeces pass out of the body.

B Name the structure that food passes along to reach the stomach.

Big Idea: Organisms 8

Moving through the digestive system

Fibre in your food isn't digested but adds bulk to the food. Muscles push against this, forcing food along the gut. Eating lots of fibre-rich foods such as vegetables and wholemeal bread helps prevent constipation.

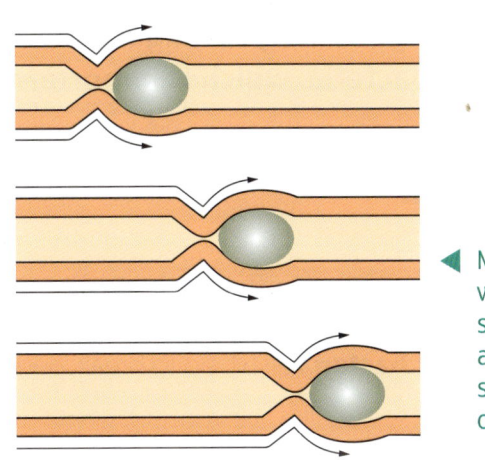

◀ Muscles in the wall of the gut squeeze food along – a bit like squeezing a tube of toothpaste.

C Describe how food moves along the gut.

Passing into the blood

The small molecules of nutrients produced during digestion pass into the bloodstream through the wall of the small intestine. They are then transported around the body.

The small intestine needs to absorb the nutrients quickly, before the undigested food passes out of the body. The small intestine is specially adapted to this function. The wall of the small intestine is thin. It is also covered with tiny structures called **villi**. These stick out of the wall and give it a big surface area. They also contain blood capillaries to carry away the absorbed food molecules.

▲ Villi in the small intestine increase the surface area so more nutrients can be absorbed.

Key Words

digestive system, digestion, gullet, stomach, small intestine, large intestine, rectum, anus, villi

Wordbank

Make a wordbank by listing all the scientific terms about digestion. You can refer to your wordbank as you progress through this topic.

Summary Questions

1 Match each organ below to its role in digestion.

stomach	food is chewed and mixed with saliva
small intestine	water is absorbed back into the body
large intestine	food is mixed with acid and digestive juices
rectum	faeces are stored here until they pass out of the body
mouth	small molecules of nutrients are absorbed into the bloodstream

(5 marks)

2 Describe the adaptations of the small intestine to its function.

(3 marks)

3 Explain why it is important to eat a fibre-rich diet.

(3 marks)

4 Describe in detail the passage of food through the digestive system.

(6 marks)

● Topic 8.4 Digestion

8.4.5 Bacteria and enzymes in digestion

Learning objectives

After this section you will be able to:

- describe the role of enzymes in digestion
- describe the role of bacteria in digestion
- describe all the events that take place in turning a meal into simple food molecules.

Have you seen the TV adverts that say that yoghurts and yoghurt drinks are good for your digestive system? They contain bacteria, which is important for digestion.

Bacteria in digestion

Your large intestine contains bacteria. These microorganisms live on the fibre in your diet. They make important vitamins such as vitamin K. These vitamins are then absorbed into your body and help to keep you healthy. The **gut bacteria** also help to break food down.

Some foods, called probiotic foods, like live yoghurt, contain these useful bacteria.

A State why bacteria are important in your digestive system.

What's in digestive juices?

Your teeth begin digestion by breaking down food into smaller pieces. The digestive juices in your gut contain **enzymes**. These are special proteins that can break large molecules of nutrients into small molecules.

Large molecules in your food like starch, a type of carbohydrate, are made of lots of smaller molecules joined together. Enzymes chop these large molecules into the smaller molecules they are made from.

◀ Enzymes chop large molecules into smaller molecules.

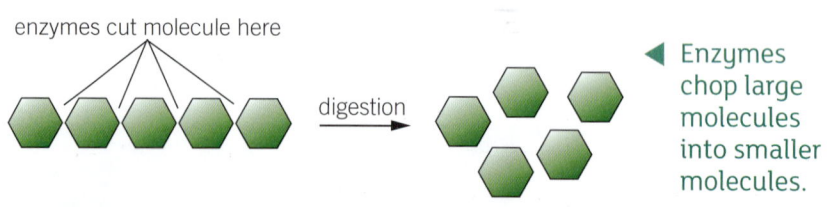

Enzymes are known as biological **catalysts** – they speed up digestion without being used up.

▲ Probiotic foods.

B State the role of enzymes in digestion.

Different types of enzyme

Different types of enzyme break down different nutrients. There are three main types of enzymes involved in digestion – **carbohydrase**, **protease**, and **lipase**.

What's in a name?
The enzymes carbohydrase, protease, and lipase are named after the type of nutrient they break down.

Big Idea: Organisms 8

Carbohydrase

Carbohydrase is an enzyme that breaks down carbohydrates into sugar molecules.

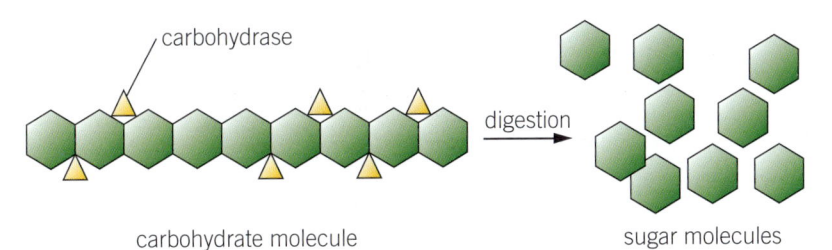

▲ Starch is broken down into sugar molecules.

Carbohydrates are digested in the mouth, stomach, and small intestine. Carbohydrase present in your saliva breaks down the starch in bread into sugar.

Protease

Protease is an enzyme that breaks down proteins into amino acids.

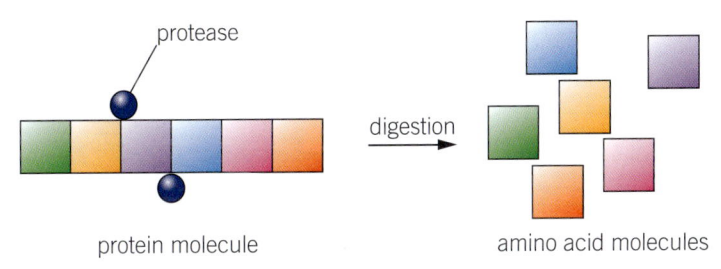

▲ Protein is broken down into amino acids.

Proteins are digested in the stomach and small intestine. Acid in the stomach helps digestion and kills harmful microorganisms in food.

Lipase

Lipase is an enzyme that breaks down lipids into fatty acids and glycerol.

Digestion of lipids takes place in the small intestine. It is helped by **bile**, a substance made in the liver. Bile breaks the lipids into small droplets that are easier for the lipase enzymes to work on.

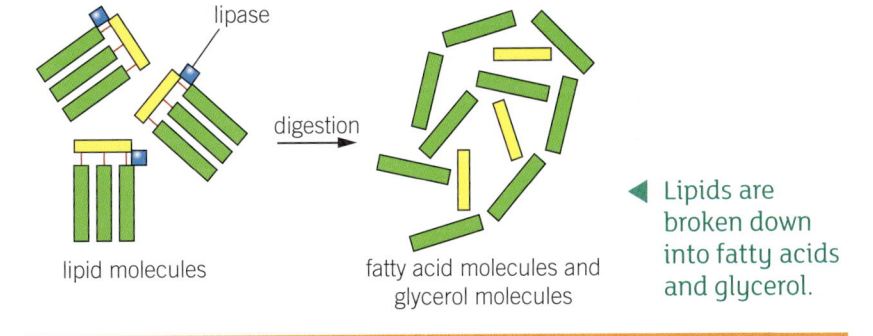

◄ Lipids are broken down into fatty acids and glycerol.

C State the function of bile.

What happens to the bread you eat?

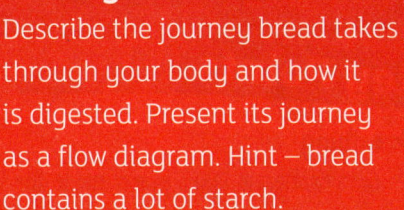

Describe the journey bread takes through your body and how it is digested. Present its journey as a flow diagram. Hint – bread contains a lot of starch.

Key Words

gut bacteria, enzyme, catalyst, carbohydrase, protease, lipase, bile

Summary Questions

1. Copy the sentences below, choosing the correct bold word.
   Carbohydrates/proteins are broken down into sugar by the enzyme **lipase/carbohydrase**. Proteins are broken down into **amino acids/lipase** by the enzyme **carbohydrase/protease**. Lipids are broken down into **lipase/fatty acids and glycerol** by the enzyme **lipase/carbohydrase**.
   (6 marks)

2. Explain why live yoghurt should be part of your diet.
   (3 marks)

3. Make a visual summary of the ideas on this page to compare the roles of enzymes and bacteria in digestion.
   (6 marks)

Topic 8.4 Digestion

8 Organisms: Summary

Key Points

Breathing
- Gas exchange takes place inside the lungs – oxygen is taken in and carbon dioxide is given out.
- Oxygen enters the body through the mouth and nose. It then travels down the windpipe, through a bronchus, then a bronchiole, into an alveolus, and diffuses into the blood.
- Exhaled air is warmer and contains more carbon dioxide and water vapour than inhaled air, but less oxygen.
- When you inhale, muscles between your ribs and the diaphragm contract. This increases the volume inside your chest. The pressure decreases and air is drawn into the lungs.
- When you exhale, muscles between your ribs and the diaphragm relax. This decreases the volume inside your chest. The pressure increases and air is forced out of your lungs.

Digestion
- Nutrients are essential substances that your body needs to survive. They are carbohydrates, lipids, proteins, vitamins, mineral, water, and fibre.
- To remain healthy you must eat a balanced diet. This means eating food containing the right nutrients in the correct amounts.
- Underweight people often lack energy. They may also suffer from a vitamin or mineral deficiency, which can cause problems like a poor immune system.
- Overweight people have an increased risk of heart disease, diabetes, and some cancers.
- During digestion large molecules like lipids and proteins are broken down into small molecules. They can then pass into the blood where they are used by the body.
- Enzymes are proteins that can break large molecules into small molecules. They are biological catalysts – they speed up digestion without being used up.

Key Words

gas exchange, lungs, ribs, respiratory system, trachea, bronchus, bronchiole, alveolus, breathing, inhale, respiration, exhale, condense, contract, diaphragm, lung volume, asthma, drug, medicinal drug, recreational drug, addiction, withdrawal symptoms, ethanol, depressant, alcoholic, unit of alcohol, passive smoking, stimulant, nutrient, carbohydrate, lipid, protein, vitamin, mineral, dietary fibre, balanced diet, food test, hypothesis, malnourishment, starvation, obese, deficiency, digestive system, digestion, gullet, stomach, small intestine, large intestine, rectum, anus, villi, gut bacteria, enzyme, catalyst, carbohydrase, protease, lipase, bile

BIG Write

Say no to drugs
You work for the NHS as a communications officer. You have been asked to produce an antidrugs leaflet. It will be given to all teenagers as part of an antidrugs campaign.

Task
Write the text that will appear in the leaflet. It should contain information on smoking, alcohol, and illegal recreational drugs.

Tips
- Make sure your points are clear, concise, and convincing – back up your arguments with scientific facts.
- Keep your audience in mind – your leaflet needs to appeal to teenagers and all scientific concepts must be explained clearly.

End-of-Big Idea questions

1. To remain healthy you must eat a balanced diet. Draw a line to match the nutrient to its function in the body.

carbohydrates	used for growth and repair
lipids	needed in small amounts to keep you healthy
proteins	provide energy
vitamins and minerals	provide a store of energy and are used to insulate the body

   (4 marks)

2. This diagram shows your digestive system.

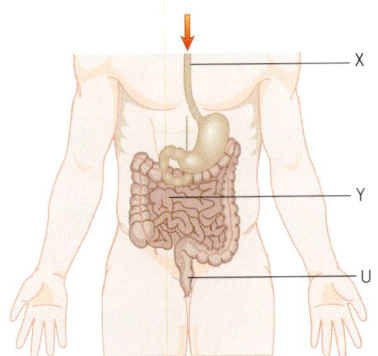

   a Name structure X. *(1 mark)*
   b State what happens in structure Y. *(1 mark)*
   c Which letter represents the structure that stores faeces until they leaves the body? *(1 mark)*
   d Describe the role of the stomach in digestion. *(2 marks)*

   (5 marks)

3. A student wants to do a food test to find out which nutrients are in crisps. She starts by making a solution of the crisps.
   a Name the piece of equipment she should use to break the crisps into small pieces. *(1 mark)*
   b Suggest **two** safety precautions the student should take before beginning the test. *(2 marks)*
   c Describe how the student should test the food solution for protein. *(3 marks)*

   (6 marks)

4. This diagram shows the main structures in the respiratory system.

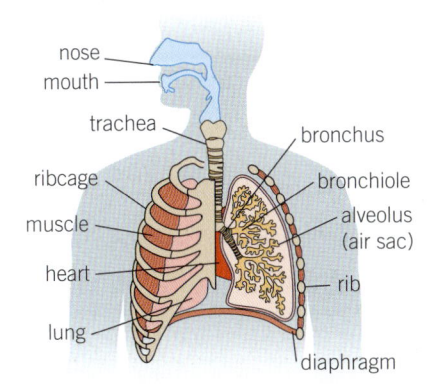

   a Name the bones that protect the lungs. *(1 mark)*
   b Name the process that occurs in the alveolus. *(1 mark)*
   c State what the diaphragm is made of. *(1 mark)*
   d Describe what happens in the lungs when you exhale. *(3 marks)*

   (6 marks)

5. Enzymes are special proteins that play a crucial rule in digestion.
   a Describe the role of enzymes in digestion. *(1 mark)*
   b Explain why enzymes are called catalysts. *(2 marks)*
   c Compare how and where carbohydrates and proteins are digested. *(4 marks)*
   d Explain how lipids are broken down and digested. *(3 marks)*

   (10 marks)

6. Compare the main differences in the composition of inhaled and exhaled air.

   (6 marks)

9 Ecosystems

How do we get energy from food? In this Big Idea, you will find out how the body transfers energy from food so it can be used for movement, growth, and repair by the process of respiration. You will also discover how anaerobic respiration in microorganisms can be used to make bread and beer. You will learn how plants produce food by the process of photosynthesis, and look in detail at the structure of a leaf and why minerals are required for healthy growth.

You already know

- The functions of different parts of flowering plants: roots, stem/trunk, leaves, and flowers.
- The requirements of plants for life and growth (air, light, water, nutrients from soil, and room to grow) and how they vary from plant to plant.
- The way in which water is transported within plants.

Q What are the main components of a cell? What is their function?

BIG Questions

- How does the body transfer energy from food by respiration?
- What is the difference between aerobic and anaerobic respiration?
- How do plants produce food by photosynthesis?

Picture Puzzler
Key Words

Can you solve this Picture Puzzler? The first letter of each of these images spells out a science word that you will come across in this book.

Picture Puzzler
Close Up

Can you tell what this zoomed-in picture is?
Clue: This allows gases to move in and out of a leaf.

Making connections

In your GCSE course you will learn in more detail about the process of anaerobic and aerobic respiration.

You will also discover how different environmental factors limit the rate of photosynthesis and how scientists exploit these to maximise photosynthesis.

You will also investigate how different environmental factors affect the rate of transpiration (movement of water through a plant).

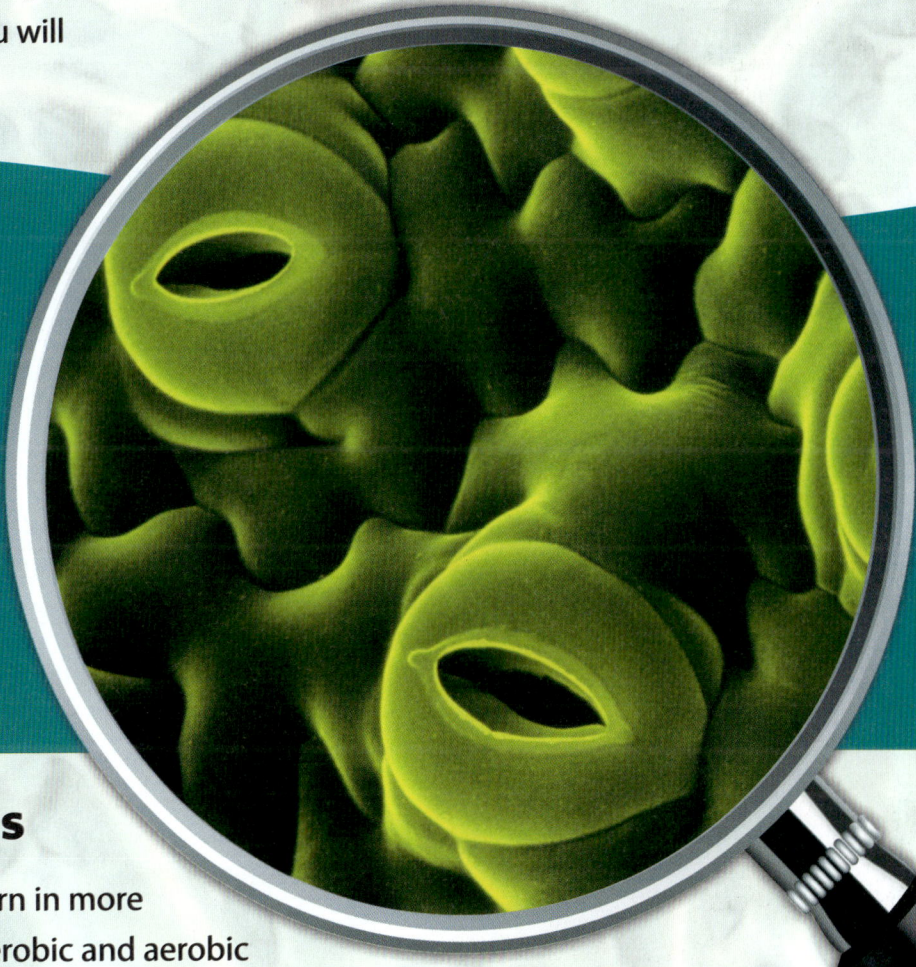

9.3.1 Aerobic respiration

Learning objectives

After this section you will be able to:
- state what happens during aerobic respiration
- use a word equation to describe aerobic respiration.

Key Words

aerobic respiration, plasma, haemoglobin

Why do you need to eat to survive? You use the glucose in your food to provide energy to perform all body processes.

How do cells transfer energy?

Your body needs energy for everything it does. You need energy to move, to grow, and to keep warm. Energy is being used constantly (even when you are asleep!) to keep your body functioning.

You get your energy from organic molecules in the food you eat. To transfer the energy stored in food, glucose reacts with oxygen in a series of chemical reactions called **aerobic respiration**. This reaction transfers energy to your cells. The waste products carbon dioxide and water are also produced.

A Name the chemical reaction that transfers energy from glucose.

The word equation for aerobic respiration is:

$$\text{glucose} + \text{oxygen} \longrightarrow \text{carbon dioxide} + \text{water} (+ \text{energy})$$
$$\text{(reactants)} \qquad\qquad \text{(products)}$$

B State the word equation for aerobic respiration.

Defining respiration

Read through the information about respiration on these pages for 3 minutes. Close the book, and produce a definition and description of aerobic respiration. Swap your ideas with a partner. Together can you improve your definition?

Link

You can learn more about mitochondria in Book 1, 8.2.2 Plant and animal cells.

▲ Physically active people like athletes need to eat lots of high-energy foods, as their bodies require energy to be transferred quickly.

Big Idea: Ecosystems 9

Where does respiration happen?

Respiration happens inside tiny structures inside your cells called mitochondria. All cells contain mitochondria but different cells contain different amounts. Muscle cells carry out lots of respiration, so they contain large amounts of mitochondria.

C State where in a cell respiration occurs.

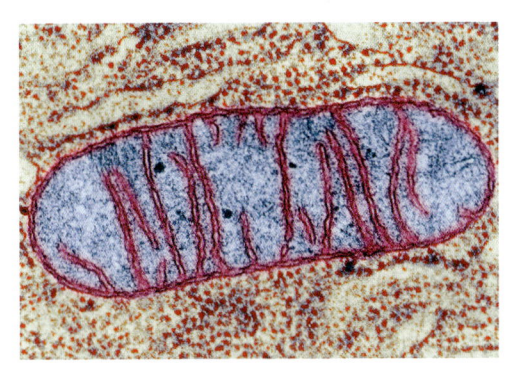

▲ A mitochondrion.

How does glucose get into cells?

Glucose is a carbohydrate found in food. Digestion breaks down food into small molecules, releasing glucose molecules. These molecules are absorbed by the wall of the small intestine, into the bloodstream.

Glucose is transported around your body in your blood. It dissolves in the liquid part of your blood called **plasma**. The dissolved glucose can diffuse into the cells that need it for respiration.

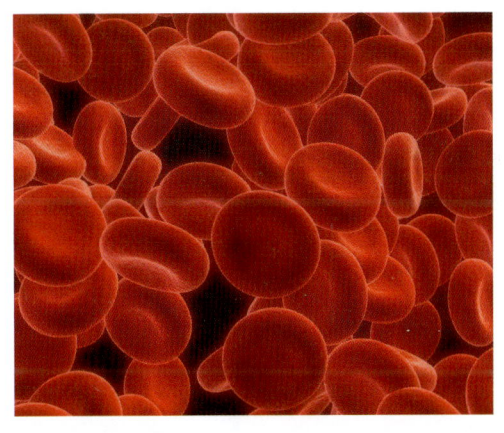

How does oxygen get into cells?

When you breathe in, air fills the alveoli in your lungs. The oxygen then diffuses into your bloodstream.

Oxygen is carried by the red blood cells in your body. Red blood cells contain **haemoglobin** (the substance that makes them red). Oxygen joins to the haemoglobin, and gets carried around the body in the blood vessels. When it reaches a cell requiring oxygen, the oxygen diffuses into the cell.

▲ Red blood cells carry oxygen to cells.

D Name the component of blood that carries oxygen around the body.

How does carbon dioxide leave the body?

If carbon dioxide remained in your body it would build up to a harmful level. You get rid of carbon dioxide when you exhale. Carbon dioxide produced during respiration diffuses out of your cells and into the blood plasma. The blood transports it to the lungs, where it diffuses into the air sacs, and is then exhaled.

E Name the component of blood that transports carbon dioxide.

Summary Questions

1. Copy and complete the sentences below.
   Energy is released in _____ inside your cells by the process of _____. _____ and oxygen react together to release _____. Carbon dioxide and _____ are produced as waste products.
   (5 marks)

2. Describe where and how respiration takes place.
   (4 marks)

3. Explain in detail how the reactants of respiration get into the cells and what happens to the products of respiration.
   (6 marks)

Topic 9.3 Respiration

147

9.3.2 Anaerobic respiration

Learning objectives

After this section you will be able to:

- state the difference between aerobic and anaerobic respiration
- use a word equation to describe anaerobic respiration
- explain why specific activities involve aerobic or anaerobic respiration.

▲ After heavy exercise you will breathe heavily, to break down lactic acid in your muscles.

Key Words

anaerobic respiration, oxygen debt, fermentation

During a sprint race athletes have very little time to breathe. Respiration must constantly supply your body with energy, even when you are unable to breathe.

How do you respire without oxygen?

Anaerobic respiration is a type of respiration that does not use oxygen. Your body uses this type of respiration to transfer energy from glucose when there is not enough oxygen for aerobic respiration to take place.

Anaerobic respiration often happens during strenuous exercise like when you sprint, as the body requires extra energy to be produced quickly. The body can transfer this extra energy for short periods of time without oxygen.

The word equation for anaerobic respiration is:

$$\text{glucose} \longrightarrow \text{lactic acid (+ energy)}$$
$$\text{(reactant)} \qquad \text{(products)}$$

The energy you get from anaerobic respiration is less than that from aerobic respiration.

A State the word equation for anaerobic respiration.

Like most living things, we normally use aerobic respiration. There are two reasons why the body normally respires aerobically:

1. Aerobic respiration transfers more energy per glucose molecule than anaerobic respiration.
2. The lactic acid produced from anaerobic respiration can cause painful cramps in your muscles.

When you have finished exercising you keep on breathing heavily. The extra oxygen you inhale breaks down the lactic acid. The oxygen needed for this process is called the **oxygen debt**.

B State two reasons why the body normally respires aerobically.

Do other organisms perform anaerobic respiration?

Like you, animals normally respire aerobically. However when they need to carry out vigorous exercise their heart and lungs are not able to get sufficient oxygen to their muscles.

Big Idea: Ecosystems 9

They switch to anaerobic respiration. For example, when a fox chases a rabbit, both organisms are likely to respire anaerobically. The rabbit needs to get out of danger and the fox needs to get food.

Plants also usually respire aerobically. Sometimes the oxygen supply to plants can run out. For example if the soil gets waterlogged. When this happens, plants' have to switch to anaerobic respiration in their roots to obtain their energy.

Some microorganisms can also respire anaerobically. This allows them to survive in environments with no or very little oxygen. For example over 90% of the bacteria in your gut perform anaerobic respiration.

Fermentation

Anaerobic respiration in plants and microorganisms produces ethanol and carbon dioxide instead of lactic acid. This process is called **fermentation**. Fermentation is a type of anaerobic respiration, as the plant or microorganism respires without oxygen.

The word equation for fermentation is:

glucose ⟶ ethanol + carbon dioxide (+ energy)

(reactant)   (products)

C State the word equation for fermentation.

Fermenting sugar
When yeast ferments sugar, carbon dioxide is produced. Design an investigation to investigate how the concentration of glucose affects the rate at which fermentation occurs.

◀ The yeast in the conical flask is carrying out fermentation. It is converting the glucose into carbon dioxide which is turning the limewater in the test tube cloudy.

▲ Yeast is a microorganism. It is a type of fungus that carries out fermentation.

Summary Questions

1. 🧪 Copy and complete the sentences below.

   _____ respiration is a type of respiration that does not use _____. Anaerobic respiration in humans causes _____ to be released from glucose. _____ _____ is produced as a waste product, which can build up in muscles and cause _____.

   Plants and microorganisms carry out a type of anaerobic respiration called _____. In this reaction carbon dioxide and _____ are produced.

   (7 marks)

2. 🧪🧪 Describe the main similarities and differences between anaerobic and aerobic respiration. *(4 marks)*

3. 🧪🧪🧪 Suggest what type of respiration is carried out by bacteria in a puncture wound (tiny hole in the skin). *(2 marks)*

4. 🧪🧪🧪 Imagine you are an athletics coach. Explain to a sprinter why they use anaerobic respiration during a race but marathon runners use aerobic respiration. *(6 marks)*

● Topic 9.3 Respiration

9.3.3 Biotechnology

Learning objectives

After this section you will be able to:
- state the word equation for fermentation
- describe how bread, beer, and wine are made.

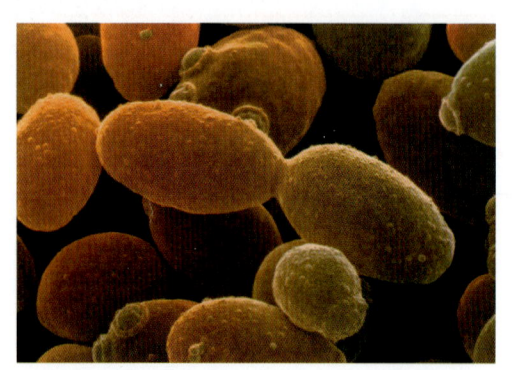

Many of the foods and drinks we consume have been made using microorganisms. For example, yeast is added to bread to make it rise. This is an example of biotechnology.

What is biotechnology?

Biotechnology is the use of biological processes or organisms to create useful products. Many of these products are foods and drinks.

A State what is meant by the term biotechnology.

What is yeast?

Yeast is a microorganism. It is used in the production of bread and many alcoholic drinks. These products are made using the chemical reaction fermentation. Fermentation is a type of anaerobic respiration – the yeast respires without needing oxygen.

The word equation for fermentation is:

$$\text{glucose} \longrightarrow \text{ethanol} + \text{carbon dioxide} (+ \text{energy})$$
$$\text{(reactant)} \qquad \qquad \text{(products)}$$

Enzymes present in the yeast speed up fermentation, making the reaction occur faster. The enzymes work best in a warm environment.

How do you make bread?

Flour, water, and yeast are mixed to make dough. The dough is then left in a warm place to rise. This is caused by the yeast respiring, changing the sugars in the flour into ethanol and carbon dioxide. The carbon dioxide gas is trapped as bubbles inside the dough, making it rise.

The dough is then baked. In the oven, the ethanol evaporates. The bubbles of gas expand, making the bread rise further.

▲ *Saccharomyces cerevisiae* is the yeast used to make bread.

▲ Before baking, the bread is left to rise.

B Name the gas that makes dough rise.

Link
You can learn more about fermentation in Book 2, 9.3.2 Anaerobic respiration.

Fantastic Fact
The world record for the longest loaf of bread is 1211.6 m. It was baked in Portugal in 2005 during the Bread and Bakers' Party.

Big Idea: Ecosystems 9

How do you make beer and wine?

▲ Alcoholic drinks are made by fermenting plant sugars.

Beer and wine are made in very similar ways. The type of alcoholic drink produced depends on the source of sugar. This determines the type of ethanol produced.

Wine is made when yeast is used to ferment grape sugar. Beer or lager is made when yeast is used to ferment sugar in malted barley. This is known as brewing.

| Plant sugar is added to a large container – often the plant needs to be crushed. | → | Yeast is added to ferment the sugar into alcohol. | → | The container is sealed to keep out oxygen and other microorganisms. |

| The mixture is left until the sugar has fermented into alcohol. | → | Sediment is removed from the liquid, often by filtration. | → | The liquid is bottled or put into barrels, ready for use. |

◀ Wine fermenters are kept warm to speed up the process of fermentation.

Key Word
biotechnology

Useful microorganisms
Using the information on this page, write a paragraph explaining how anaerobic respiration is used to produce a useful product.

Summary Questions

1. Copy and complete the sentences below.
   Yeast is a _____. It is used to make bread and _____ drinks. During _____, the _____ in yeast convert glucose into ethanol and _____ _____.
   (5 marks)

2. Some types of bread are made without using yeast. Suggest and explain how these breads would differ in appearance from bread made with yeast.
   (3 marks)

3. Cider is an alcoholic drink made from apples. Explain how cider could be produced.
   (6 marks)

Topic 9.3 Respiration

9.4.1 Photosynthesis

Learning objectives

After this section you will be able to:
- recall how plants make glucose
- describe how plants get the resources they need for photosynthesis
- use the word equation to describe photosynthesis.

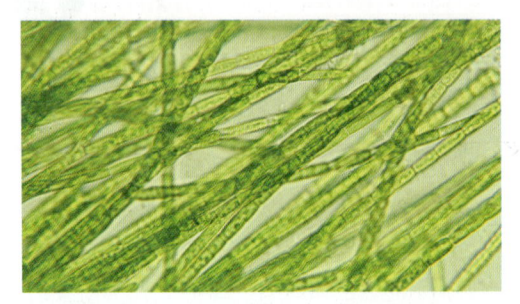

▲ Algae live in water.

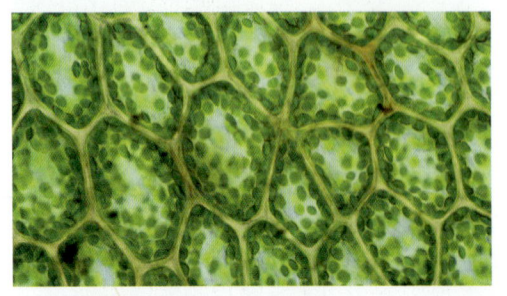

▲ Photosynthesis takes place inside chloroplasts in leaf cells.

Hypothesis

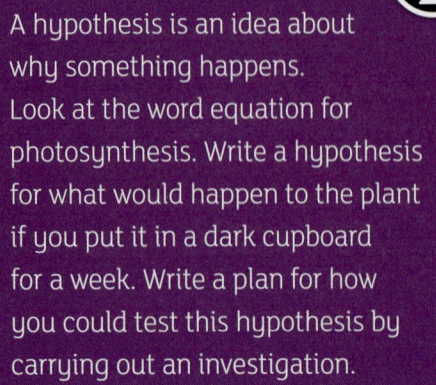

A hypothesis is an idea about why something happens. Look at the word equation for photosynthesis. Write a hypothesis for what would happen to the plant if you put it in a dark cupboard for a week. Write a plan for how you could test this hypothesis by carrying out an investigation.

Unlike animals, plants do not have to eat other organisms to survive. Instead they make their own food using sunlight. How do they do this?

What is a producer?

Plants and **algae** are called **producers** because they make their own food. They convert materials found in their environment into glucose, using sunlight. This brings energy from the Sun into the food chain.

Plants use glucose as an energy source. They also use glucose to build new tissue. Some glucose is stored to use later. This energy is passed onto consumers when they eat the producers.

Algae are like plants because they are green organisms that make their own food. However, they differ from plants in the following ways:

- They can be uni-cellular or multi-cellular organisms.
- They live underwater while most plants live on land.
- Algae do not have leaves, stems, or roots.

A State what is meant by a producer.

What is photosynthesis?

Plants make food through the process of **photosynthesis**. Photosynthesis is a chemical reaction in which plants take in carbon dioxide and water and change them into glucose. This provides the plant with food. Oxygen is also made. Oxygen is a waste product of the reaction. Oxygen is released back into the atmosphere. Plants need to use light from the Sun in this chemical reaction.

The word equation below shows the process of photosynthesis:

$$\text{carbon dioxide} + \text{water} \xrightarrow{\text{light}} \text{glucose} + \text{oxygen}$$
$$\text{(reactants)} \qquad\qquad\qquad\qquad \text{(products)}$$

B State the word equation for photosynthesis.

How are plants adapted for photosynthesis?

Plants have specifically adapted organs that allow them to obtain all the resources needed for photosynthesis. These organs are the leaves, stem, and roots.

Big Idea: Ecosystems 9

Photosynthesis mainly takes place in chloroplasts in the leaf cells, though a small amount happens in the stem. Leaves and stems are green because they contain the green pigment **chlorophyll**. Chlorophyll uses light from the Sun. The energy transferred from the Sun is needed for the plant to change carbon dioxide and water into glucose and oxygen.

Key Words

algae, producer, photosynthesis, chlorophyll

C Name the part of the cell where photosynthesis occurs.

How does water get into a plant?
Water diffuses into the root hair cells. The hairs provide a large surface area to maximise diffusion of water into the plant. The water is then transported around the plant in long hollow tubes, called xylem tubes. These run throughout the plant. As the water evaporates from the leaves, more water is drawn up through the plant. It is a bit like sucking on a straw!

How do gases get into and out of a plant?
On the underside of the leaf there are tiny holes. These allow gases to diffuse into the leaf. Carbon dioxide diffuses into the leaf, and oxygen diffuses out.

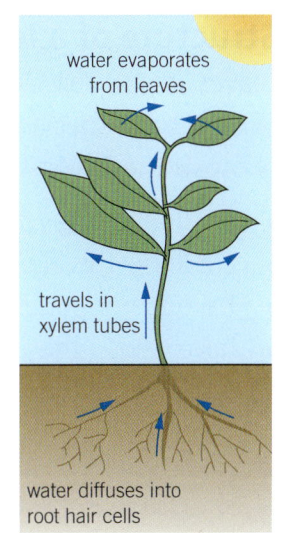

▲ Water enters the plant through the roots, then travels through the plant in the xylem tubes.

Link
You can learn more about diffusion in Book 1, 8.2.4 Movement of substances. You can learn how the structure of a root hair cell is adapted to its function in Book 1, 8.2.3 Specialised cells.

D State how the stem and root organs are adapted to obtain resources for photosynthesis.

The diagram below represents what happens during photosynthesis.

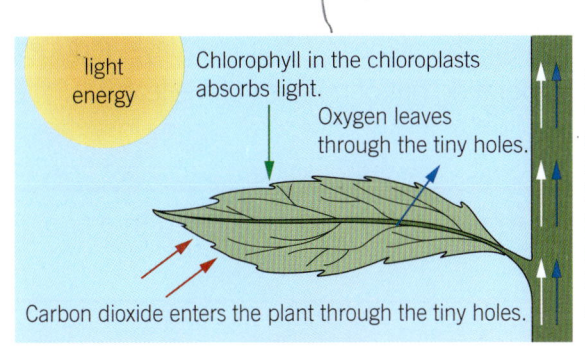

Chlorophyll in the chloroplasts absorbs light.
Oxygen leaves through the tiny holes.
Glucose is transported to all the parts of the plant. Water is transported from the roots to the stem and leaves.
Carbon dioxide enters the plant through the tiny holes.

Definitions
Using the information in the text to write a definition of the following words – producer, consumer, photosynthesis.

Summary Questions

1. Copy and complete the sentences below.
   Plants and _____ are _____. They use _____ to make their own food. They use _____ and water to make _____ and oxygen using _____ energy.
   (6 marks)

2. Explain why photosynthesis is important for all life.
   (3 marks)

3. State and explain whether photosynthesis would occur in the following situations:
   a a bright sunny day (1 mark)
   b at night (1 mark)
   c in the root hair cells. (2 marks)

4. Explain how the reactants of photosynthesis get into the leaf cells and what happens to the products of photosynthesis.
   (6 marks)

Topic 9.4 Photosynthesis

9.4.2 Leaves

Learning objectives

After this section you will be able to:
- describe the structure and function of the main components of a leaf
- explain how a leaf is adapted for photosynthesis.

Leaves come in all shapes and sizes. Most are green because they contain lots of chlorophyll but have you ever looked closely at a leaf? Some, like stinging nettles, are covered in tiny hairs.

Structure of a leaf

Leaves are specially adapted for photosynthesis. Each component of a leaf has a special function that helps it to carry out photosynthesis. Most leaves:

- are green – they contain chlorophyll, which absorbs sunlight
- are thin – this allows gases to diffuse in and out of the leaf easily
- have a large surface area – to absorb as much light as possible
- have veins – these contain xylem tubes, which transport water, and phloem tubes, which transport glucose.

A State why most leaves are green.

The underneath of a green leaf is lighter than the top. This is because the cells in the bottom of the leaf contain fewer chloroplasts, which means there is less chlorophyll. Most sunlight hits the top of the leaf so this is where the chloroplasts need to be to absorb as much sunlight as possible.

B State which part of the leaf contains the most chloroplasts.

The top of the leaf feels waxy, whereas the bottom is normally much drier. The Sun will heat up the top of the leaf. The waxy layer reduces the amount of water evaporating out of this part of the leaf.

C State why the top surface of the leaf is covered in a waxy layer.

▲ Leaves come in all shapes and sizes.

▲ The top and bottom surfaces of the leaf are normally quite different.

Key Word

stomata

How do gases get into and out of the leaf?

The tiny holes (pores) found on the bottom surface of the leaf are called **stomata** (singular: stoma). Their function is to allow gases to diffuse into and out of the leaf:

- carbon dioxide diffuses in
- oxygen and water vapour diffuse out.

Stomata are opened and closed by guard cells. These cells open the stomata during the day, and close them at night.

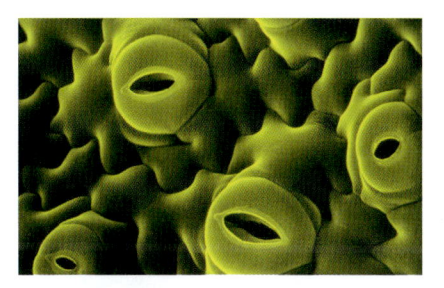

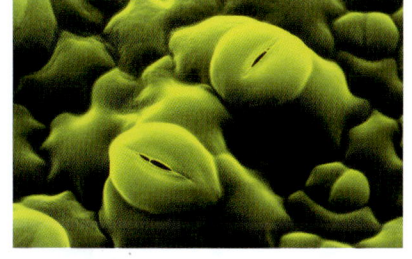

▲ Open stomata.

▲ Closed stomata.

D State the function of stomata.

What does the inside of a leaf look like?

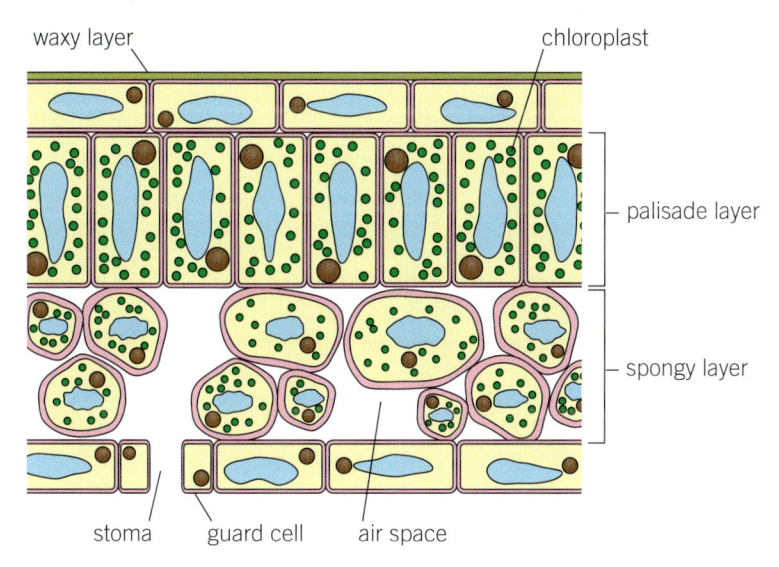

▲ Cross section of a leaf.

The leaf is divided into two main layers:

- palisade layer – contains cells packed with chloroplasts. This is where most of a plant's photosynthesis occurs.
- spongy layer – contains air spaces, allowing carbon dioxide to diffuse throughout the leaf. Oxygen diffuses out of the leaf.

• Big Idea: Ecosystems 9

Observing stomata
Draw a detailed diagram of the underside of a leaf, labelling the key structures.

Link
You can learn more about evaporation in Book 1, 5.1.5 More changes of state.

Summary Questions

1. Match the part of a leaf to its function.

stomata	reduces amount of water evaporating
waxy layer	main site of photosynthesis
guard cells	transport water to cells in leaf
veins	open and close stomata
cells in palisade layer	allow gases to diffuse into and out of the leaf

(5 marks)

2. Suggest why stomata may close during hot weather.

(1 mark)

3. Explain in detail how leaves are adapted for photosynthesis.

(6 marks)

4. Compare the movement of carbon dioxide and oxygen through stomata during the day and during the night.

(4 marks)

• Topic 9.4 Photosynthesis

9.4.3 Investigating photosynthesis

Learning objectives

After this section you will be able to:

- state the factors that affect the rate of photosynthesis
- describe how to test a leaf for starch
- show graphically how different factors affect the rate of photosynthesis.

Scientists are keen to maximise the conditions for photosynthesis. This will allow plants to grow bigger and faster.

How can you show that a plant is photosynthesising?

Plants turn glucose into starch if they do not use it immediately. This starch can be tested for using iodine.

▲ Testing leaves for starch.

To do this you should first take the leaf you are about to test and, using forceps, place it in a beaker of boiling water to kill it. Then place the leaf into a boiling tube of boiling ethanol to remove all the chlorophyll. Wash the leaf with water to remove the ethanol and soften the leaf, and spread it out on a white tile. Add a few drops of **iodine** solution onto the leaf. If starch is present, the iodine will turn from yellow-brown to blue-black.

▲ A giant tomato.

A Suggest why you need to remove the chlorophyll from the leaf when testing for starch.

How can you measure the rate of photosynthesis?

You can measure how fast a plant is growing by measuring the amount of oxygen it produces in a given time. There are two ways to do this.

Place an upturned test-tube over an aquatic plant such as pondweed. This will collect the gas given off by the plant. You can then:

- count the number of bubbles given off in a specific time period
- time how long it takes to collect a specific volume of gas.

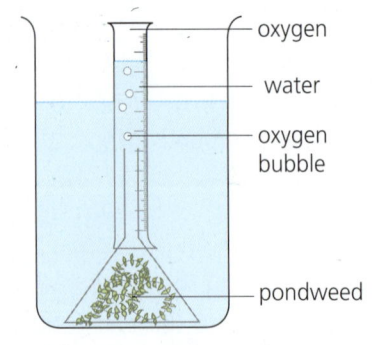

▲ Collecting oxygen produced by photosynthesis.

You can test that the gas given off is oxygen. When you have collected a full tube of gas, place a glowing splint in the test-tube. The splint will relight because of the oxygen present.

B Describe how you test for the presence of oxygen.

Which factors affect the rate of photosynthesis?
Light intensity, carbon dioxide, and temperature affect the rate of photosynthesis. If light or carbon dioxide is in short supply, or if the temperature is too low, then the rate of photosynthesis will be slower than it could be.

C State three factors which affect the rate of photosynthesis.

How does light intensity affect the rate of photosynthesis?
The higher the light intensity, the faster the rate of photosynthesis. It will get faster until photosynthesis reaches its maximum rate. In very low light levels, or if there is no light, photosynthesis stops.

How does carbon dioxide affect the rate of photosynthesis?
Carbon dioxide is one of the reactants of photosynthesis. The greater the concentration of carbon dioxide, the faster the rate of reaction.

How does temperature affect the rate of photosynthesis?
In general, the higher the temperature, the faster the rate of photosynthesis. This is because photosynthesis involves enzymes, which speed up the reaction as the temperature increases. However, at a certain temperature the enzymes stop working, so photosynthesis stops.

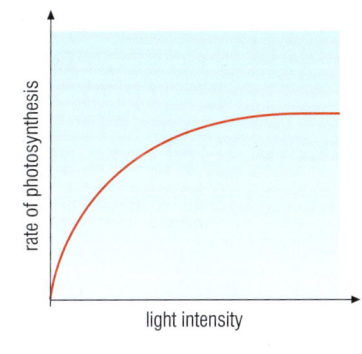

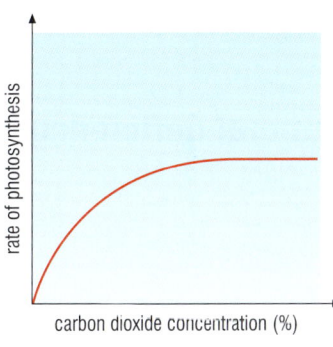

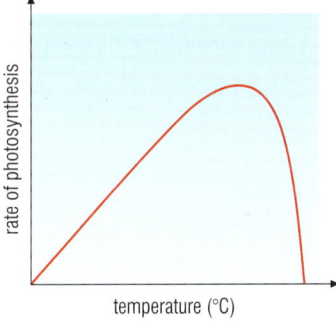

Key Word
iodine

▲ Farmers artificially increase the amount of carbon dioxide in greenhouses. This increases rates of photosynthesis.

Summary Questions

1 Copy and complete the sentences below.

To test a leaf for starch you need to place it in boiling _____. Then place the leaf in boiling _____ to remove the _____. After washing the leaf, add a few drops of _____. If starch is present the iodine will turn _____.

(5 marks)

2 Explain why plants grow more in summer than in winter.

(2 marks)

3
   a Design an investigation using pondweed to study how light intensity affects the rate of photosynthesis.

(6 marks)

   b Sketch a graph of the predicted results.

(1 mark)

● Topic 9.4 Photosynthesis

9.4.4 Plant minerals

Learning objectives

After this section you will be able to:
- state what fertilisers are used for
- describe how a plant uses minerals for healthy growth
- explain the role of nitrates in plant growth.

Link
You can learn more about the importance of minerals in 8.4.1 Nutrients.

▲ Organic farmers return minerals to the soil by spreading manure on their fields.

▲ A nitrate deficiency results in poor growth.

Farmers and gardeners regularly check their plants for signs of poor health. If your plants start to wilt they need watering. What does it mean if the leaves turn yellow? Just like people, plants need minerals for healthy growth.

What minerals do plants need?
For healthy growth, plants need four important minerals:
- **nitrates** (contain nitrogen) – for healthy growth
- **phosphates** (contain phosphorus) – for healthy roots
- **potassium** – for healthy leaves and flowers
- **magnesium** – for making chlorophyll.

A Name four minerals that plants need for healthy growth.

Where do plants get minerals from?
Plants get the minerals they need from the soil. The minerals are dissolved in soil water. They are absorbed into the root hair cells, and are then transported around the plant in the xylem tubes.

B State how minerals enter plants.

Mineral deficiency
If a plant does not get enough minerals, its growth will be poor. This is called a mineral **deficiency**. Different mineral deficiencies have different symptoms:
- nitrate deficiency – plant will have poor growth and older leaves are yellowed
- phosphorus deficiency – plant will have poor root growth, and younger leaves look purple
- potassium deficiency – plant has yellow leaves, with dead patches
- magnesium deficiency – plant leaves will turn yellow.

C State what is meant by a mineral deficiency.

Big Idea: Ecosystems 9

Mineral deficiency
Produce a leaflet for farmers that could help them to decide which mineral their plant is missing. You should include an image of a healthy plant that farmers can compare to their own.

Nitrates are involved in making amino acids. The amino acids join together to form proteins. These proteins are needed for cell growth, to grow leaves and shoots.

The chlorophyll molecule, which makes plants green, contains magnesium. If a plant does not get enough magnesium it can't make as much chlorophyll as it needs. This results in yellow leaves.

Why do farmers use fertilisers?
When crops are harvested, minerals are removed from the ground. These would normally be replaced when the plant dies, or when leaves are shed. To prevent future crops suffering from a mineral deficiency, farmers add chemicals to the soil to replace missing minerals – these chemicals are called **fertilisers**.

D State what is meant by a fertiliser.

NPK is a common fertiliser. It contains three of the important minerals needed for healthy plant growth: nitrogen (N), phosphorus (P), and potassium (K).

▲ Farmers use fertilisers to add minerals to their crops.

▲ Magnesium deficiency results in yellow leaves.

Key Words
nitrates, phosphates, potassium, magnesium, deficiency, fertiliser

Summary Questions

1. Copy and complete the sentences below.
   To remain healthy, plants need to absorb _____ from the soil. They are absorbed through the root _____ cells and then travel around the plant in the _____ tubes.
   The mineral _____ is needed to make chlorophyll, and _____ are needed to make amino acids.
   (5 marks)

2. Explain the role of nitrates in plant growth.
   (3 marks)

3. Explain in detail why farmers have to add fertiliser to soil to ensure good crop yields year after year.
   (6 marks)

● Topic 9.4 Photosynthesis

9 Ecosystems: Summary

Key Points

Respiration
- To transfer energy from glucose, aerobic respiration takes place inside mitochondria.
- Aerobic respiration: glucose + oxygen → carbon dioxide + water (+ energy)
- If no oxygen is present, energy can be transferred from glucose using anaerobic respiration.
- Anaerobic respiration: glucose → lactic acid (+ energy)
- Fermentation is a type of anaerobic respiration performed by microorganisms. It is used in bread- and beer-making.
- Fermentation: glucose → ethanol + carbon dioxide (+ energy)

Photosynthesis
- Photosynthesis: carbon dioxide + water → glucose + oxygen
- Photosynthesis takes place in chloroplasts. Chloroplasts contain chlorophyll, which traps the light needed for photosynthesis.
- Stomata allow gases to enter and leave a leaf. Guard cells open the stomata during the day and close them at night.
- Plants need minerals for healthy growth. For example, nitrates are needed to make amino acids. Amino acids join together to form proteins, which are used for growth.

BIG Write

Banana power

Many tennis players eat a banana during a match to give them a boost of energy. The energy transferred to them from the banana has started off in the Sun. Almost all life on Earth depends on the transfer of the Sun's energy to plants and algae in photosynthesis.

Task

Write a short essay explaining how the energy was transferred into the banana from the Sun, and what happens inside the tennis player's body to transfer this energy to his muscles.

Tips
- Make sure you use as many scientific terms as possible.
- Use word equations to represent reactions that take place.

Key Words

aerobic respiration, plasma, haemoglobin, anaerobic respiration, oxygen debt, fermentation, biotechnology, algae, producer, photosynthesis, chlorophyll, stomata, iodine, nitrates, phosphates, potassium, magnesium, deficiency, fertiliser

End-of-Big Idea questions

1
  a Name the reaction that your body uses to transfer energy from glucose. *(1 mark)*
  b State where in a cell this reaction happens. *(1 mark)*
  c Complete the word equation below to represent this process:

  glucose + _____ → _____ + water (+ energy) *(2 marks)*
  (4 marks)

2
  a For the following statements state whether they apply to aerobic or anaerobic respiration.
   i takes place when oxygen is present
   ii is also known as fermentation
   iii can result in lactic acid building up
   iv releases more energy per glucose molecule. *(4 marks)*
  b State and explain one situation in which you may respire anaerobically. *(2 marks)*
  (6 marks)

3 This equipment can be used to study photosynthesis.

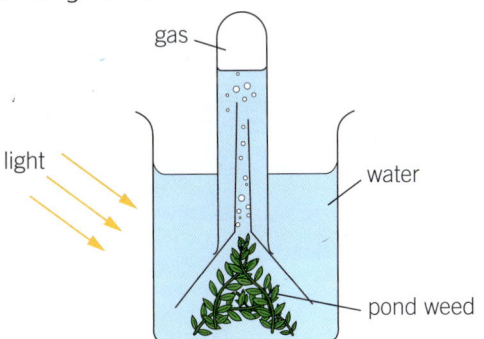

  a Name the gas given off by the plant. *(1 mark)*
  b State the **two** reactants needed for photosynthesis. *(2 marks)*
  c Explain what would happen to the number of bubbles if the plant was placed in the dark. *(3 marks)*
  d Describe the role of stomata in photosynthesis. *(2 marks)*
  (8 marks)

4 The following graph shows how the level of carbon dioxide affects the rate of photosynthesis.

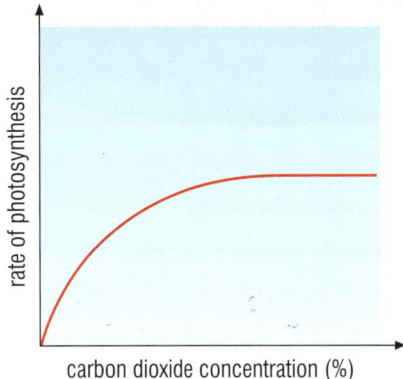

  a State the structure through which carbon dioxide enters the plant. *(1 mark)*
  b Describe the trend shown by the graph. *(2 marks)*
  c Farmers who grow plants in greenhouses often artificially increase the levels of carbon dioxide present. Explain how this would affect the rate of photosynthesis. *(3 marks)*
  (6 marks)

5 To remain healthy plants need minerals.
  a Explain how a plant absorbs minerals and transports them to different parts of the plant. *(3 marks)*
  b Plants lacking in magnesium have yellow leaves. Explain why this means they carry out less photosynthesis. *(2 marks)*
  c Explain how the structure of a leaf is adapted to maximise sunlight absorption. *(3 marks)*
  (8 marks)

6 Explain how fermentation is used in food production. **(6 marks)**

10 Genes

The world is full of lots of different types of living things. In this Big Idea you will find out how the organisms that exist today have evolved, and how scientists are trying to prevent further species from becoming extinct and preserve biodiversity. You will also learn about how you inherit characteristics from your parents through genetic material, and how genetic material in some organisms is being modified.

You already know

- Animals and plants are adapted to suit their environment in different ways. Adaptation may lead to evolution.
- Living things have changed over time, and fossils provide information about living things that inhabited the Earth millions of years ago.
- Living things produce offspring of the same kind, but normally offspring vary and are not identical to their parents.

Q What are the main adaptations of a polar bear and a cactus?

BIG Questions

- What is the theory of evolution by natural selection?
- How do you inherit characteristics from your parents?
- What is the likelihood of you inheriting a characteristic?

Picture Puzzler
Key Words

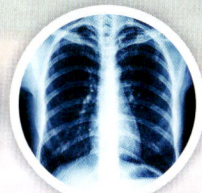

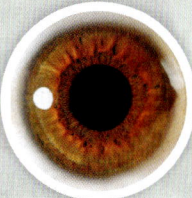

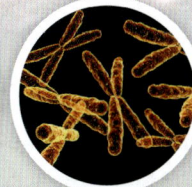

Can you solve this Picture Puzzler?

The first letter of each of these images spells out a science word that you will come across in this book.

Picture Puzzler
Close Up

Can you tell what this zoomed-in picture is?

Clue: This contains all the information to needed to make an organism.

Making connections

In your GCSE course you will learn how mutations in DNA can create variation.

You will also discover how environmental changes and the impact of humans have resulted in a loss of biodiversity, as well as the steps being taken to prevent this occurring further.

You will also study how scientists genetically engineer organisms to display desired characteristics.

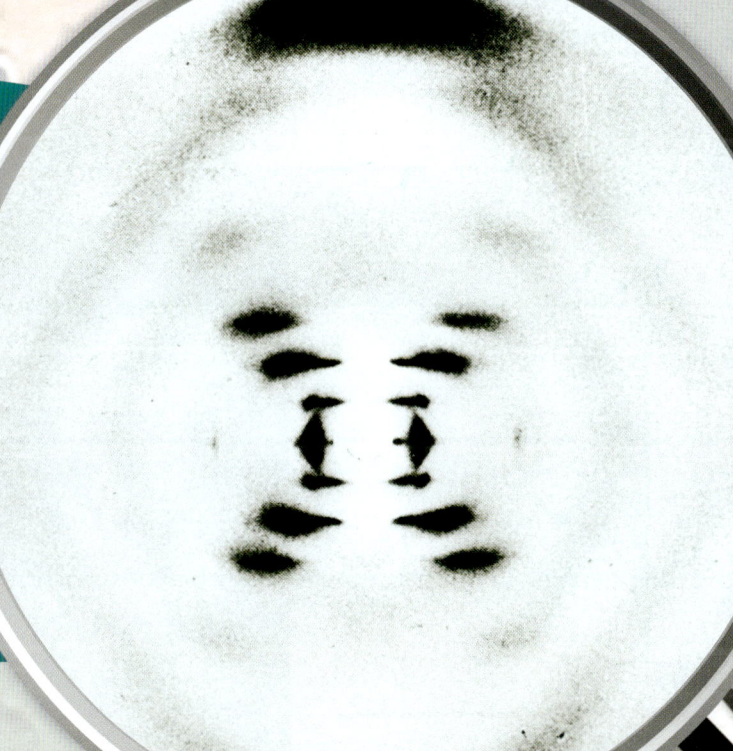

10.3.1 Natural selection

Learning objectives

After this section you will be able to:
- describe the theory of natural selection
- explain why species evolve over time.

Fantastic Fact

More proof for evolution comes from your DNA. You share about 97% of your DNA with a gorilla and 50% with a banana! This is evidence that all living things evolved from the same ancestor.

Key Words

evolution, fossil, natural selection

Evolution cartoon

Produce a cartoon strip showing the evolution of an organism of your choice – this could be a real organism or a made-up one.

Have you heard the phrase 'survival of the fittest'? It means that organisms that are best adapted to a situation will survive, and those that are not will die. This is how scientists think that all organisms on Earth have developed.

What is evolution?

Scientists believe that the species we see on Earth today have gradually developed over millions of years. This is called the theory of **evolution**.

Evolution started with uni-cellular organisms. These organisms, similar to bacteria, lived in water more than three billion years ago. Over time they evolved to become multi-cellular organisms. Eventually, this process resulted in organisms that could live on land and in the air.

A State what is meant by evolution.

▲ A dinosaur fossil.

The **fossil** record provides most of the evidence for evolution. Fossils are the remains, or traces, of plants or animals that lived many years ago. They have been preserved by natural processes. The fossil record provides evidence of species that no longer exist, such as dinosaurs.

B Describe what a fossil is.

Big Idea: Genes 10

How do organisms evolve?

Organisms evolve through the process of **natural selection**. They change slowly over time, to become better adapted to their environment. The process takes many years, sometimes millions, as it happens over a number of generations.

C Describe the process of natural selection.

Peppered moths

Living organisms are continually evolving to adapt to their environment. Evolution usually happens slowly over many years. However, dramatic changes in an organism's environment can result in evolution happening quickly. Peppered moths evolved in this way during the 19th century.

Before the Industrial Revolution, most peppered moths in Britain were pale coloured. This was helpful to the moths, as they blended in with tree bark. A few peppered moths were dark coloured. This was a disadvantage, as they were easily seen by birds, and eaten. The pale moths were more likely to survive and reproduce, so most of the peppered moth population was pale coloured.

After the Industrial Revolution many trees were covered in soot, turning the bark black. This meant that the dark moths were camouflaged. More dark peppered moths survived and reproduced than pale moths. After several years, the population of dark peppered moths in towns and cities became much higher than the population of pale peppered moths.

▲ Before the Industrial Revolution, pale peppered moths were highly camouflaged against tree bark. Dark moths were easily seen.

▲ After the Industrial Revolution, dark peppered moths were more camouflaged against soot-blackened trees and pale moths were easily seen.

Natural selection

Organisms in a species show variation – this is caused by differences in their genes.

⬇

The organisms with the characteristics that are best adapted to the environment survive and reproduce. Less well adapted organisms die. This process is known as 'survival of the fittest'.

⬇

Genes from successful organisms are passed to the offspring in the next generation. This means the offspring are likely to possess the characteristics that made their parents successful.

⬇

This process is then repeated many times. Over a period of time this can lead to the development of a new species.

Summary Questions

1. Copy and complete the sentences below.

   All living organisms have _____ from a common ancestor. This process has taken _____ of years. _____ provide evidence for evolution. These are the _____ of plants or animals that died long ago, which have turned to _____.

   (5 marks)

2. Describe the process of natural selection.

   (3 marks)

3. Explain in detail how peppered moths evolved as a result of the Industrial Revolution.

   (6 marks)

● Topic 10.3 Evolution

10.3.2 Charles Darwin

Learning objectives

After this section you will be able to:
- describe the process of peer review
- evaluate the evidence that Darwin used to develop his theory of natural selection.

Have you heard of the scientist Charles Darwin? One of the most famous scientists of all time, Darwin developed the theory of natural selection.

Darwin's theory

Darwin's theory states that organisms evolve as a result of natural selection. Darwin realised that organisms best suited to their environment are more likely to survive and reproduce, passing on their characteristics to their offspring. Gradually, a species changes over time. We now know that these characteristics are passed on through genes.

A Name the process by which organisms evolve.

How did Darwin come up with his theory?

Darwin was born in 1809. At that time, most people believed that the Earth and all the organisms on it were created by God.

In 1831, Darwin joined Captain Robert FitzRoy's scientific expedition to the Galapagos Islands. While on HMS Beagle, Darwin read Lyell's 'Principles of Geology'. This suggested that fossils were actually evidence of animals that had lived millions of years ago. Modern scientists agree with this.

▲ Charles Darwin, author of 'On the Origin of Species'. Darwin's theory of evolution took over 20 years to develop.

1. Geospiza magnirostris. 2. Geospiza fortis.
3. Geospiza parvula. 4. Certhidea olivacea.

▲ Darwin noticed that finches on different islands had different beaks. The shape of the beak was adapted to the food the finch ate.

Big Idea: Genes 10

Darwin noticed that different islands had different types of finch. The birds' beaks and claws were different sizes and shapes. Darwin realised that the size and shape were linked to the type of food available on each island.

B Name the organism that Darwin studied on the Galapagos Islands.

Darwin concluded that if a bird was born with a beak suited to the food available on its island, it would survive for longer. Therefore, it would have more offspring. Over time the population of birds on that island would all have this characteristic. Darwin called this process natural selection.

Another scientist, Alfred Wallace, was working on his own theory of natural selection and evolution. Wallace and Darwin read each other's unpublished work. This is an early example of **peer review**, where a scientist's work is checked by another scientist who works in a similar area of science. Darwin's and Wallace's ideas were so similar that they jointly published the theory of evolution in a scientific paper.

▲ Alfred Wallace gathered his evidence for the theory of evolution from the wildlife of South America and Asia.

Key Word

peer review

C State what is meant by peer review.

A year later, in 1859, Darwin published his book 'On the Origin of Species'. The book was extremely controversial – the theory of evolution went against the view that God had created all of the life on Earth. As a result of Darwin's theory, people learnt that humans were simply a type of animal, and had evolved from apes.

Do people still disagree with Darwin?

Darwin's theory of evolution is now widely accepted, though not by everyone. Evidence for his theory includes:

- the fossil record – which provides evidence that organisms have changed over time
- changes that have been observed in microorganism populations – for example, the development of antibiotic-resistant bacteria
- extinction – species that do not adapt to environmental changes die out.

Natural selection
Imagine you are a newspaper reporter at the time of the publication of Darwin's 'On the Origin of Species'. Write a front-page article about the theory of evolution.

Summary Questions

1. Copy and complete the sentences below.

   Charles _____ came up with the theory of _____ by natural _____. Before they published their theory, Darwin and Wallace checked each other's work. This is called _____ _____.

   (4 marks)

2. Describe three pieces of evidence in support of Darwin's theory of natural selection.

   (3 marks)

3. Describe the process of peer review.

   (2 marks)

4. Explain how Darwin's observations of finches in the Galapagos Islands supply evidence for the theory of natural selection.

   (6 marks)

Topic 10.3 Evolution

10.3.3 Extinction

Learning objectives

After this section you will be able to:

- state some factors that may lead to extinction
- describe the importance of biodiversity in maintaining plant and animal populations
- explain why a species has become extinct
- explain how a lack of biodiversity can affect an ecosystem.

Can you think of any species that no longer live on the Earth? You might think of dinosaurs – millions of years ago these organisms were found all over the Earth. There are many other animal and plant species that have completely died out.

What does extinction mean?

If a species is not adapted to its environment, it will not survive. Organisms will die before reproducing. Eventually, by this process of natural selection, the species becomes **extinct**. A species becomes extinct when there are no more individuals of that species left anywhere in the world. An extinct species has gone forever – no new organisms can be created.

A State what is meant by the word extinct.

How do we know other species existed?

The fossil record shows that many species have become extinct. For example, you may have seen fossils of ammonites. These animals existed at around the same time as the dinosaurs. They had spiral shells and could be up to 2 m wide.

How do organisms become extinct?

There are a number of factors that can cause a species to become extinct, including:

- changes to the organism's environment
- destruction of habitat
- outbreak of a new disease
- introduction of new predators
- increased **competition** for resources.

▲ An ammonite fossil. These animals lived in the sea and could grow up to 2 m wide.

B State three causes of extinction.

Extinction occurs naturally. For example, most scientists believe that dinosaurs became extinct due to a dramatic change in the Earth's climate, after a meteor hit the Earth. Dinosaurs could not adapt to these changes in their environment and died out.

▲ A woolly mammoth – this animal became extinct about 4000 years ago.

Humans can make extinction more likely. For example, the dodo lived on the island of Mauritius, which was an uninhabited island. It had no natural predators. In the 17th century people arrived on the island, and dodos were hunted for food. Rats that came on the ships ate the dodos' eggs. In less than a century, the dodo became extinct.

C Name two organisms that have become extinct.

Extinction is still happening today, in many cases as a result of human activity. Humans compete with other organisms for space, food, and water, and are also very successful predators.

Climate change has resulted in many organisms losing their habitat. For example, the size of the polar ice caps is shrinking. If a species that lives in these habitats cannot adapt successfully, or find somewhere else to live, it could become extinct.

How does extinction affect the populations of other organisms?

When a species becomes extinct, **biodiversity** is reduced. Biodiversity is a measure of the variety of all the different species of organisms on Earth or within a particular ecosystem.

D State what is meant by biodiversity.

Biodiversity is vital for maintaining **populations**. The greater the variation within a species the more likely some members of the population will survive environmental changes. This will reduce the likelihood of that particular species becoming extinct.

Having many different species in an ecosystem ensures resources are available for other populations, such as humans. If a forest only contained one type of tree, animals may lose their only source of food and shelter if that type of tree died out. However, if a variety of trees are present, the animals could survive on a different food source.

▲ The dodo was a large, flightless bird.

Key Words

extinct, competition, biodiversity, population

Summary Questions

1. Copy and complete the sentences below.

   A species becomes _____ when there are no more individuals of that species left _____ in the world.

   Changes in a species' _____ or the introduction of new _____ can cause a species to become extinct.

   (4 marks)

2. Explain how a lack of biodiversity can affect an ecosystem.

   (4 marks)

3. Using evidence and a named example, explain in detail how a species could become extinct.

   (6 marks)

● Topic 10.3 Evolution

10.3.4 Preserving biodiversity

Learning objectives

After this section you will be able to:

- describe what is meant by an endangered species
- describe some techniques used to prevent extinction
- describe how preserving biodiversity benefits humans.

Several million years ago, dinosaurs roamed the planet. These species are now extinct. Did you know that other species are becoming extinct today?

Can we prevent extinction?

Species that are at risk of extinction are called **endangered species**. This means that there are very few of the species left. An example is the giant panda. Their numbers have been severely reduced by loss of habitat, and by being killed by poachers.

A State why the panda is an endangered species.

There are a number of ways that scientists are trying to prevent extinction. These include:

- **conservation**
- **captive breeding**
- **gene banks**

What is conservation?

Conservation means protecting a natural environment, to ensure that habitats are not lost. Protecting an organism's habitat increases their chance of survival, allowing them to reproduce.

As well as reducing the risk of a particular species becoming extinct, conservation also:

- reduces disruption to food chains and food webs
- makes it possible for medicinal plant species to be discovered.

The UK has over 4000 conservation areas where habitats are protected. These are known as Sites of Special Scientific Interest (SSSI) and cover around 8% of the nation's land.

▲ The black rhino has become endangered due to poachers killing them for their horns.

▲ It is estimated that there are fewer than 2000 giant pandas living in the wild.

B State what is meant by conservation.

What is captive breeding?

Captive breeding means breeding animals in human-controlled environments. Scientists working on captive-breeding programmes aim to:

- create a stable, healthy population of a species
- gradually re-introduce the species back into its natural habitat.

Captive-breeding debate
Hold a debate to discuss the pros and cons of captive breeding.

C List the aims of captive breeding.

Big Idea: Genes 10

Unfortunately there are also problems associated with captive breeding.
- Maintaining genetic diversity can be difficult. Only a small number of breeding partners are available.
- Organisms born in captivity may not be suitable for release in the wild. For example, predators bred in captivity may not know how to hunt for food.

What are gene banks?

Gene banks store genetic samples from different species. In the future they can be used for research, or to produce new individuals.

There are a number of different types of gene bank. These include:
- seed banks – dried seeds of plants are stored at low temperatures
- tissue banks – buds and other cells from plants are stored
- cryobanks – a seed or embryo is preserved at very low temperatures, normally in liquid nitrogen; sperm and egg cells from animals can also be stored in this way
- pollen banks – pollen grains are stored.

▲ Nearly half of the medicines used by doctors today are based on plant extracts that have come from the rainforests.

Key Words

endangered species, conservation, captive breeding, gene bank

◀ Seeds in the Millennium Seed Bank.

How does biodiversity benefit humans?

Preserving biodiversity not only ensures that a species survives but can provide useful products and services for humans. For example, plants in the rainforest are the basis of many medical drugs. Ensuring species are not lost may ensure that new cures for disease can still be discovered.

Maintaining biodiversity also ensures that we have a rich and varied food supply. For example, protecting insect habitats will ensure plants are pollinated. Preventing overfishing of certain species ensures populations remain at a level at which they can continue to reproduce and can provide a food supply for generations to come.

D State two ways preserving biodiversity benefits humans.

Summary Questions

1. Copy and complete the sentences below.
   Scientists are using a number of techniques to try to prevent _____ species becoming _____. These include storing seeds in seed _____, breeding animals in _____, and protecting habitats through _____.
   (5 marks)

2. Describe the role of gene banks in preventing extinction.
   (3 marks)

3. Describe two advantages and two disadvantages of captive-breeding programmes.
   (4 marks)

4. Discuss how humans can have a positive or a negative effect on the population of a species.
   (6 marks)

● Topic 10.3 Evolution

10.4.1 Inheritance

Learning objectives

After this section you will be able to:

- describe how characteristics are inherited
- describe the relationship between DNA, genes, and chromosomes
- explain how a DNA mutation may affect an organism and its future offspring.

▼ The shape of DNA is a double helix – a bit like a twisted ladder.

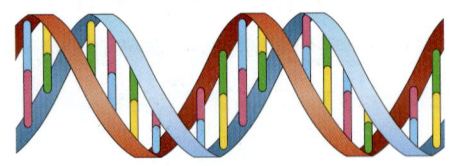

▼ DNA is bundled up and twisted into long strands called chromosomes.

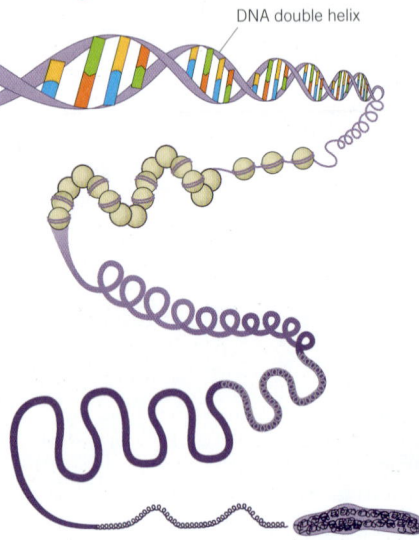

DNA double helix

chromosome

▼ A gene is a section of the chromosome that holds information to produce a characteristic.

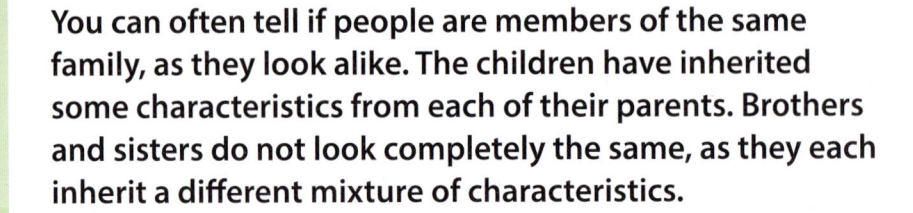

gene

You can often tell if people are members of the same family, as they look alike. The children have inherited some characteristics from each of their parents. Brothers and sisters do not look completely the same, as they each inherit a different mixture of characteristics.

How do you inherit characteristics?

Your **inherited characteristics** come from your parents through genetic material stored in the nucleus of your cells. This material is a chemical called **DNA** (deoxyribonucleic acid). DNA contains all the information needed to make an organism.

A State what DNA is.

Chromosomes

Inside the nucleus, your DNA is arranged into long strands called **chromosomes**. Different species have a different number of chromosomes in their nucleus. Humans have 46 chromosomes; whereas cats have 38 chromosomes.

You inherit half of your chromosomes from your mother and half from your father. This is why you share some of your characteristics with your mother and some with your father.

B State what a chromosome is.

Genes

Each chromosome is divided into sections of DNA. The sections that hold the information to produce a characteristic are called **genes**. For example, one gene contains the information that sets your eye colour, while a different gene sets your hair colour. Each chromosome contains thousands of genes.

C State what a gene is.

How is genetic material inherited?

Inside the nucleus of your cells, the 46 chromosomes are arranged into 23 pairs. One copy of the chromosome of each pair comes from your mother, and the other comes from your father.

Big Idea: Genes 10

Egg and sperm cells (gametes) are the only cells to contain 23 chromosomes. They only have one copy of each chromosome. During fertilisation, the egg and sperm cells join together. When their nuclei join, their chromosomes pair up, producing an embryo with 46 chromosomes.

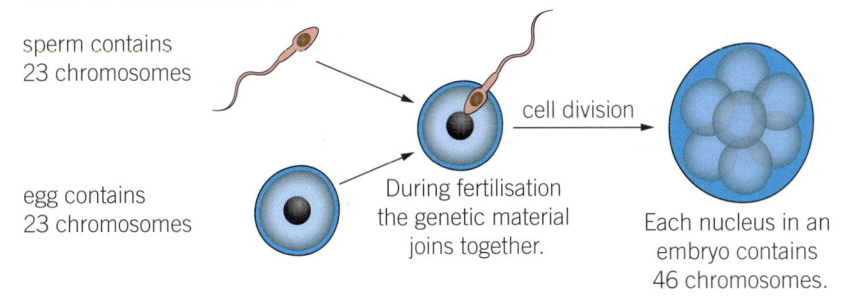

sperm contains 23 chromosomes

egg contains 23 chromosomes

During fertilisation the genetic material joins together.

cell division

Each nucleus in an embryo contains 46 chromosomes.

▲ You get half of your genetic material from your mother, and half from your father.

D State the number of chromosomes present in a normal human body cell.

What happens if DNA becomes damaged?

When DNA is copied to make new cells it can become damaged. This change in the DNA is known as a **mutation**.

If a change occurs in a gene it can affect that organism's characteristics. However, your body normally detects these changes and tries to mend them. If undetected they can lead to disease.

If a mutation occurs in a gamete cell, then this altered form of DNA may be passed onto the organisms' offspring.

Most mutations are harmful if undetected, but occasionally they can be beneficial. For example, in some species of bacteria a mutation has resulted in them becoming resistant to antibiotics. This is good for the bacteria as the antibiotic can no longer kill them, but not good for us.

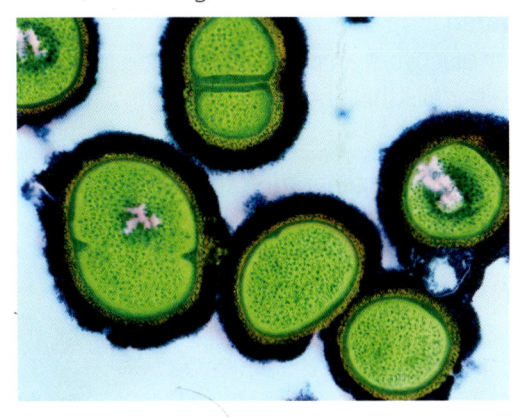

◀ Methicillin-resistant *Staphylococcus aureus* (MRSA) is resistant to antibiotics.

Key Words

inherited characteristics, DNA, chromosome, gene, mutation

Summary Questions

1. 🧪 Copy and complete the sentences below.
   Genetic material in the body is stored in the _____ of a cell.
   _____ is the name of the chemical that contains the instructions needed to make an organism.
   _____ are made of long strands of DNA.
   The sections of DNA that hold the information for a _____ are called _____.

   (5 marks)

2. 🧪🧪 Arrange these objects in order of size, starting with the smallest.

   cell   chromosome   gene   DNA   nucleus

   (2 marks)

3. 🧪🧪 Explain how a DNA mutation may affect an organism and its future offspring.

   (4 marks)

4. 🧪🧪🧪 Explain in detail why you share some characteristics with your mother and some with your father.

   (6 marks)

● Topic 10.4 Inheritance

10.4.2 DNA

Learning objectives

After this section you will be able to:
- describe the structure of DNA
- describe how scientists worked together to discover the structure of DNA.

Everyone's DNA is unique, except for identical twins. Identical twins have the same DNA. You have lots of DNA which is identical to that of your parents, and your siblings.

What does DNA look like?

DNA has three main features:

1. It is made up of two strands.
2. The strands are joined together by four different chemicals called DNA bases. The bases are normally referred to by the letters A (adenine), T (thymine), C (cytosine), and G (guanine).
3. The strands are twisted together to form a double-helix shape.

A Describe three features of a DNA molecule.

B State the only individuals who have identical DNA.

How did scientists discover DNA?

Many scientists have worked together to discover the structure and function of DNA. Although we have discovered lots of information about DNA, research is still continuing. It is hoped that this will lead to the prevention and cure of many diseases in the future.

The table shows some of the main steps in the discovery of DNA.

▲ DNA is a double helix. It contains four chemical bases – A (adenine), T (thymine), C (cytosine), and G (guanine).

1866	**Certain characteristics are inherited** Gregor Mendel carries out experiments using peas. He notices that certain characteristics such as height and colour are passed on from parents to their offspring.
1869	**Nuclein is discovered** Friedrich Miescher discovers an acidic substance in the nucleus of a cell. He calls this substance nuclein. This chemical is now called DNA.
1944	**Genes are passed from one generation to the next** Oswald Avery transfers the ability to cause disease from one type of bacteria to another. He proves that genes are sections of the DNA molecule.

Big Idea: Genes 10

1950	**DNA base pairs are discovered** Erwin Chargaff finds out that, even though different organisms have different amounts of DNA, all DNA contains equal quantities of the bases A and T, and equal quantities of the bases C and G.
1952	**DNA crystals are photographed** Maurice Wilkins and Rosalind Franklin use X-rays to take an image of DNA crystals.
1953	**Double-helix structure of DNA is identified** James Watson and Francis Crick, working at another university, were also studying DNA. When they saw Wilkins and Franklin's image it told them that DNA had a helical shape. Through further investigations, Watson and Crick worked out that the structure of DNA is like a twisted ladder. This is known as a double helix.
1953–2000	**Advances in genetics** Individual genes that code for genetically inherited disorders such as cystic fibrosis are discovered. The production of genetically engineered food and animal cloning also begin.
2003	**Human genome project completed** Scientists working across the globe identify around 24 000 genes – the complete set of genes in the human body.

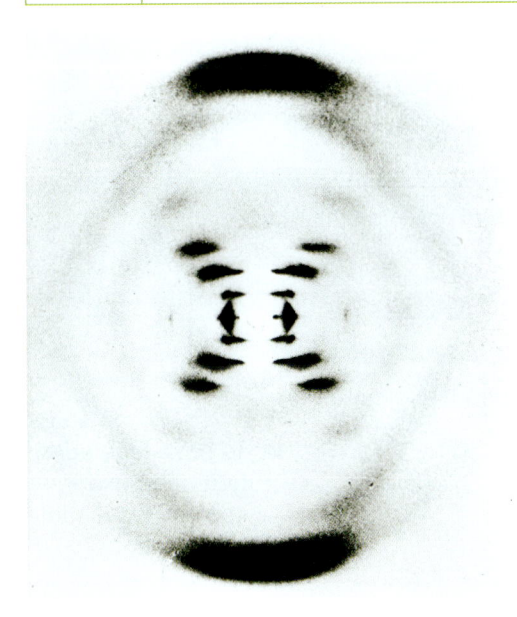

▲ Wilkins and Franklin's famous 'Photo 51' revealed the helical structure of DNA to Watson and Crick. The fuzzy X-shape suggests a helical structure.

C Name the four scientists involved in developing a model of the structure of DNA.

Team work
The scientists who discovered the structure of DNA did so by working together. Communication is very important so that scientists can share their ideas and carry out investigations. Watson and Crick were able to work out the structure of DNA by building on the work of Franklin and Wilkins.

Fantastic Fact
The police use a technique called DNA fingerprinting to prove the presence, or absence, of a suspect at a crime scene.

Summary Questions

1. Copy and complete the sentences below.
   DNA is made up of two _____ that are twisted together to form a double _____. The strands are held together by four _____, called A, T, _____, and G.
   (4 marks)

2. Draw a timeline showing the key steps in the discovery of DNA.
   (4 marks)

3. Explain how scientists worked together to discover the structure and function of DNA.
   (6 marks)

4. Suggest three benefits from scientists knowing all the genes in the human genome.
   (3 marks)

Topic 10.4 Inheritance

10.4.3 Genetics

Learning objectives

After this section you will be able to:
- describe the difference between dominant and recessive alleles
- use a Punnett square to show how genes are inherited
- explain why offspring are not identical to their parents.

Have you ever wondered why brothers and sisters often have a similar appearance? It's all down to the genes they inherit from their parents.

Which characteristics will you inherit?

For each characteristic, like blood group or eye colour, you have two genes. One gene is inherited from your mother, and one from your father. These two genes may be the same, or different. Different forms of the same gene are called **alleles**.

A State what is meant by an allele.

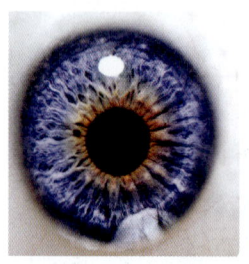

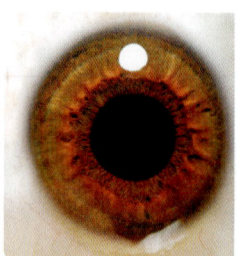

How is eye colour inherited?

Some alleles will always produce a characteristic in an organism. These are called **dominant** alleles. You only need one copy of a dominant allele for the characteristic to appear in the organism. This allele is said to be 'expressed' in the organism.

▲ The gene for eye colour has an allele for blue eye colour and an allele for brown eye colour.

B Name the type of allele that will always produce a characteristic in an organism.

Link

You can learn more about genes in 10.4.1 Inheritance.

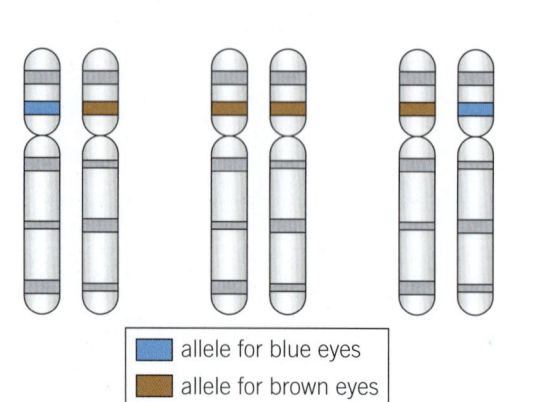

For example, the allele for brown eyes is a dominant allele. If you inherit this allele from your mother, your father, or both parents, you will have brown eyes.

The allele for blue eye colour is a **recessive** allele. You need two copies of a recessive allele for the characteristic to be expressed in the organism.

For example, you will only have blue eyes if you inherit this allele from both your mother and your father.

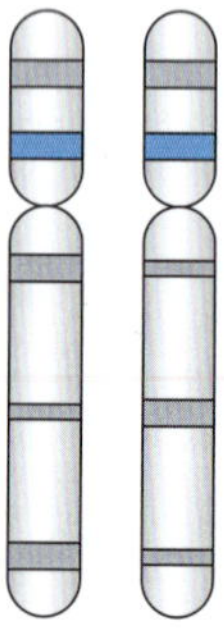

▲ To have blue eyes, you need two copies of the allele for blue eyes.

- allele for blue eyes
- allele for brown eyes

▲ These pairs of genes show three different ways a person could inherit brown eyes.

C State how many copies of a recessive allele are needed for it to be expressed.

Key Words

allele, dominant, recessive, Punnett square

Big Idea: Genes 10

Can characteristics be predicted?
When a sperm fertilises an egg, genes from the mother join with genes from the father. This results in the combination of alleles present in the offspring. Scientists are able to predict what an organism's offspring will look like by carrying out a genetic cross.

How do you perform a genetic cross?
In a genetic cross, alleles are represented by letters. The dominant allele is represented by a capital letter, and the recessive allele by the same, lowercase letter.

When studying eye colour, 'B' is used to represent the dominant allele for brown eyes, and 'b' represents the recessive allele for blue eyes.

Scientists use a **Punnett square** to show what happens to the alleles in the genetic cross. In this example, a mother with blue eyes (bb) is crossed with a father with brown eyes (BB).

Mother: blue eyes   Father: brown eyes   A sperm and egg cell only contain one copy of each gene.

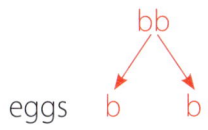

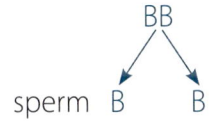

bb   BB

eggs b   b   sperm B   B

A Punnett square is actually a simple table. To produce a Punnett square, put the possible alleles from one parent across the top of the square, and the alleles from the other parent down the side.

	Father	
	B	B
Mother b		
b		

Use the square to work out the possible combinations of alleles in the offspring.

In this example, all offspring produced will have brown eyes. This is because the dominant allele is present in all possible combination of the parents' alleles.

	Father	
	B	B
Mother b	Bb	Bb
b	Bb	Bb

If the father's alleles are Bb, he will still have brown eyes but now it is possible that the offspring will have blue eyes.

	Father	
	B	b
Mother b	Bb	bb
b	Bb	bb

In this example, two of the four combinations are bb, which means there is a 2 in 4 chance that the offspring will have blue eyes, and a 2 in 4 chance it will have brown eyes.

Genetic-cross outcomes
Scientists often display the possible outcomes from a genetic cross as the probability of a characteristic being expressed. This could be in the form of a ratio, a percentage, or a fraction. For example, a 1 in 5 probability is 1/5 = 0.2 = 20%.

Write each of the following as a fraction and a percentage:

0 in 4   1 in 4   2 in 4
3 in 4   4 in 4

Summary Questions

1. Copy and complete the sentences below.
   Different forms of the same gene are known as _____. _____ alleles will always be expressed if they are present. _____ alleles will only be expressed if two copies are present.
   (3 marks)

2. In mice, black fur is dominant and white fur is recessive. State the fur colour a mouse would have with the following allele combinations:
   a BB **b** bb **c** Bb *(3 marks)*

3. Explain why offspring from the same parents look similar but are not usually identical. *(3 marks)*

4. Use a Punnett square to calculate and explain the chance of a person inheriting freckles if their mother has the alleles Ff and their father has the alleles Ff. Freckles are a dominant characteristic. *(6 marks)*

● Topic 10.4 Inheritance

10.4.4 Genetic modification

Learning objectives

After this section you will be able to:
- describe how a product is produced using genetic modification
- describe some advantages of genetic modification.

Have you ever seen fish that glow in the dark? Scientists have altered the genes of one type of fish to make them fluoresce (glow) by genetic modification. The aim was to produce a fish that would glow in the presence of polluted water.

What is genetic modification?

When farmers selectively breed plants and animals to produce offspring with desired characteristics, they are choosing organisms' genes. However, this is a slow process that takes place over many generations. It is also not very precise.

Scientists are now able to alter an organism's genes to produce an organism with desired characteristics. For example, crops can be produced that are resistant to disease. This is called **genetic modification** (or genetic engineering).

A State what is meant by genetic modification.

This is a very precise process, as single genes can be targeted. It can also happen in one generation. Therefore, it is a much quicker process than selective breeding, which can take many years.

B State an advantage of genetic modification.

Examples of genetic modification

Many organisms have been genetically modified. For example:
- cotton – to produce high yields
- corn – to produce toxins (poison) that kill insects
- bacteria – to produce medicinal drugs.

▲ GloFish.

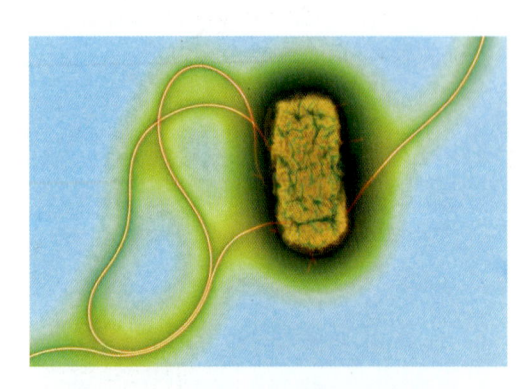

▲ *Escherichia coli* is genetically engineered to produce insulin. Some people do not produce insulin, and must inject this chemical daily to control their blood sugar levels.

How can you alter an organism's genes?

To create an organism with a desired characteristic, scientists take genes from another organism that shows this characteristic. These are known as foreign genes. The foreign genes are put into plant or animal cells at a very early stage of the organism's development. As the organism develops, it will display the characteristics of the foreign genes.

Frost-resistant tomatoes

The flounder is a fish that lives in very cold waters, and contains a gene to prevent it freezing. Scientists have created frost-resistant tomatoes by inserting the flounder's antifreeze gene into the cells of a tomato plant. This type of genetically modified tomato plant is no longer destroyed by frost, which is very beneficial for farmers.

▲ Flounders produce antifreeze chemicals that allow them to live in very cold water.

▲ Tomatoes can be made frost resistant by adding the flounder's antifreeze gene.

Genetically modified bacteria

Bacteria can be genetically modified to produce many useful chemicals, including vaccines and antibiotics. As bacteria reproduce very quickly, they can be used to produce large amounts of the chemical in a very short period.

C Name two useful chemicals produced by genetically modified bacteria.

Are there any disadvantages of genetic modification?

Some people believe that it is unethical to interfere with an organism's genetic material and therefore the use of this technique should be banned.

Other people are worried that there may be unwanted risks of creating genetically modified organisms. For example, they may trigger allergic reactions or long-term health problems. There is no evidence to suggest that this is true.

Another concern is that if the genetically modified organisms bred with other species it could result in new pathogens or superweeds being created.

Key Word
genetic modification

GM cartoon strip
Select one example of genetic modification. Produce a cartoon strip that explains simply how an organism can be genetically modified to produce a desired characteristic. Write a short caption for each step of the cartoon strip.

Summary Questions

1. Copy and complete the sentences below.
   Scientists can insert _____ genes into organisms to produce desired _____. This is called _____ modification. For example, bacteria can be modified to produce _____.
   (4 marks)

2. Describe the advantages of genetic modification over selective breeding.
   (3 marks)

3. Suggest two arguments for and two arguments against genetic modification.
   (4 marks)

Topic 10.4 Inheritance

10 Genes: Summary

Key Points

Evolution
- Charles Darwin and Alfred Wallace came up with the theory of evolution by natural selection.
- All living organisms have evolved from a common ancestor, through the process of natural selection.
- Fossils provide evidence for evolution.
- If a species is not adapted to its environment, it will not survive. Eventually a species can become extinct.
- To prevent endangered species becoming extinct, scientists store genetic samples in gene banks, breed animals in captivity, and protect habitats through conservation.

Inheritance
- You inherit characteristics from your parents in your DNA.
- DNA (deoxyribonucleic acid) is made up of two strands twisted together to form a double helix. The strands are held together by bases. There are four bases – A, T, C, and G.
- DNA is arranged into long strands called chromosomes. Each chromosome is divided into sections of DNA. The sections of DNA that contain the information to produce a characteristic are called genes.
- Watson, Crick, Franklin, and Wilkins worked together to produce a model of the structure of DNA.

BIG Write

Explaining natural selection
Imagine that you have to teach the process of natural selection to other members of your year group.

Task
Produce a presentation that explains how peppered moths evolved as a response to the Industrial Revolution. You need to explain what genes are, and how they are passed on.

Tips
- Make sure your slides are clear and cover topics in a logical order.
- Remember to explain all scientific terms clearly.

Key Words

evolution, fossil, natural selection, peer review, extinct, competition, biodiversity, population, endangered species, conservation, captive breeding, gene bank, inherited characteristics, DNA, chromosome, gene, mutation, allele, dominant, recessive, Punnett square, genetic modification

End-of-Big Idea questions

1
   a Scientists are trying to prevent endangered species becoming extinct. Tick the cells in the table to show what type of organism the technique is used for. *(3 marks)*

Technique	Plants	Animals	Both
captive breeding			
seed bank			
conservation			

   b Describe the difference between an endangered organism and an extinct organism. *(2 marks)*
   (5 marks)

2
Rosalind Franklin   Louis Pasteur
Charles Darwin   Francis Crick
Edward Jenner   Joseph Lister

From the list of scientists above identify:
   a The scientist that developed the theory of evolution. *(1 mark)*
   b One of the scientists that took an X-ray of DNA. *(1 mark)*
   c One of the scientists who developed the model of DNA based on the X-ray image. *(1 mark)*
   (3 marks)

3 Characteristics are passed on from parents to their children through genetic material.
   a Name the cell component that stores genetic material. *(1 mark)*
   b Name the chemical that contains all the information needed to make an organism. *(1 mark)*
   c Describe the difference between a gene and a chromosome. *(2 marks)*
   d Describe how genetic material is passed from parents to their children. *(4 marks)*
   (8 marks)

4 Dinosaurs were animals that lived on Earth millions of years ago.
   a State **one** piece of evidence that proves dinosaurs existed. *(1 mark)*
   b State what is meant by the word extinction. *(1 mark)*
   c State and explain **two** reasons that could cause an organism to become extinct. *(4 marks)*
   d Describe the role of gene banks in helping to prevent extinction. *(3 marks)*
   (9 marks)

5 Gregor Mendel was a famous scientist who carried out experiments on peas to find out how characteristics are inherited. He found that peas could be rounded or wrinkled, and that round peas were always dominant to wrinkled peas.

Use a Punnett square to calculate the chance of a pea plant producing wrinkled peas if both parent plants carry the alleles Rr. *(6 marks)*

6 Explain the process of natural selection and the role it plays in the evolution of species. *(6 marks)*

Glossary

addiction A need to keep taking a drug in order to feel normal.
aerobic respiration Breaking down glucose with oxygen to release energy and producing carbon dioxide and water.
air resistance The force on an object moving through air that causes it to slow down, also known as drag.
alcoholic A person who is addicted to alcohol.
algae Green uni-cellular or multi-cellular organisms that perform photosynthesis and live underwater.
alkali metals The elements in the left column of the Periodic Table, including lithium, sodium, and potassium. Also called Group 1.
allele Different forms of a gene.
alveolus Small air sacs found at the end of each bronchiole where gas exchange takes place with the blood.
anaerobic respiration Releasing energy from the breakdown of glucose without oxygen, producing lactic acid (in animals) and ethanol and carbon dioxide (in plants and microorganisms).
anus Muscular ring through which faeces pass out of the body.
argumentation Using logical reasoning, debate, and negotiation to reach conclusions.
asthma A lung disorder in which inflammation (swelling) causes the bronchi to swell and narrow the airways, creating breathing difficulties.
atmosphere The mixture of gases surrounding the Earth.
atmospheric pressure The pressure caused by the weight of the air above a surface.
atom The smallest part of an element that can exist.
audience The person or people who will read what you write or hear what you say.
balanced diet Eating food containing the right nutrients in the correct amounts.
balanced symbol equation In a balanced symbol equation, chemical formulae represent the reactants and products. The equation shows how atoms are rearranged and joined together differently, and gives the relative amounts of reactants and products.
benefit Something good or helpful.
bias When the views of an experimenter affects the outcome, or when a journalist favours a point of view.
bile Substance that breaks fat into small droplets.

biodiversity A measure of the variety of all the different species of organisms on earth or within a particular ecosystem.
biotechnology The use of biological processes or organisms to create useful products.
breathing The movement of air in and out of the lungs.
bronchiole Small tube in the lung.
bronchus One of two tubes which carry air into the lungs.
captive breeding Breeding animals in human-controlled environments.
carbohydrase Enzyme that breaks down carbohydrates into sugar molecules.
carbohydrates Nutrients that provide the body's main source of energy. There are two types: simple (sugars) and complex (starch).
carbon cycle The carbon cycle shows carbon sinks, and summarises how carbon and its compounds enter and leave the atmosphere and these sinks.
carbon sink Areas of vegetation, the ocean or the soil, which absorb and store carbon. Carbon and its compounds may remain in carbon sinks for many years.
carbonate A compound that includes carbon and oxygen atoms, as well as a metal element. There are three atoms of oxygen for every one atom of carbon.
catalyst Substances that speed up chemical reactions but are unchanged at the end.
catalytic converter A part of a car between the engine and exhaust pipe that converts harmful sustances made in the engine into less harmful ones.
centre of gravity The point in an object where the force of gravity seems to act.
centre of mass The point in an object where all the mass of an object seems to act.
chemical bond Force that holds atoms together in molecules.
chemical formula A formula that shows the elements present in a compound and their relative proportions.
chemical properties Features of the way a substance reacts with other substances.
chemical reaction A change in which a new substance is formed. In a chemical reaction, atoms are rearranged and joined together differently.

chemical symbol A one- or two-letter code for an element that is used by scientists in all countries.

chlorophyll Green pigment in plants and algae which absorbs light energy.

chromosome Thread-like structure containing tightly coiled DNA. It contains many genes.

circuit breaker A device that uses an electromagnet to break a circuit if the current is too big.

claim A statement that says something is true.

climate change A long-term change in weather patterns.

combustion A chemical reaction in which a substance reacts quickly with oxygen and gives out light and heat. Also called burning.

competition When two or more living things struggle against each other to get the same resource.

compound Pure substances made up of atoms of two or more elements, strongly joined together.

compression Force squashing or pushing together, which changes the shape of an object.

condense The change of state from gas to liquid.

conduction Transfer of thermal energy by the vibration of particles.

conservation Protecting a natural environment, to ensure that habitats are not lost.

conservation of mass In a chemical reaction, the total mass of reactants is equal to the total mass of products. This is conservation of mass. Mass is conserved in chemical reactions and in physical changes.

conserved When the quantity of something does not change after a process takes place.

contact force A force that acts when an object is in contact with a surface, air, or water.

contract To get shorter or smaller.

convection Transfer of thermal energy when particles in a heated fluid rise.

convection current The movement of heated fluids where hot fluid moves upwards, and cold fluid moves downwards.

core (electromagnet) Soft iron metal which the solenoid is wrapped around.

decomposition A chemical reaction in which a compound breaks down to form more than one product.

deficiency A lack of minerals that causes poor growth.

deform When an object is stretched or squashed, which requires work.

deformation Changing shape due to a force.

dependent variable What you measure or observe in an investigation.

depressant A drug that slows down the body's reactions by slowing down the nervous system.

diaphragm A sheet of muscle found underneath the lungs which is used in breathing.

dietary fibre Parts of plants that cannot be digested. It helps the body to eliminate waste by provinging bulk to keep food moving through the digestive system.

digestion Process in which large molecules are broken down into small molecules.

digestive system Group of organs that work together to break down food.

displacement The distance an object moves from its original position.

DNA A molecule found in the nucleus of cells that contains genetic information.

dominant (allele) A dominant allele will always be expressed if it is present.

drag force The force acting on an object moving through air or water that causes it to slow down.

drug Chemical substance that affects the way your body works.

elastic limit The point beyond which a spring will not return to its original length when the force is removed.

electric bell A device that uses an electromagnet to make sound using a 'make and break' circuit.

electrolysis Using electricity to split up a compound into its elements.

electromagnet A non-permanent magnet turned on and off by controlling the current through it.

electromagnetic spectrum The range of wavelengths of radiation produced by the Sun and other sources.

elements Substances that all other materials are made up of, and which contain only one type of atom. An element cannot be broken down into other substances.

endangered species A species with only small numbers of organisms left in the world.

endothermic reaction An endothermic reaction takes in energy, usually as heat. In other words, it transfers energy from the surroundings.

energy level diagrams Diagram showing the relative energies of the reactants and products. It shows whether a reaction is endothermic or endothermic.

enzyme Substances that speed up the chemical reactions of digestion resulting in large molecules being broken into small molecules.

equilibrium State of an object when opposing forces are balanced.

ethanol The drug found in alcoholic drinks.
evidence Measurements or observations offered to support or oppose a theory.
evolution Theory that the animal and plant species living today descended from species that existed in the past.
exhale Breathing out, to remove carbon dioxide.
exothermic reaction An exothermic reaction gives out energy, usually as heat or light. In other words, it transfers energy to the surroundings.
extension The difference between the original length of an object and the length when you apply a force.
extinct When no more individuals of a species remain anywhere in the world.
extraction Separation of a metal from a metal compound.
fermentation A type of anaerobic respiration in which glucose is converted into ethanol, carbon dioxide, and energy.
fertiliser Chemicals containing minerals that plants need to build new tissues.
fluid A substance with no fixed shape, a gas or a liquid.
food test Chemical test to detect the presence of particular nutrients in a food.
fossil The remains or traces of plants and animals that have turned to stone.
fossil fuel A fuel made from the remains of animals and plants that died millions of years ago. Fossil fuels include coal, oil, and natural gas.
friction Force opposing motion which is caused by the interaction of surfaces moving over one another. It is called 'drag' if one is a fluid.
fuel A substance that stores energy in a chemical store which it can release as heat.
funder Organisation or person that pays for scientific research.
gamma rays Waves with the highest frequency in the electromagnetic spectrum.
gas exchange The transfer of gases between an organism and its environment.
gas pressure The force exerted by air particles when they collide with a surface.
gene A section of DNA that determines an inherited characteristic.
gene bank A store of genetic samples, used for research and to try to prevent extinction.

genetic modification A technique in which scientists insert foreign genes into organisms to change their characteristics.
global warming The gradual increase in the average surface temperature of the Earth.
greenhouse effect When energy from the Sun is transferred to the thermal energy store of gases in Earth's atmosphere. The greenhouse effect keeps the surface of the Earth warmer than it would otherwise be.
greenhouse gas A gas that contributes to the greenhouse effect, such as carbon dioxide.
group A column of the Periodic Table. The elements in a group have similar properties.
Group 0 Group 0 is on the right of the Periodic Table. Group 0 elements include helium, neon, argon, and krypton. Also called the noble gases.
Group 1 The elements in the left column of the Periodic Table, including lithium, sodium, and potassium. Also called the alkali metals.
Group 7 Group 7 is second from the right of the Periodic Table. Group 7 elements include fluorine, chlorine, bromine, and iodine. Also known as the halogens.
gullet Tube that food travels down into the stomach.
gut bacteria Microorganisms that naturally live in the intestine and help food break down.
haemoglobin The substance in blood that carries oxygen around the body.
halogen The name for elements in the group that is second from the right of the Periodic Table. Halogens include fluorine, chlorine, bromine, and iodine. Also known as the Group 7 elements.
Hooke's Law A law that says that if you double the force on an object, the extension will double.
hydroxide A compound that includes hydrogen and oxygen atoms, as well as a metal element. There is one atom of oxygen for every one atom of hydrogen.
hypothesis An explanation you can test which includes a reason and a 'science idea'.
incompressible Cannot be compressed (squashed).
independent variable What you change in an investigation to see how it affects the dependent variable.
infrared (radiation) Radiation given off by the Sun and other objects that brings about energy transfer.
inhale Breathing in, to take in oxygen.

inherited characteristic Features that are passed from parents to their offspring.

input force The force you apply to a machine.

iodine Indicator used to test for the presence of starch.

ionisation The removal of an electron from an atom.

journal Magazine which publishes science research for others (usually scientists) to read.

large intestine Lower part of the intestine from which water is absorbed and where faeces (solid waste of undigested food) are formed.

law A theory that you can express with a concise statement.

law of moments An object is in equilibrium if the clockwise moments equal the anticlockwise moments.

lever A type of machine which is a rigid bar that pivots about a point.

line of best fit A straight or curved line drawn to show the pattern of data points.

linear relationship When two variables are graphed and show a straight line which goes through the origin, and they can be called proportional.

lipase Enzyme that breaks down lipids into fatty acids and glycerol.

lipids Nutrients that provide a store of energy and insulate the body. Found in butter, milk, eggs, nuts.

liquid pressure The pressure produced by collisions of particles in a liquid.

longitudinal wave A wave in which the direction of vibration is the same as that of the wave.

loudspeaker A device that uses an electromagnet to make sound from a varying potential difference. Turns an electrical signal into a pressure wave of sound.

lubrication A substance that reduces friction between surfaces when they rub together.

lung volume Measure of the amount of air breathed in or out.

lungs The organ in which gas exchange takes place.

magnesium A mineral needed by plants for making chlorophyll. It is an element in group 2 of the Periodic Table.

magnet A material with a magnetic field around it in which a magnetic material experiences a force.

magnetic field A region in which there is a force on a magnet or magnetic material.

magnetic field lines Imaginary lines that show the direction of the force on a magnetic material.

magnetic force Non-contact force from a magnet on a magnetic material.

magnetic poles The ends of a magnetic field, called north-seeking and south-seeking poles.

magnetise To make a material magnetic.

malnourishment Eating the wrong amount or wrong types of food.

medicinal drug Drug that has a medical benefit to your health.

microphone Turns the pressure wave of sound hitting it into an electrical signal (potential difference).

microwaves Waves of the electromagnetic spectrum used for heating and for communicating.

mineral (biology) Essential nutrient needed in small amounts to keep you healthy.

mineral (chemistry) Naturally occurring metals, and their compounds.

model A way of representing something that is too difficult to display, usually because it is too big, too small, or too complicated.

molecule A group of two or more (up to thousands) atoms strongly joined together. Most non-metal elements exist either as small or giant molecules.

moment A measure of the ability of a force to rotate an object about a pivot.

mutation Change to DNA that can cause disease.

natural polymer A polymer made by plants or animals. Examples include starch, wool, cotton, and rubber.

natural resources Materials from the Earth, its atmosphere, and the oceans, which act as raw materials for making a variety of products.

natural selection Process by which species change over time in response to environmental changes and competition for resources. The organisms with the characteristics that are most suited to the environment survive and reproduce, passing on their genes.

newton Unit for measuring forces (N).

newton metres The unit of moment.

newtons per metre squared A unit of pressure.

nitrate (chemistry) A compound that includes nitrogen and oxygen atoms, as well as a metal element. There are three atoms of oxygen for every one atom of nitrogen.

nitrates (biology) Minerals containing nitrogen for healthy growth.

noble gases The name for elements in the group on the right of the Periodic Table. Noble gases include helium, neon, argon, and krypton. Also known as the Group 0 elements.

non-renewable Energy resources that have a limited supply and that cannot be replaced within a short timeframe.

nutrient Essential substance that your body needs to survive, provided by food.

obese Extremely overweight.

ore A naturally occurring rock that contains enough of a mineral to make it worth getting the mineral – and then the metal it includes – out of the rock.

output force The force that is applied to the object moved by the machine.

oxygen debt Extra oxygen required after anaerobic respiration to break down lactic acid.

passive smoking Breathing in other people's smoke.

peer review The evaluation of a scientist's work by another scientist.

period A row of the Periodic Table. There are trends in the properties of the elements across a period.

Periodic Table A table which shows all the elements arranged in columns and rows. Elements with similar properties are grouped together.

permanent magnet An object that is magnetic all of the time.

phosphates Mineral containing phosporus for healthy roots.

photosynthesis The process plants and algae use to make their own food, glucose. In photosynthesis, carbon dioxide and water react together to make glucose and oxygen.

physical change One that changes the physical properties of a substance, but no new substance is formed. A physical change is reversible.

physical properties Features of a substance that can be observed without changing the substance itself.

pivot The point about which a lever or see-saw balances or rotates.

plasma Liquid that transports blood cells and other materials around the body.

polymer A molecule made by joining up thousands of smaller molecules in a repeating pattern. Plastics are synthetic polymers, and starch is a natural polymer.

population Group of organisms of the same kind living in the same place.

potassium A mineral needed by plants for healthy leaves and flowers.

pressure The ratio of force to surface area, in N/m^2, and how it causes stresses in solids.

pressure wave An example is sound, which has repeating patterns of high-pressure and low-pressure regions.

producer Organism that make its own food using photosynthesis.

products Substances that are formed in a chemical reaction, shown on the right of the arrow in a chemical equation.

protease Enzyme that breaks down proteins into amino acids.

protein Nutrient your body uses to build new tissue for growth and repair. Sources are meat, fish, eggs, dairy products, beans, nuts, and seeds.

Punnett square A diagram used to show the possible combinations of alleles inherited from the parents.

radiation The transfer of energy as a wave.

radio waves Waves with the lowest frequency in the electromagnetic spectrum, used for communicating.

rarefaction The part of a longitudinal wave where the air particles are spread out.

reactants Substances that react together, shown on the left of the arrow in a chemical equation.

reaction (physics) The support force provided by a solid surface like a floor.

reasoning Your ideas about what the evidence means, in the form of an argument for or against the claim.

recessive A recessive allele will only be expressed if two copies are present.

recreational drug Drug that is taken for enjoyment.

rectum Faeces are stored here, before being passed out of the body.

recycling Collecting and processing a material so that it can be used again.

renewable A fuel that can be easily replaced within a short timeframe.

repeatable When repeat readings are similar.

respiration The process that transfers energy in plants and animals. In respiration, glucose reacts with oxygen to make carbon dioxide and water.

respiratory system Organ system which replaces oxygen and removes carbon dioxide from the blood.

resultant force Single force which can replace all the forces acting on an object and have the same effect.

ribs   Bones which surround the lungs to form the ribcage and protect the lungs.
secondary data   Results that have already been collected by another person.
simple machine   A machine such as a lever or pulley system which changes the size of the force by moving a force over a bigger or smaller distance.
small intestine   Upper part of the intestine where digestion is completed and nutrients are absorbed by the blood.
solenoid   Wire wound into a tight coil, part of an electromagnet.
starvation   Extreme case of not eating enough food.
stimulant   A drug that speeds up the body's reactions by speeding up the nervous system.
stomach   Organ where food is mixed with acidic juices to start the digestion of protein and kill microorganisms.
stomata   Pores in the bottom of a leaf which open and close to let gases in and out.
streamlined   Shaped to reduce resistance to motion from air or water.
stress   The effect of a force applied to a solid, found using stress = force/area.
sulfate   A compound that includes sulfur and oxygen atoms. There are four atoms of oxygen for every one atom of sulfur.
superpose   When waves join together so that they add up or cancel out.
synthetic polymer   A polymer made by people, often in a factory. Examples include poly(ethene) and poly(propene).
temperature   A measure of the motion and energy of particles.
tension   Force extending or pulling apart.
theory   An explanation for patterns that we see in observations or data that is supported by evidence.
thermal conductor   Material that allows heat to move quickly through it.
thermal decomposition   A chemical reaction in which a compound breaks down on heating to form more than one product.
thermal energy store   The store containing energy due to the vibration or movement of particles of a substance.
thermal imaging camera   A camera that absorbs infrared and produces a (false colour) image.
thermal insulator   Material that only allows heat to travel slowly through it.

thermometer   Instrument used to measure temperature.
trachea   Tube which carries air from the mouth and nose to the lungs.
transmission   Where waves travel through a medium rather than being absorbed or reflected.
transverse wave   A wave in which the direction of vibration is perpendicular to that of the wave.
trend   A pattern in properties, such as an increase or decrease.
ultrasound   Sound waves with frequencies higher than the human auditory range.
ultraviolet   Waves with frequencies higher than those of light, which human eyes cannot detect.
unit of alcohol   10 ml of pure alcohol.
unreactive   Elements that take part in few chemical reactions are unreactive.
upthrust   The upward force that a liquid or gas exerts on a body floating in it produced by the collisions of the particles in the liquid or gas.
villi   Tiny projections in the small intestine wall that increase the area for absorption.
visible light   The band of frequencies of light that we can detect with our eyes.
vitamin   Essential nutrients needed in small amounts to keep you healthy.
water resistance   The force on an object moving through water that causes it to slow down, also known as drag.
wave   Vibrations that transport energy from place to place without transporting matter.
withdrawal symptom   Unpleasant symptom a person with a drug addition suffers from when they stop taking the drug.
work   The transfer of energy when a force moves an object through a distance, in joules.
X-rays   Waves of the electromagnetic spectrum used for producing images of bones and tissue.

Index

absorption 62
addiction 127, 128
aerobic respiration 146–147
air resistance 20–21
alcohol
    effects 128–129
    ethanol 93, 128–129, 134–135, 149, 150, 151
    fermentation 150–151
alcoholics 128
algae 152
alkali metals (Group 1) 80–81
alleles 176
aluminium 114, 115, 116–117
alveolus 122
anaerobic respiration 148–149
analysing data 4–5
anus 139
area, stress forces 30, 31
argumentation 16, 17
asthma 125
atmosphere 51, 61, 93, 108
atmospheric pressure 27
atoms
    compounds 72–76
    elements 70–71
    ionisation 61
    reactions 90–91, 96–97
    sizes 79
audience 6–7

bacteria 140, 149, 173, 179
balanced diet 132, 136
balanced forces (equilibrium) 21, 24–25
balanced symbol equations 97
benefits and risks 12–13, 61, 126, 179
bias 9
bile 141
biodiversity 169, 170–171
biotechnology 150–151
    see also genetic modification
blood 122, 147
boiling points 73, 81, 82, 84
bond energies 102–103
breadmaking 150
breathing 122–125
bronchiole 122
bronchus 122
burning (combustion) 92–93, 96–97, 100–101, 110

captive breeding 170–171
carbohydrase 140–141
carbohydrates 132, 134, 135
carbon
    cycle 110–111
    metal extraction 114–115
    sinks 110

carbonates 75, 94–95
carbon dioxide
    aerobic respiration 146, 147
    breathing out 123
    burning fuels 92–93, 110
    carbon cycle 110–111
    fermentation 149–150
    global warming 108–109, 112–113
    molecules 74–75
    photosynthesis 152, 153, 157
    thermal decomposition 94–95
catalysts 103, 140
catalytic converters 78, 103
centre of gravity (centre of mass) 25
changes of state
    energy level diagrams 100
    see also boiling; freezing; melting
changing ideas 16–17
chemical bonds 102–103
chemical formula 75, 97
chemical properties of elements 81, 83
chemical reactions 83, 88–105
chemical symbols 69, 97
chlorophyll 153, 154, 159
chromosomes 172
circuit breakers 40–41
claims 10
climate change 108–113
combustion (burning) 92–93, 96–97, 100–101, 110
communication 6–7
competition 168
compounds 72–73
compression 22, 58
condensation 123
conduction of heat 50–51
consequences 12–13
conservation of atoms 91
conservation of biodiversity 170
conservation of mass 96–97
contact forces 20–21
contracting muscles 124
convection 50, 51
convection currents 51
cores of electromagnets 38–39

Darwin, Charles 166–167
data analysis 4–5
data collection 2–3, 10
    see also experiments; investigations
decomposition reactions 94–95
deficiencies in diet 137
deficiencies in plant nutrition 158
deform/deformation 22–23, 46
dependent variables 3

depressants 128–129
depth and pressure 28–29
diaphragm 124
diet see balanced diet; nutrition
dietary fibre 133
digestion/digestive system 138–141
displacement of objects 46–47
displacement reactions 83
DNA 172–175
dominant alleles 176
drag forces 20–21
drugs 126–131

Earth
    atmosphere 27, 51, 61, 93, 108
    climate 106–113
    magnetic field 37
    mineral resources 114–117
ecosystems 144–161
elastic limit 23
electric bell 40
electricity from renewable sources 59, 113
electrolysis 115
electromagnetic spectrum 60–61
electromagnetic waves/radiation 60–61, 63
electromagnets 34, 38–42
elements 68–71, 78–85
endangered species 170
endothermic reactions/changes 98, 100, 102–103
energy 44–55
    bond energies 102–103
    dietary 137
    heat 48–53
    renewable and non-renewable sources 93
    work and machines 46–47
energy level diagrams 100–101
energy transfer
    changes of state 100
    endothermic/exothermic processes 98–101, 103
    heat 49–53
    particles 50–51
    respiration 147
    thermal radiation 52–53
    waves 56–65
enquiry processes 2–16
enzymes 140–141, 150, 157
equilibrium 21, 24–25
ethanol 93, 128–129, 134–135, 149, 150, 151
evidence 8–11, 14–17
evolution 164–167
exhaling 123
exothermic reactions/changes 99, 101, 102–103

experiments 2–3, 5, 10, 14
extension 22–23
extinction 168–169
extracting metals 114–115

fermentation 149
fertilisers 159
fibre, dietary 133, 139
floating 29
fluid pressure 26–29
food
    diet 132–137
    digestion 138–141
    tests 134
forces 18–33
    magnetism 36–41
    movement 20–25, 46–47
    pressure 26–31
fossil fuels 93, 110, 112
fossils 164
freezing 100
frequency 60, 63
friction 20–21
fuels 92–93
funder of research 9

gamma rays 60, 61
gas exchange 122–123
gas pressure 26–27
gene banks 170, 171
genes 162, 165, 172, 176–179
genetic modification/genetic engineering 178–179
genetics 176–177
global warming 108–113
gold 68, 69, 71
graphs 4, 5, 23, 109, 113, 137
greenhouse effect/greenhouse gases 93, 108–109, 113, 115
Group 0 elements 84–85
Group 1 elements 80–81
Group 7 elements 82–83
groups of periodic table 78, 80–85
gullet 138
gut 138–141
gut bacteria 140

haemoglobin blood 147
halogens (Group 7 elements) 82–83
healthy eating 132–133, 136–137
heat
    energy transfer 49–53
    fuels 92–93
    temperature 48–49, 52
    see also thermal...
Hooke's Law 23
hydroxides 75, 81
hypotheses 3, 8, 134, 152

illegal drugs 126–127
incompressible 28
independent variables 3
infrared (IR) 52–53, 60, 61
inhaling 123
inheritance 172–173, 176–177
input forces 47
insulation, heat 50–51, 53
intestines 138–140
investigations 2–8, 156–157
iodine 156
ionisation 61
IR *see* infrared

journals 6, 8, 9, 10

large intestine 138
law of moments 24–25
laws in science 14
leaves 152, 153, 154–155
levers 47
light 52, 60–61
    photosynthesis 152–153, 157
linear relationships 23
line of best fit 4
lipase 140, 141
lipids 132, 134–135
liquid pressure 28–29
longitudinal waves 62, 63
loudspeakers 41, 58–59
lubrication 21
lungs 122–125, 131

machines 46–47
magnesium 158–159
magnetic fields/field lines 36–39
magnetic forces 36–41
magnetic poles 36
magnetising steel 38–39
magnets 34–43
malnourishment 136
matter 66–87
medicinal drugs 126
melting 100
melting points 76, 79, 80, 82
metals
    alkali/Group 1 80–81
    extraction 114–115
methane 109
microphones 58–59
microwaves 60, 61
minerals
    dietary 132, 133, 137
    metal ores 114
    plants 158–159
models 14
molecules 72–77
    bond energies 102–103
    reactions 90–91
moments of turning forces 24–25
mutations 60, 173

natural polymers 76–77
natural resources 114
natural selection 164–167

newton metres 24–25
newtons 20
newtons per metre squared 30–31
nitrates 75, 95, 158–159
noble gases (Group 0 elements) 84–85
non-renewable energy sources 93
    see also fossil fuels
non-renewable resources 116
nutrients/nutrition 132–137

obesity 136
opinions 11
ores 114
organisms 120–143
output forces 47
oxides 74–75, 90–94
oxygen 27, 72, 123, 143, 146, 147, 152, 156–157
    see also combustion
oxygen debt 148

particles, energy transfer 50–51
passive smoking 130–131
peer review 8, 167
periodic table 68, 78–85
periods of periodic table 79
permanent magnets 36–37
phosphates 158, 159
photosynthesis 110, 152–157
physical changes
    conservation of mass 96
    endothermic/exothermic 98–100
physical properties
    elements 78, 80, 82, 84
    molecules 76
pivots 24–25
planning enquiries 2–3
plants 152–159
plasma 147
poles of a magnet 36
poly(ethene) 76, 77
polymers 76–77
populations 169
potassium 158, 159
pregnancy 129, 130
pressure
    gases 26–27
    liquids 28–29
    solids 30–31
    waves 58
producers 152
products 90, 97, 100–101
protease 140, 141
proteins 132, 133, 135
pulleys 47
Punnett square 177

radiation 60–61
radiation of heat 50, 52–53
radio waves 60, 61
rarefaction 58
reactants 90, 97, 100–101
reaction forces 22

reactions, chemical 83, 88–105
reasoning 10
recessive alleles 176
recreational drugs 126–131
rectum 138
recycling 116–117
reflection 62, 63
refraction 63
reliability of evidence 8–9
renewable energy sources 59, 93, 113, 115
repeatable experiments 3
respiration 110, 123, 144–147
respiratory system 122–125
resultant forces 21
ribs 122
risks and benefits 12–13, 61, 126, 179

salt 73
scientific laws 14
secondary data 5
see-saws 25
silicon 70
simple machines 46–47
sinking 29
small intestine 138, 139, 141
smoking 130–131
solenoids 38–39
solids, pressure 30–31
sound waves 58–59, 63
springs 22–23
squashing 22
starvation 136
stimulants 131
stomach 138
stomata 155
streamlined 21
stress 30–31
stretching 22–23
sulfates 75
superposed waves 63
synthetic polymers 77

temperature 48–50, 52
    photosynthesis 157
tension 22
theories 14–17
thermal conductors 50
thermal decomposition 94–95
thermal energy stores 48
thermal imaging cameras 53, 60, 61
thermal insulators 50–51, 53
thermometers 48
tobacco 130–131
trachea 122
transmission of waves 62
transverse waves 62, 63
trend in periodic table 79, 80, 81, 83
turning forces 24–25

ultrasound 59
ultraviolet (UV) 60, 61

units of alcohol 128–129
unreactive elements 85
upthrust 29
UV *see* ultraviolet

villi 139
visible light 60, 61
vitamins 132, 133, 137
volume of lungs 125

water
    drinking 133
    molecules 72–73
    photosynthesis 153
    waves 59, 63
water resistance 20–21
wave energy 59
wavelength 60, 62, 63
waves 56–65
    electromagnetic 52, 60–61, 63
    energy transfer 56–65
    modelling 62–63
    sound 58–59, 63
    water 59, 63
withdrawal symptoms 127
work and energy 46–47

X-rays 60, 61

yeast 149–151

Periodic Table

1	2											3	4	5	6	7	0
						1 **H** hydrogen 1											4 **He** helium 2
7 **Li** lithium 3	9 **Be** beryllium 4											11 **B** boron 5	12 **C** carbon 6	14 **N** nitrogen 7	16 **O** oxygen 8	19 **F** fluorine 9	20 **Ne** neon 10
23 **Na** sodium 11	24 **Mg** magnesium 12											27 **Al** aluminium 13	28 **Si** silicon 14	31 **P** phosphorus 15	32 **S** sulfur 16	35.5 **Cl** chlorine 17	40 **Ar** argon 18
39 **K** potassium 19	40 **Ca** calcium 20	45 **Sc** scandium 21	48 **Ti** titanium 22	51 **V** vanadium 23	52 **Cr** chromium 24	55 **Mn** manganese 25	56 **Fe** iron 26	59 **Co** cobalt 27	59 **Ni** nickel 28	63.5 **Cu** copper 29	65 **Zn** zinc 30	70 **Ga** gallium 31	73 **Ge** germanium 32	75 **As** arsenic 33	79 **Se** selenium 34	80 **Br** bromine 35	84 **Kr** krypton 36
85 **Rb** rubidium 37	88 **Sr** strontium 38	89 **Y** yttrium 39	91 **Zr** zirconium 40	93 **Nb** niobium 41	96 **Mo** molybdenum 42	[98] **Tc** technetium 43	101 **Ru** ruthenium 44	103 **Rh** rhodium 45	106 **Pd** palladium 46	108 **Ag** silver 47	112 **Cd** cadmium 48	115 **In** indium 49	119 **Sn** tin 50	122 **Sb** antimony 51	128 **Te** tellurium 52	127 **I** iodine 53	131 **Xe** xenon 54
133 **Cs** caesium 55	137 **Ba** barium 56	139 **La*** lanthanum 57	178 **Hf** hafnium 72	181 **Ta** tantalum 73	184 **W** tungsten 74	186 **Re** rhenium 75	190 **Os** osmium 76	192 **Ir** iridium 77	195 **Pt** platinum 78	197 **Au** gold 79	201 **Hg** mercury 80	204 **Tl** thallium 81	207 **Pb** lead 82	209 **Bi** bismuth 83	[209] **Po** polonium 84	[210] **At** astatine 85	[222] **Rn** radon 86
[223] **Fr** francium 87	[226] **Ra** radium 88	[227] **Ac*** actinium 89	[261] **Rf** rutherfordium 104	[262] **Db** dubnium 105	[266] **Sg** seaborgium 106	[264] **Bh** bohrium 107	[277] **Hs** hassium 108	[268] **Mt** meitnerium 109	[271] **Ds** darmstadtium 110	[272] **Rg** roentgenium 111	[285] **Cn** copernicium 112	[286] **Uut** ununtrium 113	[289] **Fl** flerovium 114	[289] **Uup** ununpentium 115	[293] **Lv** livermorium 116	[294] **Uus** ununseptium 117	[294] **Uuo** ununoctium 118

key

relative atomic mass
atomic symbol
name
atomic (proton) number

*The lanthanides (atomic numbers 58–71) and the actinides (atomic numbers 90–103) have been omitted.
Relative atomic masses for **Cu** and **Cl** have not been rounded to the nearest whole number.

COVER: Science Photo Library / Alamy Stock Photo; pzAxe / Shutterstock **p2:** Ammit Jack/Shutterstock; **p4:** Artem Zakharov/Shutterstock; **p6:** Colin Cuthbert/Science Photo Library; **p7b:** Mikkel Juul Jensen/Science Photo Library; **p7t:** Spencer Grant/Science Photo Library; **p8b:** Art Directors & Trip/Alamy Stock Photo; **p8t:** Prath/Shutterstock; **p9:** Ragma Images/Shutterstock; **p10b:** Robert Brook/Science Photo Library; **p10t:** Castleski/Shutterstock; **p11l:** Saturn Stills/Science Photo Library; **p11r:** Peter Kotoff/Shutterstock; **p12:** Wk1003mike/Shutterstock; **p13:** Yauhen D/Shutterstock; **p14b:** Martyn F. Chillmaid/Science Photo Library; **p14m:** Alfred Pasieka/Science Photo Library; **p14t:** Photosani/Shutterstock; **p15:** Noam Armonn/Shutterstock; **p16bl:** Mikkel Juul Jensen/Science Photo Library; **p16bm:** Toeytoey/Shutterstock; **p16br:** Steve Gschmeissner/Science Photo Library; **p16t:** Science Photo Library; **p17b:** Tomasz Bidermann/Shutterstock; **p17t:** Paul D Stewart/Science Photo Library; **p18-19:** Joggie Botma/Shutterstock; **p18t:** Brave Rabbit/Shutterstock; **p18b:** Stas Vulkanov/Shutterstock; **p19tl:** Castleski/Shutterstock; **p19tml:** Andrey Pavlov/Shutterstock; **p19tm:** Lukasz Janyst/Shutterstock; **p19tmr:** Vit Kovalcik/Shutterstock; **p19tr:** Keith Levit/Shutterstock; **p19b:** Mike Taylor/Shutterstock; **p20t:** Velychko/Shutterstock; **p20b:** Willyam Bradberry/Shutterstock; **p22:** Brave Rabbit/Shutterstock; **p23:** Stas Vulkanov/Shutterstock; **p24t:** Leo Brogioni/Shutterstock; **p24bl:** Benedektibor/Shutterstock; **p24br:** GI Photo Stock/Science Photo Library; **p26:** Ted Kinsman/Science Photo Library; **p27l:** Charles D. Winters/Science Photo Library; **p27r:** Charles D. Winters/Science Photo Library; **p28:** DR Ken Mac Donald/Science Photo Library; **p30t:** Castleski/Shutterstock; **p30b:** Dmitry Kalinovsky/Shutterstock; **p31t:** Daxiao Productions/Shutterstock; **p31bl:** Racheal Grazias/Shutterstock; **p31br:** Bigchen/Shutterstock; **p32t:** Castleski/Shutterstock; **p32b:** Stas Vulkanov/Shutterstock; **p32-33** Stas Vulkanov/Shutterstock; **p34-35:** Hung Chung Chih/Shutterstock; **p34t:** Alexandre Dotta/Science Photo Library; **p34b:** Chrislofotos/Shutterstock; **p35:** Vova Shevchuk/Shutterstock; Arnoud Quanjer/Shutterstock; Pippee Contributor/Shutterstock; Sea photo art/Shutterstock; Mark Doherty/Shutterstock; Bakounine/Shutterstock; Emrahselamet/Shutterstock; Studio on line/Shutterstock; Philip Image/Shutterstock; **p36:** Oliver Hoffmann/Shutterstock; **p37t:** Cordelia Molly/Science Photo Library; **p37b:** Mark Garlick/Science Photo Library; **p38:** Trevor Clifford Photography/Science Photo Library; **p39:** Alexandre Dotta/Science Photo Library; **p40t:** Hung Chung Chih/Shutterstock; **p40b:** Rido/Shutterstock; **p41:** Kyrylo Glivin/Shutterstock; **p42t:** Trevor Clifford Photography/Science Photo Library; **p42b:** Oliver Hoffmann/Shutterstock; **p42-43** Mark Garlick/Science Photo Library; **p44-15:** Mr Segui/Shutterstock; **p44t:** Alter Ego/Shutterstock; **p44b:** Tony Mcconnell/Science Photo Library; **p45:** Sarunyu foto/Shutterstock; Milsi Art/Shutterstock; Brat82/Shutterstock; Daxiao Productions/Shutterstock; Imfoto/Shutterstock; Bikeriderlondon/Shutterstock; Michael Rosskothen/Shutterstock; Hanafi Latif/Shutterstock; **p46t:** Matteo Gabrieli/Shutterstock; **p46b:** Pung/Shutterstock; **p47:** Philip Image/Shutterstock; **p48t:** Mr Segui/Shutterstock; **p48m:** Nikkytok/Shutterstock; **p48bl:** Alter Ego/Shutterstock; **p48bm:** Bikeriderlondon/Shutterstock; **p48br:** Pavlo Loushkin/Shutterstock; **p50t:** NREL/US Department Of Energy/Science Photo Library; **p50b:** Bill Ingalls/NASA; **p51:** Guido Amrein Switzerland/Shutterstock; **p52t:** GI Photo Stock/Science Photo Library; **p52bl:** NOAO/Science Photo Library; **p52br:** Edward Kinsman/Science Photo Library; **p53:** Dario Sabljak/Shutterstock; **p54t:** Bill Ingalls/NASA; **p54b:** Dario Sabljak/Shutterstock; **p54-55** Alter Ego/Shutterstock; **p56t:** Paul Rapson/Science Photo Library; **p56b:** GI Photo Stock/Science Photo Library; **p56-57:** Science Photo Library; **p57:** Lifetime Stock/Shutterstock; Vinicius Tupinamba/Shutterstock; Narongsak Nagadhana/Shutterstock; Andrew Brookes/National Physical Laboratory/Science Photo Library; Oskari Porkka/Shutterstock; Bikeriderlondon/Shutterstock; Erik Wollo/Shutterstock; Artem Furman/Shutterstock; Dirk Ercken/Shutterstock; **p58:** Monty Rakusen/Cultura Creative (RF)/Alamy Stock Photo; **p59b:** Science Photo Library; **p59t:** Paul Rapson/Science Photo Library; **p60t:** NASA; **p60b:** Tony Mcconnell/Science Photo Library; **p61:** Scientifica, Visuals Unlimited/Science Photo Library; **p62t:** Sputnik/Science Photo Library; **p62b:** Andrew Lambert Photography/Science Photo Library; **p63:** Science Photo Library; **p64b:** Paul Rapson/Science Photo Library; **p64t:** Science Photo Library; **p64-65** Tony Mcconnell/Science Photo Library; **p66-67:** Iren Lo/Shutterstock; **p66b:** North western University/Science Photo Library; **p66t:** Martyn F. Chillmaid/Science Photo Library; **p67b:** Philippe Plailly/Science Photo Library; **p67tmr:** Tfox Foto/Shutterstock; **p67tr:** StepanPopov/Shutterstock; **p67tl:** Oleg Doroshin/Shutterstock; **p67tml:** Mevans/iStock/Getty Images; **p68:** Akhenaton Images/Shutterstock; **p69l:** Vetkit/Shutterstock; **p69m:** Chalermsak/Shutterstock; **p69r:** Borysevych.com/Shutterstock; **p70b:** North western University/Science Photo Library; **p70t:** Dsmsoft/Shutterstock; **p71:** Ksander/Shutterstock; **p72:** Pavel Semenov/Shutterstock; **p73:** ESB Professional/Shutterstock; **p76bl:** Hasnuddin/Shutterstock; **p76br:** Vidguten/Shutterstock; **p76ml:** Rangizzz/Shutterstock; **p76mr:** Ananaline/Shutterstock; **p76tl:** Adrian T Jones/Shutterstock; **p76tr:** Sensay/Shutterstock; **p77:** Vladimir Melnik/Shutterstock; **p78:** Dien/Shutterstock; **p80b:** Andraž Cerar/Shutterstock; **p80tl:** Hadrian/Shutterstock; **p80tm:** simazoran/iStockphoto; **p80tr:** Pavel Vakhrushev/Shutterstock; **p81l:** Andrew Lambert Photography/Science Photo Library; **p81r:** Martyn F. Chillmaid/Science Photo Library; **p82:** Andrew Lambert Photography/Science Photo Library; **p83b:** Andrew Lambert Photography/Science Photo Library; **p83t:** Andrew Lambert Photography/Science Photo Library; **p84b:** baranozdemir/iStockphoto; **p84tl:** Djburrill/Dreamstime; **p84tm:** Anatoly Vartanov/Shutterstock; **p84tr:** Iren Lo/Shutterstock; **p85bl:** Iren Lo/Shutterstock; **p85br:** Stock solutions/Shutterstock; **p85t:** Mastering Microstock/Shutterstock; **p86-87** Dsmsoft/Shutterstock; **p86b:** Martyn F. Chillmaid/Science Photo Library; **p86t:** Hasnuddin/Shutterstock; **p88-89:** Fer Gregory/Shutterstock; **p88b:** Andrew Lambert Photography/Science Photo Library; **p88t:** Simon Pedersen/Shutterstock; **p89b:** Adam J/Shutterstock; **p89tl:** Francisco Amaral Leitao/Science Photo Library; **p89tml:** Paul Rapson/Science Photo Library; **p89tmr:** Chuyuss/Shutterstock; **p89tr:** Andrey Pavlov/Shutterstock; **p90:** Lena Pan/Shutterstock; **p92b:** Simon Pedersen/Shutterstock; **p92m:** Martin Bond/Science Photo Library; **p92t:** Cylonphoto/Shutterstock; **p94b:** Andrew Lambert Photography/Science Photo Library; **p94m:** Bonzodog/Shutterstock; **p94t:** Quirex/Istockphoto; **p95:** Dlogger/Shutterstock; **p96b:** Andrew Lambert Photography/Science Photo Library; **p96t:** wolv/iStockphoto; **p98:** Andrey Popov/Shutterstock; **p99:** Levente Gyori/Shutterstock; **p100:** Dima Sobko/Shutterstock; **p102:** Uleiber/Shutterstock; **p103:** Slavoljub Pantelic/Shutterstock; **p104-105:** Bonzodog/Shutterstock; **p104b:** Andrew Lambert Photography/Science Photo Library; **p104t:** Lena Pan/Shutterstock; **p106-107** Songsak P/Shutterstock; **p106t:** Florida Stock/Shutterstock; **p106b:** Bondgrunge/Shutterstock; **p107tl:** Eyeidea/Shutterstock; **p107tm:** Kristi Dodo/Shutterstock; **p107tr:** Marcel Clemens/Shutterstock; **p107b:** Dirk Wiersma/Science Photo Library; **p110t:** grafikeray/iStockphoto; **p110b:** kamisoka/iStockphoto; **p111:** Douglasmack/Shutterstock; **p112tr:** Smereka/Shutterstock; **p112tm:** Mironov/Shutterstock; **p112tl:** Olesia Bilkei/Shutterstock; **p112m:** AC Rider/Shutterstock; **p112b:** OMMB/Shutterstock; **p114t:** Oneinchpunch/Shutterstock; **p114b:** Bjoern Wylezich/Shutterstock; **p116t:** Tana R/Shutterstock; **p116bl:** Anthony Berenyi/Shutterstock; **p116br:** Sputnik/Science Photo Library; **p117:** Philippa Gardom Hulme; **p118t:** Perfect Lazybones/Shutterstock; **p118b:** Ondrej Prosicky/Shutterstock; **p118-119** Victor Lauer/Shutterstock; **p120b:** CP DC Press/Shutterstock; **p120m:** Steve Gschmeissner/Science Photo Library; **p120t:** Puwadol Jaturawutthichai/Shutterstock; **p121:** Power And Syred/Science Photo Library; Dencg/Shutterstock; Tatiana Makotra/Shutterstock; Mharzl/Shutterstock; Ninell/Shutterstock; Raj Creationzs/Shutterstock; Dudarev Mikhail/Shutterstock; **p122:** Puwadol Jaturawutthichai/Shutterstock; **p123:** Nokdue/Shutterstock; **p126:** TTshutter/Shutterstock; **p127l:** Sam Jonah/Shutterstock; **p127r:** Oxford University Press; **p129:** Arthur Glauberman/Science Photo Library; **p130:** Pe3k/Shutterstock; **p131:** James Stevenson/Science Photo Library; **p132b:** Valentyn Volkov/Shutterstock; **p132t:** Evgenia Sh./Shutterstock; **p133b:** CP DC Press/Shutterstock; **p133t:** Africa Studio/Shutterstock; **p134:** Andrew Lambert Photography/Science Photo Library; **p135b:** Martyn F. Chillmaid/Science Photo Library; **p135tl:** Andrew Lambert Photography/Science Photo Library; **p135tr:** Andrew Lambert Photography/Science Photo Library; **p136:** Elena Schweitzer/Shutterstock; **p137:** Bio Photo Associates/Science Photo Library; **p139:** Steve Gschmeissner/Science Photo Library; **p140:** Cordelia Molloy/Science Photo Library; **p142-143:** ANDREW Lambert Photography/Science Photo Library; **p142b:** Pe3k/Shutterstock; **p142t:** Evgenia Sh./Shutterstock; **p144-145:** John Durham/Science Photo Library; **p144b:** Sawaddeebenz/Shutterstock; **p144t:** Paul Cowan/Shutterstock; **p145:** Chad Zuber/Shutterstock; DR Jeremy Burgess/Science Photo Library; Katrina Leigh/Shutterstock; Bigone/Shutterstock; Oksana Shufrych/Shutterstock; Elenamiv/Shutterstock; Armin Rose/Shutterstock; Puwadol Jaturawutthichai/Shutterstock; **p146:** Stephen Mcsweeny/Shutterstock; **p147b:** Sebastian Kaulitzki/Shutterstock; **p147t:** CNRI/Science Photo Library; **p148:** Sawaddeebenz/Shutterstock; **p149b:** Martyn F. Chillmaid/Science Photo Library; **p149t:** Power And Syred/Science Photo Library;

p150b: Paul Cowan/Shutterstock; **p150t**: Power And Syred/Science Photo Library; **p151b**: Iakov Filimonov/Shutterstock; **p151t**: Christian Draghici/Shutterstock; **p152b**: John Durham/Science Photo Library; **p152t**: Videologia/Shutterstock; **p154b**: Vvoe/Shutterstock; **p154t**: Andre Nantel/Shutterstock; **p155l**: DR Jeremy Burgess/Science Photo Library; **p155r**: DR Jeremy Burgess/Science Photo Library; **p156l**: Ocskay Mark/Shutterstock; **p156r**: Science Photo Library; **p157**: Den Edryshov/Shutterstock; **p158b**: Nigel Cattlin/Science Photo Library; **p158t**: Kondor83/Shutterstock; **p159b**: Kaband/Shutterstock; **p159t**: Nigel Cattlin/Science Photo Library; **p160-161**: Power And Syred/Science Photo Library; **p160b**: Sebastian Kaulitzki/Shutterstock; **p160t**: John Durham/Science Photo Library; **p162b**: Marcio Jose Bastos Silva/Shutterstock; **p162t**: Eco Print/Shutterstock; **p163**: Andrew Lambert Photography/Science Photo Library; Science Photo Library; Kim D. Lyman/Shutterstock; Puwadol Jaturawutthichai/Shutterstock; Andre Nantel/Shutterstock; Anemone/Shutterstock; Evan Lorne/Shutterstock; Sebastian Kaulitzki/Shutterstock; **p164**: Marcio Jose Bastos Silva/Shutterstock; **p165l**: Michael W. Tweedie/Science Photo Library; **p165r**: Michael W. Tweedie/Science Photo Library; **p166l**: Everett Historical/Shutterstock; **p166r**: Paul D Stewart/Science Photo Library; **p167**: Science Photo Library; **p168b**: The Natural History Museum/Alamy Stock Photo; **p168t**: Ann Baldwin/Shutterstock; **p169**: Morphart Creation/Shutterstock; **p170b**: Leungchopan/Shutterstock; **p170t**: EcoPrint/Shutterstock; **p171b**: Frans Lanting, Mint Images/Science Photo Library; **p171t**: Timothy Epp/Shutterstock; **p173b**: DR Kari Lounatmaa/Science Photo Library; **p173**: DR Kari Lounatmaa/Science Photo Library; **p175**: Science Photo Library; **p176**: Anemone/Shutterstock; **p178b**: Centre for Infections/Public Health England/Science Photo Library; **p178t**: Grigorev Mikhail/Shutterstock; **p179l**: Helle/Shutterstock; **p179r**: Zelenskaya/Shutterstock; **p180-181**: Marcio Jose Bastos Silva/Shutterstock; **p180b**: Centre for Infections/Public Health England/Science Photo Library; **p180t**: Ann Baldwin/Shutterstock; **p181**: Leungchopan/Shutterstock;

OXFORD
UNIVERSITY PRESS

Great Clarendon Street, Oxford, OX2 6DP, United Kingdom

Oxford University Press is a department of the University of Oxford.
It furthers the University's objective of excellence in research,
scholarship, and education by publishing worldwide. Oxford is a
registered trade mark of Oxford University Press in the UK and in
certain other countries

© Oxford University Press 2017

The moral rights of the authors have been asserted

First published in 2017

All rights reserved. No part of this publication may be reproduced,
stored in a retrieval system, or transmitted, in any form or by any
means, without the prior permission in writing of Oxford University
Press, or as expressly permitted by law, by licence or under terms agreed
with the appropriate reprographics rights organization. Enquiries
concerning reproduction outside the scope of the above should be sent
to the Rights Department, Oxford University Press,
at the address above.

You must not circulate this work in any other form and you must
impose this same condition on any acquirer

British Library Cataloguing in Publication Data
Data available

978 0 19 840825 3

10 9 8 7 6 5 4 3 2

Paper used in the production of this book is a natural, recyclable
product made from wood grown in sustainable forests.
The manufacturing process conforms to the environmental regulations
of the country of origin.

Printed in Great Britain by Bell and Bain Ltd. Glasgow.

Activate author acknowledgements
The authors would like to thank Yon-Hee Kim for keeping everything on
track, as well as for her great patience and attention to detail. You have
done an excellent job.

Philippa Gardom Hulme would like to thank Barney Gardom, Catherine
Gardom, and Sarah Gardom for their help, support, and patience. She is
also grateful to the man in the computer shop who sold her the biggest
computer monitor ever.

Jo Locke would like to thank her husband Dave for all his support,
encouragement, and endless cups of tea, as well as her girls Emily and
Hermione who had to wait patiently for Mummy 'to just finish this
paragraph'.

Helen Reynolds would like to thank Michele, Janet, Liz and Carol,
and all at OUP.

Andy Chandler-Grevatt would like to thank the editorial team at OUP,
the awesome author team, and Geoff.

Although we have made every effort to trace and contact all copyright
holders before publication, this has not been possible in all cases.
If notified, the publisher will rectify any errors or omissions at the
earliest opportunity.